vnD//CKb

ps 86 Duck River
87/84 Blue River
158 Civil war
* 178 Warren/map

Blue Water Creek and the First Sioux War, 1854–1856

Campaigns and Commanders

Campaigns and Commanders

GENERAL EDITOR

Gregory J. W. Urwin, *Temple University, Philadelphia, Pennsylvania*

ADVISORY BOARD

Blue Water Creek and the First Sioux War, 1854–1856

R. Eli Paul

University of Oklahoma Press : Norman

Also by R. Eli Paul

(with Richard E. Jensen and John E. Carter) *Eyewitness at Wounded Knee* (Lincoln, 1991)
(coeditor, with Thomas R. Buecker) *The Crazy Horse Surrender Ledger* (Lincoln, 1994)
(editor) *Autobiography of Red Cloud: War Leader of the Oglalas* (Helena, 1997)
(editor) *The Nebraska Indian Wars Reader, 1865-1877* (Lincoln, 1998)

This book is published with the generous assistance of The McCasland Foundation, Duncan, Oklahoma.

Blue Water Creek and the First Sioux War, 1854-1856 is Volume 6 in the Campaigns and Commanders series.

Library of Congress Cataloging-in-Publication Data

Paul, R. Eli, 1954–
    Blue Water Creek and the first Sioux war, 1854–1856 / R. Eli Paul.
       p.   cm. — (Campaigns and commanders ; 6)
    Includes bibliographical references and index.
    ISBN 0-8061-3590-5
     1. Blue Water Creek, Battle of, Neb., 1855—Personal narratives.
    2. Dakota Indians—Wars—Sources. 3. Dakota Indians—Government relations. 4. Little Thunder, Chief. 5. Harney, William S. (William Selby), 1800–1899. I. Title. II. Series

E83.854.P38 2004
973.6'6—dc22

2004047884

1 2 3 4 5 6 7 8 9 10

*To Clyde Eli Paul and Lucy Evalene Keck Paul
and their children, Clyde Alan, Roberta Jean,
Linda Ruth, and Lizabeth Jo*

Contents

Illustrations

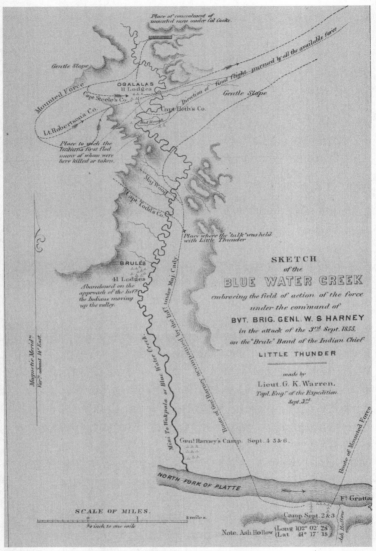

Blue Water Creek battlefield. Expertly sketched by Lieut. G. K. Warren of
the Topographical Engineers immediately after the 1855 fight, this version
appeared in a later report of his explorations. Nebraska State Historical Society
Photograph Collections.

Preface

"It is the nature of great events to obscure the great events that came before them."

FRANCIS PARKMAN

The great American historian of the nineteenth century, Francis Parkman, was referring to a topic near and dear to his heart, the French and Indian War, and how the subsequent American Revolution had overshadowed that story. He tried to rectify that. The same has happened, apparently, in another, smaller arena—the first violent conflict between the United States and the Lakota people. The great events of 1854–1856 have been obscured by later struggles, in particular, the Sioux wars along the Platte River road in 1864–1865, the Bozeman Trail War, also known as Red Cloud's War, of 1866–1868, and the Great Sioux War of 1876–1877.[1] The Civil War, too, and the careers it made or broke, easily overshadowed the frontier military exploits of the previous decade. This book, a retelling of the events of the First Sioux War, its mundane causes, violent consequences, and lingering effects, attempts to rectify that.

First, an explanation of the title: Blue Water Creek comes from a translation of the Lakota *mini wakpala* (water + blue), usually written as "Blue Water" by the writers of the day, and today simply as Blue Creek. The stream originates in Crescent Lake, a Sand Hills lake in northern Garden County, Nebraska. It flows south in a twisted, tortured fashion, by an impressive range of bluffs to its west, until emptying in the North Platte

River. Reaching the summit of one flat-topped butte in particular, "the sentinel of the valley," as one visitor called it, gives
a magnificent view of Blue Creek valley.[2] From these heights,
soldiers saw the climax of this first war with the Sioux.

Not being seers, chroniclers of the war did not use the
term First Sioux War, the other half of this book's title.
Although everyone knew this was the first such conflict, no
one predicted the ones to follow. Its conclusion seemed to
preclude that. The official term of that day was the Sioux
Expedition, itself a name of subsequent military campaigns
yet unimagined.

This was a military campaign staged during an era of
intense letter writing, diary keeping, and record filing. Hence
a wealth of surviving documentary sources generated by the
white participants exists that one can draw on to recount major
events. The same cannot be said for the Indian side. Many
stories by Lakota witnesses to "Little Thunder's disaster" and
other incidents undoubtedly have been lost or never recorded;
others await discovery. Nevertheless, a goal of this book has
been to find and use new sources of Lakota history, as well as
to distill old accounts, in order to tell this story thoroughly,
concisely, and fairly.

The narrative presented here depends largely on such
accounts and on contemporary eyewitnesses—those who saw
the events rather than individuals present in the general area
who heard about the events. My version also emphasizes accounts
recorded relatively soon afterwards rather than reminiscences
written down decades later. Unpublished accounts have been edited
for clarity and consistency, especially regarding spelling and
punctuation.

Blue Water Creek and the
First Sioux War, 1854–1856

Chapter 1
Origins

Captain Oscar F. Winship began his long, improbable trip to Fort Laramie on the North Platte River by taking a steamboat up the Mississippi. Winship's roundabout route, though, made sense in May 1854, when he departed St. Louis, Missouri, for points north, not west. His superiors had ordered him, in his capacity as assistant adjutant general, to tour eight government forts of the Department of the West, United States Army, and report on the "usual objects of military inspection." Three of the forts—Ridgely, Ripley, and Snelling—were located in Minnesota Territory, the last reached most conveniently by Mississippi steamer. Five more lay far to the southwest, the nearest being Fort Leavenworth on the similarly navigable Missouri River in soon-to-be Kansas Territory. Completion of this "very interesting tour" would involve several hundred miles of overland travel to Forts Riley, Atkinson, and Laramie before returning, via Fort Kearny, to the States. The entire trip would take months and an unexpected turn.[1]

On May 1, 1854, Brig. Gen. David E. Twiggs, the commander of the Department of the West, served as the conduit for orders originating from the headquarters of the Army, located in New York City, and from Winfield Scott, its commanding general. In response, only four days later, Winship took passage alone on the steamboat *Prairie State* for Galena, Illinois. He then transferred to *War Eagle* for St. Paul, Minnesota, a slow trip of nine days against the current. There he began his work with an inspection of Fort Snelling, "deviating from the order" in which the posts occurred in his instructions, but generally following a routine that repeated itself at the stops to follow.

Winship commented on the general—the site, its defensibility against Indians, and the strategic lay of the land—and on the specific—the arms, accoutrements, and clothing of the garrison, as well as the quarters, hospital, guardhouse, stables, commissary, quartermaster and ordnance storehouses, and their stores. Mundane bookkeeping details did not escape his attention. He specifically noted that the clothing of Company K, Sixth Infantry, was of "the old pattern," the men mandated to wear it out before they could receive current issue. Economy was always on the military mind. More importantly, Winship witnessed the infantry company's ability to carry out group field maneuvers and individual bayonet exercises, both of which received his high praise. Satisfied, he moved on to Fort Ripley, 125 miles northwest.

That small garrison consisted entirely of Company A, Sixth Infantry, a mere forty-five men. The company, which would be at war in little over a year, was described as "very deficient" in military instruction. Charitably, Winship gave the commanding officer, Capt. John B. S. Todd, some benefit of the doubt when he added in his report that, after needing soldiers to guard, farm, garden, and cut wood for fuel, it only left a handful at any one time to drill. To the garrison's credit, the government buildings were "neat, orderly, and comfortable." More significantly, perhaps, Captain Todd had become somewhat accomplished in his peaceful dealings with the area Chippewa and Winnebago Indian tribes.

On May 28, Winship reached Fort Ridgely, on the Minnesota River about twenty miles from New Ulm, Minnesota, in the land of the Dakota, or eastern Sioux. "The country," observed Winship before returning to the task at hand, "is being peopled more rapidly, perhaps, than any other of the United States territories, and both the Indians and the frontier posts must perforce recede before this overwhelming tide of emigration." He made no elaboration on where either could go.

Garrisoned by two companies of Sixth Infantry, a labor force of 120 busily engaged in pressing construction projects, and commanded by an officer absent on leave, the men's appearance was "respectable but by no means remarkable." As for their abilities, "[b]oth companies were evidently unaccustomed to drilling in their knapsacks." But again came the same excuse. "Men cannot play soldiers and day-laborers at the same time. . . ."

Thus, by visiting just three posts in the Department of the West and his assignment hardly half finished, Captain Winship had witnessed the panoply of problems commonly experienced by the country's little frontier army, any one of which was more serious than out-of-date uniforms. The "multipurpose" army seemed preoccupied with decidedly nonmilitary activities. Would he find the peacetime garrisons on the Great Plains also victims of limited manpower, sporadic military training, and a contradictory mission?[2] Winship would soon find out. He returned to St. Louis on June 10, hurriedly arranged his travel, and left on the Missouri River steamer *F. X. Aubrey* on June 14. Six days later, he set foot on the grounds of Fort Leavenworth, arguably the department's most important post.

Geography had determined the post's location and purpose. It served as the military depot for the other posts in Kansas, Nebraska, and New Mexico territories. Men and supplies from the East were carried in bulk by water to Fort Leavenworth, the latter stored and then transported west by land. Trains, employing hundreds of wagons, teams, and teamsters destined for Forts Kearny and Laramie, followed the Oregon-California Trail, designated by military correspondence as the

"Oregon Route," or just "O.R.," or they took the Santa Fe Trail to the Southwest. But, just as the frontier was so fluid in Minnesota, Winship could see the same process unfolding here. Fort Riley, established a year earlier on the Kansas River some one hundred twenty-five miles west, was seen as the heir apparent to Leavenworth. Besides being that much closer to the other installations, Fort Riley could help open new routes west along the Republican and Smoky Hill rivers, tributaries of the Kansas. And already there was talk of establishing yet another depot higher up on the Missouri.

Once again, though, Winship turned to his assigned duties, here focusing more on the capabilities of mounted troops. The several cases of cholera in the post hospital warranted a mention, although to his greater consternation he found the regimental band of the First Dragoons unable to perform mounted! "A band which cannot perform on horseback is, of course, unfit for a Regiment of Dragoons," he sniffed. More substantively, he again saw resource deficits that needed correcting. Company G, Fourth Light Artillery, was "deplorably deficient in men and horses," a chronic condition "obvious to any one acquainted with the history of our light batteries since the Mexican War. They have been mounted and dismounted until . . . they now hardly know whether they are on foot or on horseback." Regarding the two companies of dragoons, "[I]n my experience as a Cavalry officer, I have often seen it take three or even four companies to form a minimum squadron," which was Winship's preferred size of mounted force. A year later, these words would be heeded, long after his criticisms of military musicians were forgotten.

On June 30 at Fort Riley, Winship found a garrison largely composed of raw recruits, infantrymen who made "a sorry appearance," and quickly dismissed them to their more customary duties of "stone quarrying, stone cutting, and hod carrying." Undeterred, he moved on to the storehouses where he stumbled across a large cache of firearms taken by the commanding officer at Fort Atkinson from an Indian agent, originally intended by the latter official for issuing to his Indians.[3] Apparently Winship's interest lay only with their continued safekeeping.

Now Winship's own security became a concern; he traveled to Fort Atkinson with an escort of five men, reaching the infantry camp on the Arkansas River on July 11. The nearby fort, originally established to protect the Santa Fe Trail, had been abandoned as a permanent post in fall 1853. The "immediate neighborhood," as Winship termed it in his report, had been reoccupied only a month before. Companies F and H, Sixth Infantry, guarded this portion of the military lifeline, located midway between Fort Leavenworth and Santa Fe, but also "near the center of the great buffalo range of the Arkansas, . . . consequently central to the various tribes of Indians which meet here to hunt. . . ." Winship was finally, officially, in the heart of Indian country.

In his opinion, prospects had improved for addressing the problem of training. Without a permanent post to build and maintain, the troops could "devote their whole time to military exercises and instruction." Unfortunately, the soldiers had not been there long enough for this "devotion" to take effect, although their officers were endeavoring to make it so. Encouraged, Winship claimed he saw progress during his stay. He recommended further that the camp be abandoned before winter set in, and the men withdrawn to Riley or Leavenworth. Here were the makings of an adaptive military strategy: units stationed at moving, but strategic points on the Plains, as fluid and flexible as their potential foes.[4]

Winship spent more time at this camp than he cared for, but he had a good reason. John W. Whitfield, agent for many of the southern Plains tribes in this region, was making a stop here to distribute annuities under a treaty negotiated with the government the previous year.[5] Winship saw the advantage of traveling with him. Wherever the agent went this season, hundreds, if not thousands, of Indians for Winship to observe were sure to congregate. Since Whitfield needed to wait for the tardy Comanches and Kiowas to pick up their portion, he, his employees, and his wagonloads of goods could not leave until July 24. Winship and an escort of four soldiers accompanied him, all headed for Fort St. Vrain, a fur trade post on the South Platte River, and then to Fort Laramie.

The 539-mile, basically uneventful, trip to Fort Laramie generally took the party on a route now known as the Cherokee Trail.[6] It passed by the ruins of George Bent's "Old Fort" on the Arkansas and his thriving "New Fort" before paralleling north along the Front Range of the Rocky Mountains. At Fort St. Vrain, near present Gilcrest, Colorado, members of the Cheyenne and Arapaho tribes were assembled to receive their annuities from Whitfield. This took five days. Branching off from the Cherokee Trail and away from the South Platte River, the government train now continued north to Fort Laramie on the Trappers Trail, the longtime highway between Taos, New Mexico, and the North Platte.[7] At Fort Laramie, Winship had another garrison to inspect, and Whitfield expected more Cheyennes and thousands of awaiting Sioux. The pair reached their destination on August 26, alerted beforehand by persons coming from Fort Laramie that their days of bureaucratic tedium this season had ceased.

* * *

Geography had also determined Fort Laramie's location and purpose and had set in motion the collision of two expansionist powers. Sitting on a critical choke point, the fort played a central role in the movement of two peoples across a continent.[8]

Founded in 1834 as a fur trade post initially named Fort William, its roots lay with its intimate ties to the Lakota, or western Sioux. Seven tribes that shared a common culture and language—Blackfeet, Brulé, Hunkpapa, Miniconjou, Oglala, Sans Arc, and Two Kettles—formed this Lakota "nation." Their origins began in the Great Lakes region, but their destinies lay west and south. So intertwined were the traders and these Indians that who influenced whom to make the Platte River drainage their home became something of a mystery.[9]

Good historical evidence can be found that traders drew the Oglalas, one of the more southernmost of the Lakota tribes, southward to the North Platte area almost immediately after the fort's establishment. Equally good testimony shows that the Oglalas already ranged the area, particularly during the summer. Apparently, both arguments are correct. Fort William and the economic opportunities it afforded, plus abundant buffalo herds, encouraged a year-round Oglala presence and a significant one at that (initially some two thousand persons). Soon Fort William, later known by its more famous name of Fort Laramie, became the most important post on the central Plains, the nucleus of the buffalo robe trade between Bent's Fort on the southern Plains and American Fur Company establishments on the northern. Shortly, the Brulé tribe, another Lakota division, would join their aggressive kinsmen in this inexorable tribal migration that had begun near the Great Lakes woodlands over a century before. By the 1840s, their numbers, supplemented by the Miniconjou tribe, yet another Lakota division on the move, stood at about eight thousand, a formidable power base.[10] Other tribes had retreated before this advance; only the Americans posed a threat to continued Lakota domination.

Threats came via a transcontinental road across the Plains that bisected the newly acquired Lakota territory, and from an inevitable recognition of Fort Laramie's importance by westward-looking and empire-building Americans. By 1845, the United States, in the midst of its own expansionist dreams, responded with a major military expedition, one led by Stephen Watts Kearny that presaged another by William Selby Harney a decade later.[11]

The march overland to South Pass by Colonel Kearny, accompanied by 250 mounted men, marked the greatest, most westerly incursion by the U.S. Army to date. Depending on one's reading of such saber-rattling efforts, the expedition's purpose was to subtly impress and awe the native peoples or to blatantly warn and threaten them, particular the Lakota. Either way, the expedition produced the immediate benefit of protecting that year's emigration to Oregon, California, and Utah, the largest so far with three thousand persons heading to Oregon alone.[12] Most observers, though, failed to notice that the real game being played was not with the Sioux nation, but with the Mexican. A war for empire was looming (and soon erupted in 1846), and any army reconnaissance of these western lands could pay immediate intelligence dividends. In fact, Kearny's return to Fort Leavenworth took him south to the Santa Fe Trail and closer to Mexico.

Nevertheless, in mid-June 1845, Kearny held council with Oglala and Brulé leaders at Fort Laramie, who were accompanied by twelve hundred followers probably more interested in trading than treating. The commander told the Lakotas that they must not hinder the overlanders in their travels. This was almost a moot point because the Lakotas were generally peaceful and friendly toward the whites, even without the imposing presence of the dragoons.

While at Laramie, Kearny directed Capt. Philip St. George Cooke, First Dragoons, to examine the site with an eye for a permanent post.[13] Neither was impressed, mostly for philosophical reasons. Kearny, a dedicated cavalryman, preferred action in the form of this patrol to its alternative, a chain of passively fixed forts. The dragoon ride of 2,200 miles in ninety-nine days had proved, at least to Kearny's satisfaction, that mounted forces could operate on the seemingly inhospitable Plains. Although the debate, "forays versus forts," continued for years, all agreed that the army possessed the wherewithal to project its power throughout the West.[14]

By 1849, the Mexican-American War had come and gone, and the federal government could play a demonstrably greater role in the westward migrations. In the spring, Lt. Col. William W. Loring did the dragoon class of 1845 one better and marched an even larger force—starting with over six hundred men, most of the army's regiment of mounted riflemen—all the way to the West Coast. General Kearny, dead in 1848, lent his name to a new fort at the head of the Grand Island on the Platte River, one of the static, ineffectual posts that he so despised. The second fort with his name, but the first at a meaningful location, Fort Kearny sat where all the trunk lines of the Oregon-California trail converged in central Nebraska. Also, contrary to Kearny's earlier recommendations, the government purchased Fort Laramie in 1849 from its private owners, the American Fur Company, and assigned some of Loring's troops to garrison this, the second permanent installation on the Oregon route, just in time for them and their Lakota neighbors to witness the wildest emigration seasons yet.[15]

It may be a stretch to conclude that, after James Marshall saw those first flecks of gold at Sutter's Mill on January 24, 1848, the first Sioux war became inevitable. Those two developments were not associated at the time, and maybe the latter did not have to happen, even though Francis Parkman had presciently observed in 1846 that the Indians' "wonder is now giving way to indignation." But the dynamic of the overland trail had abruptly changed and intensified. An irresistible wave of over one hundred thousand forty-niners passed over Fort Laramie in 1849 and 1850, a population in excess of all but the greatest American cities. This crowd changed demographically, too. Generally, overlander parties, composed of families destined for Oregon farms, were superseded by single males destined for California mining camps. They cut wood, killed buffalo, and fouled waterholes, and they brought with them the scourge of disease. Cholera claimed thousands of emigrant lives on the trail in 1849–1850, hundreds among the Brulés; other tribes suffered similarly. Violent conflicts between Lakotas and whites remained negligible, but with these pressures and strains swirling about, the harmony was not likely to continue.[16]

One anonymous correspondent writing from Fort Laramie called for another military overture and recalled helpfully that "General Kearny's expedition . . . had immense influence on the Indians." Another anonymous Fort Laramie letter writer— probably a military man—saw the situation from a different perspective: "The Platte Sioux . . . are the best Indians on the prairies. Look at their conduct during the past summer. Of the vast emigration, which rolled through their country this year, not a person was molested, not an article stolen. Such good conduct deserves reward."[17]

As early as 1846 the Sioux, tolerant as they seemingly were, had complained about the emigrants killing their game and demanded recompense for this loss.[18] By 1850, wiser heads saw the merit in this argument and the need quickly for a diplomatic, rather than a military, solution.

To no one's surprise they chose Fort Laramie, "the key of communication between East and West," as the meeting place of the Indian and American nations.[19] The result in September 1851, the Fort Laramie Treaty Council, turned out to be one of the grandest, most majestic events on the Plains. Somewhat a misnomer, the council really occurred over thirty miles east at the mouth of Horse Creek, a North Platte tributary, although David D. Mitchell, the superintendent of Indian affairs and the chief government negotiator, wanted it moved even farther east to Ash Hollow.[20] At Horse Creek, grazing and water proved sufficient to accommodate ten thousand Plains Indians. Tribal representatives, as well as whole villages, gathered for the talk, as much to mediate disputes among themselves as with the United States. Arapahos, Arikaras, Assiniboines, Cheyennes, Crows, Gros Ventres, Mandans, and Shoshones congregated "in union, harmony and amity," but the vast majority were Lakotas, a testament to their awesome strength. This was perhaps the height of Sioux power.[21]

Samuel Cooper, a lieutenant colonel and assistant adjutant general, witnessed the council of an estimated five hundred principal men of the different bands. He recorded this succinct overview of the proceedings in his diary: "The object of the council was made known to them, . . . the reconciling the several tribes with each other, the interchange of friendly relations, and a treaty of amity. . . ."[22] Cooper may have overstated the government's benevolence when he stated that the council was being held for the Indian's "own benefit" and not for any advantage the government might derive. In exchange for an annual payment of fifty thousand dollars worth of goods, the tribes would tolerate the roads that already existed and the traffic that they generated. This sum also took into account the damages such activity had on their hunting grounds. Later, the U.S. Senate, which ratified all treaties with other governments and nations, reduced this figure for annuities to ten thousand dollars a year.[23]

Cooper witnessed the establishment of geographical boundaries of territory between the several tribes, and with these artificial lines came the responsibility of the tribes to prevent "outrages" on whites passing through their lands. In his diary,

Cooper states, "[T]o this end, they were required to designate and appoint a principal chief for each tribe, with whom the Government of the United States might hereafter, and always, transact business for the whole tribe."

This selection did occur later in the proceedings, but only after some Lakota leaders had expressed concern about the difficulty in making a head chief to represent their entire nation.[24]

To break the deadlock, Mitchell nominated Conquering Bear of the Wazhazha band of the Brulés, an obviously surprised candidate although he came from a prominent family. A man in his thirties and not yet a chief, Conquering Bear, "a brave of the highest reputation," impressed the white delegation. Furthermore, among the whites "he bears an unspotted reputation for honesty, courage, and good behavior." After collecting himself, Conquering Bear spoke modestly to Mitchell of his youth and inexperience, that "[t]here are men who know the white man longer than I have. . . ." And he realized that this lofty political position came with great risk. "If I am not a powerful chief, my opponents will be on my trail all the time. I do not fear them. I have to sleep [die] on the prairies some time."[25]

To cement his new authority, one of his peers harangued the others, especially the young men, to open their eyes and look upon the chief of the nation, and also "to have their ears bored, that they might listen to his words. . . ." To seal the deal, a convoy of more than two-dozen wagons, loaded with presents, arrived on September 20. With the booming of a soldier cannon as a friendly signal, the division of the presents among the tribesmen commenced. As one result, for all the lofty talk of peace and friendship, the name the pragmatic Lakota gave the great gathering at Horse Creek was "The Big Issue."[26]

But how Conquering Bear's tenure would play out, lay in the future. For now, all sides had a treaty by which to abide, an agreement that proved favorable to the Lakota tribes in terms

of territory and recognition. All sides realized that, as a nego-
tiating point, the overland road—called effusively by the Belgian
Jesuit, Father Pierre-Jean De Smet, "the broadest, longest, and
most beautiful road in the whole world"—was off the table,
forever a permanent fixture of the landscape.[27] Surprisingly,
neither side seemed to grasp the dangers of a continued
Lakota presence along the trail during the travel season, specifically the council's decision to conduct the future issuance of
annuity goods at Fort Laramie.[28] If an intention of the 1851
treaty was to reduce Indian-white interaction on the trail, this
seemingly minor provision scuttled that. The unintended consequences soon followed.

❋ ❋ ❋

The 1851 season had been a slow one for emigration, due
to difficulties in travel and the reported disillusionment of many
gold-seekers after their travails at the diggings. But numbers
on the trail were expected to jump in 1852. Father De Smet,
who traveled among the western tribes extensively and who
had witnessed the treaty council, proclaimed, "It will be the
commencement of a new era for the Indians—an era of peace."
Long-standing enmity between the Crow tribe and at least
a significant segment of the Lakota had noticeably ebbed.[29]
The words of peace spoken at Horse Creek appeared to have
taken hold.

But the peace between the United States and the Lakota
lasted only until June 15, 1853, when a small skirmish erupted
between some Fort Laramie soldiers and Miniconjous.[30] On
that day, 1st Lt. Richard B. Garnett, the commanding officer
of the small garrison of Sixth infantrymen, sent 2nd Lt. Hugh B.
Fleming, a young, inexperienced officer, along with an interpreter of the Lakota language and a small detachment of troops,
to a nearby village of eighty or a hundred lodges, some one
thousand persons. Miniconjou men were accused of harassing

some emigrants and forcibly expropriating the ferry at a North Platte crossing. Worse, one had fired upon one of Garnett's sergeants after the soldier took back the boat from them.

Leading the severely outnumbered force of twenty-three to the village, Lieutenant Fleming demanded that its leaders turn over the shooter, an order with which they could not or would not comply. Talks breaking down, Fleming's group was fired upon from a ravine with "guns and arrows," to which it returned fire. The skirmish lasted but a moment. "Perhaps thirty shots were fired on both sides," reported Fleming, but the retreating Indians had left four or five of their brethren dead. Fleming took two hostages, as ordered by Garnett if failing to arrest the particular culprit, and he returned to the fort.

Days later, Garnett met with Little Brave, the chief of the Miniconjou village, and expressed regret, but promised "that under similar circumstances" he would "always act precisely in the same manner." Garnett warned against the Lakotas escalating the violence because "though they might escape at the time, and even for years, . . . the day of retribution would certainly come." Although Little Brave diplomatically offered the olive branch by admitting that Garnett's actions were "perhaps right, according to the manner of the whites," Garnett lacked the skills in Lakota political culture to recognize an opportunity to soothe these troubled waters. He released the innocent hostages and apparently dropped his demand for the shooter, but when requested to give presents—clearly to be passed along to the bereaved members of the slain Miniconjous—Garnett refused. He later discussed the episode with Conquering Bear, who "appeared to be quite friendly and well satisfied." Gratuitously, Garnett added that Conquering Bear's followers "look upon the 'Minny-Kon-joes' as interlopers and regard them with considerable distrust." To Garnett's mind, the matter was settled, and so it appeared through the remainder

of the year. The lull almost lasted until Captain Winship and
Agent Whitfield's arrival in August 1854.[31]

The relentless emigration to California, Oregon, and Utah
continued unabated in 1854, with those destined for the first
two locations having passed by Fort Laramie by mid-July. As
usual, the yearly Mormon emigration extended the travel season.
Since their destination was hundreds of miles shorter, parties
to Utah could delay their Missouri River departure by several
weeks. Hence, emigrants still could be encountered near the
fort in August.

Once again, the fort had proven its worth, its strategic
location praised by Winship in his report, its advantages uncon-
testable: "It is situated on one of the only routes which are
practicable through the first barrier of the Rocky Mountains,
besides being in the centre of many of the most powerful and
hostile tribes of the plains, such as the various bands of the
southern Sioux. . . ." Winship also noted that the fort's location placed it where the Indians were not only at their most
numerous, "but where they can do the most mischief." To handle
this responsibility were Lieutenant Fleming, now in command
during Garnett's absence on recruiting duty, and Company G,
Sixth Infantry. The fifty men present for Winship's August
inspection "[i]n personal appearance, soldierly bearing, disci-
pline, and tactical instruction, . . . exceeded any that I had yet
visited in this Department. . . ."[32]

Winship had harsh words, though, for the resident civilian
population of the fort, "a class of men who, whether good or
evil, have more influence over them [the Indians] than the
Government. . . ." However, their sway and that of the American
Fur Company, their major employer, was evaporating. "[I]ts
influence is no longer one founded on the mutual interests of
both parties, as formerly, but rather one of prestige, which must
soon decline, now that that company can find but little more

to pay the expense of maintaining that influence." James Bordeaux, an American Fur Company competitor married into the Brulé tribe, could have attested to the limited leverage he and his position as a trading post proprietor exerted. The annual issuance of government annuities now drew the Lakotas to Fort Laramie, much like the robe trade had in earlier days.

* * *

Indians, soldiers, traders, emigrants, and one footsore cow, all added to the stew that boiled over and ended the relative peace. On August 18, 1854, a member of a Salt Lake City-bound wagon train composed of Danish converts to Mormonism complained to Lieutenant Fleming that the Indians had expropriated the man's property. Specifically, a Sioux individual had killed and butchered one of his cows, a lame ox.[33] The same day, Conquering Bear reported the circumstances of the incident to Fleming and offered his services to help settle the matter; in essence, to help Fleming bring in the offender, identified as High Forehead, a Miniconjou man.[34] Fifteen lodges of Miniconjous were nestled in the much larger Brulé village near Bordeaux's establishment. Conquering Bear offered to pay the emigrant for his loss, but this did not assuage either him or Fleming, who concluded the chief could not or would not turn over the offender without the use of troops.

The next day Fleming responded by dispatching John Lawrence Grattan, a brevet second lieutenant just a year out of West Point, along with Lucien Auguste, an interpreter of the Lakota language, and a wagonload of infantrymen, to the nearby village, about eight miles away. Grattan had finished in the middle of his graduating class at the U.S. Military Academy, a couple of notches below classmate Philip H. Sheridan; his worst grades had been in infantry tactics, his best in French. He now sat cooling his heels at Fort Laramie, awaiting his lieutenant's commission and next assignment in the regular army.[35]

He led a severely outnumbered force of twenty-nine soldiers and two cannons on field carriages, requisitioned from Ordnance Sgt. Leodegar Schnyder.[36]

Man Afraid of His Horses, a preeminent Oglala leader present at Fort Laramie on another matter, witnessed the troops' preparations. His account, and those of other Lakotas, provide a dramatic narrative not often found in dispassionate, secondhand military reports.[37] "The next thing I saw was a wagon go over to the Adobe Fort, and next [I] saw the soldiers draw a cannon out of the fort. . . .[I] stood by the cannon. . . .Then I saw them clean out the cannon preparing to load it. . . .The interpreter said to me, 'It is my place to do as the captain [Fleming] tells me. I suppose the Sioux will want to kill me or think hard of me.' [T]hey were going to get the Indian who killed the cow."

Man Afraid of His Horses advised against going against so many Sioux, but he was ignored and joined this party, which also included Obridge Allen, an inquisitive and literate civilian who had only arrived at Fort Laramie the day before.[38] Together, they left the fort on the trail east that led to the massive Indian encampment. Man Afraid again tried to reason with Grattan, but the existence of large numbers of Sioux had no effect. Grattan remarked that "if any other Indians wanted to interfere, for me to tell them to stay to one side." When they beheld the tipi village, Man Afraid told Grattan, "Look, my friend, do you not see a heap of lodges?" The words fell on deaf ears, and those of the interpreter, that "[A]ll the Sioux were women," hardly helped. After traveling five miles down the North Platte they all paused at Gratiot's trading house, the American Fur Company establishment, where the soldiers loaded their guns.[39] The officer, through the interpreter, told Man Afraid that he would ask Conquering Bear to hand over the culprit.[40]

They passed Man Afraid's lodge in the Oglala village and continued toward Bordeaux's trading house, three miles from Gratiot's, and the nearby Brulé village that stretched along the river. Grattan paused during the trip to instruct his troops. He told them that the Indian must be taken "at all hazards," although "he did not expect . . . to be compelled to fire a single gun. . . ." But if that order came, "you may fire as much as you damned please."[41]

When the soldiers reached Bordeaux's, Grattan ordered the gunners to load the cannons. Bordeaux himself joined the chorus and cautioned Grattan to have an Indian leader talk to the offender about giving himself up, advice that the lieutenant would take. Conquering Bear, Little Thunder, and Big Partisan, the latter two noted Brulé chiefs, joined the group. Big Partisan, a key eyewitness to the events that followed, recalled precisely where he was on August 19 when Grattan arrived.[42] "I was in a lodge, and the first news I heard of the soldiers coming, they were close to this place. We all thought that they were bringing us word that the agent had arrived."

Big Partisan immediately realized from the interpreter's words that this was not a friendly visit from the soldiers. "They were to kill the Minneconjous," exclaimed Auguste. "[A]ll the Sioux were women." At Bordeaux's, young Grattan informed the Indian leaders of his intentions: to arrest the Indian who killed the cow, to take him to the fort, and to imprison him until the agent arrived.[43] Allen heard harsher words from the officer. "I have come down here for that man, and I'll have him or die." Grattan then ordered his men towards the village.[44] Allen discreetly remained with Bordeaux at his post. Twenty minutes later an Indian messenger came for Bordeaux, and Allen and Antoine Reynal, a Bordeaux employee, adjourned to the rooftop to view the proceedings. A frightened Bordeaux soon returned.[45]

During that interim, Auguste, reportedly drinking during
the entire trip and now quite drunk, was riding about saying
"[T]oday you are all women," and that "he was going to kill a
Minneconjou." Tensions ran high between the Indian leaders
as well. Conquering Bear turned to Man Afraid of His Horses
and asked, "You are a brave. What do you think of it?" Man
Afraid, who may have still nursed some resentment from being
passed over at Horse Creek as the headman of all the Sioux
three years before, retorted, "You are the chief. What do you
think?"[46] Grattan sent off Conquering Bear as his emissary,
but Conquering Bear turned back before entering the Miniconjou lodge. Grattan then asked Man Afraid, who went into
the lodge of the Miniconjou man. He found six men, all naked,
their hair tied up, and loading their guns. One said, "Last
year the soldiers killed three of us. . . .Our chief, the Little
Brave, is dead, and we want to die also." Man Afraid returned
to Grattan with yet another warning, "If you go, they will
shoot at you." Big Partisan added more details of Conquering
Bear's conversation with High Forehead. The accused said
that "he did not think the whites wanted to kill him for a poor
lame cow that was left on the road and could not travel any
farther, that he had killed the cow because he was hungry."[47]
Little Thunder added, "[The] Bear returned and said to [Grat-
tan], there he was, and pointed him out" and that "he could not
take him [because] he was determined to die and would kill
any person that would approach him."[48]

Conquering Bear pleaded further with Grattan not to place
his cannon where he might shoot some of his people. "Now
for once, take my advice, and go back to the fort and tell the
chief [Fleming] to think the matter over."[49] An exasperated
and seemingly powerless Conquering Bear continued, saying
"today the soldiers had made him ashamed." He concluded,

"For all I tell you, you will not hear me. Today you will meet something that will be very hard."[50]

Man Afraid challenged Conquering Bear to use his power as head chief and do "something that will be good."[51] But the time for solving this impasse with words had apparently passed.

Bordeaux, who had been summoned a second time for his linguistic and diplomatic skills, almost reached Grattan and the Indians. His eyes took in the following scene: The two cannons now formed a nucleus, with the soldiers divided in half on either side of them, and the determined Miniconjous stood in front of their lodge, about sixty yards away from Grattan, loading their guns. His mind may have rightly concluded that Grattan had foolishly decided to follow the same course—"under similar circumstances"—his peer Fleming had taken the previous year.[52]

Man Afraid saw the interpreter and Grattan exchange words, and "then one soldier came out and fired his gun, and I saw one Indian fall."[53] A puzzled Little Thunder, standing in the group's midst, saw much the same and assumed Grattan had ordered the soldiers to fire.[54] Big Partisan, though, saw who fired first. "[T]he soldiers, one of them a tall man, fired and shot an Indian in the mouth and another in the hand. After that two others fired, and then all the small arms, or most of them, were fired and wounded two, also the Bear and his brother, the Red Leaf."[55]

The scene had devolved into chaos; neither friend nor foe was distinguished. After the soldiers had fired their guns: "[T]he Minniconjous still stood looking at the soldiers. The officer was going back and forth on his horse talking to his soldiers. He then got off and stood with me [Man Afraid] and the interpreter. . . .I saw the Bear walking off and looking back. At this time the Minniconjous fired. The officer pointed towards the Bear and talked a great deal. The soldiers turned and fired at the Bear. The officer turned his cannon towards the lodge of the Minniconjous, and as I saw the fire lighted, I went around it and stood off a little distance."[56]

From his rooftop perch, Allen saw and heard the discharge of both cannons, less than a minute after the initial small arms exchange. In his statement, Big Partisan remembered the sequence of events differently, in particular, the cannon volley. "After the cannon was fired, the first Indian I saw fire was the one that killed the cow. He shot a soldier, which staggered for some distance and fell. All the other soldiers threw themselves on the ground, and when they raised, they commenced getting into the wagon and started. . . ."

Man Afraid saw that the rout of Grattan's command had begun. The soldiers in their wagon, the interpreter on horse-back, and another soldier on Grattan's horse attempted to flee. Most of the Indians chased the horsemen.

Now alongside Allen, Bordeaux could witness the final moments of Grattan's command play out. The Frenchman saw the second cannon fired personally by Grattan, who then fell.[57] After the firing of the cannon, Allen observed that Auguste and the other rider were overtaken a half mile away. The wagon soon halted, its occupants also surrounded and killed.

Big Partisan's attentions, though, lay with his fallen comrade, Conquering Bear. He put his arm under Conquering Bear's head and heard him say he "hoped that they had killed them all [because] he loved the whites and wanted to go with them." Big Partisan unbuttoned his friend's coat, saw his wound, and heard Conquering Bear say that, "he could not live."[58]

Conquering Bear's wounds proved fatal. He lingered for a few days, surely oblivious to the turmoil that now engulfed the Fort Laramie area; then he died. The Lakota had lost more than their most prominent public spokesman. The army had lost more than one officer, one civilian employee, twenty-nine enlisted men, twelve mules and their harness, and one horse. (The cannons and the wagon were soon recovered.) More importantly and irretrievably, all had lost the peace. The first shots in the First Sioux War had been fired.

* * *

Lakota rage at Grattan's actions did not dissipate with his inglorious demise. Before the shooting had ceased, James Bordeaux realized that the lives of all whites were in immediate peril and prepared his post to withstand an attack. He and such allies as Big Partisan worked ceaselessly through the night to calm the mob and to protect life and property. This became even more difficult when a soldier, the last survivor of Grattan's command, unexpectedly turned up. Pvt. John Cuddy had escaped unnoticed, although terribly wounded, during the mayhem and had hidden out in some underbrush until retrieved by Swift Bear. Brought to Bordeaux's post by the Brulé leader, Cuddy remained hidden from most of the crowd in the blacksmith's shop, safe from further harm. He died on August 21, however, before he could tell his tale.[59]

Elsewhere, leaders Little Thunder and Man Afraid of His Horses returned to their villages and urged their people to abstain from further killings. The most calming influence, though, may have come from the Lakota women. They took matters in their own hands when, as soon as the fighting had commenced, they struck camp and sought safety for themselves and their children. Both the Brulé and Oglala camps eventually crossed the North Platte and moved a few miles away.[60]

All these actions notwithstanding, on the next day, August 20, the Brulés succumbed to the harangue of some of their own to return for their government annuities, swayed no doubt by the argument that "it was on their account that this first commenced and was the cause of all their trouble." The Brulés were not alone; members of the other Lakota tribes also helped overrun Gratiot's establishment and take the annuities by force. This did little to satisfy the crowd because on August 21 it returned to the site to take or destroy fur company property as well. This seizure came over the objections of Man Afraid of His Horses. On August 23, their collective anger seemingly satiated or more likely realizing that they were in trouble, the Indians left the North Platte valley for their northern range. Among them was High Forehead, the killer of the emigrant's ox, who had apparently escaped the fighting without injury.[61]

Obviously, word of the Grattan debacle commenced a desperate time for Lieutenant Fleming and the Fort Laramie garrison. The meager remnants of his command sought refuge that evening behind the walls of the old adobe fort—described in better days as a penitentiary without the windows—and waited out the night.[62] The next day, August 20, Fleming sent word of the disaster to the world, via an eastern courier to Fort Kearny. On that same day he had the presence of mind—or was it the inflexibility?—to ask Bordeaux to retrieve Grattan's corpse and to bury those of the enlisted men in the field. Bordeaux counted twenty-four arrows in Grattan's body, with one through his head.[63]

News would move west and south as well, along less official lines. Officially, the U.S. mail arrived at Salt Lake City on Sept. 28, but rumors of "some difficulty" at Fort Laramie preceded it. From the south, Captain Winship and Agent Whitfield worked their way and encountered a few retreating Indians. After their arrival, the massacre did surprisingly little to prevent the duo of government employees from discharging their assigned duties.[64]

Whitfield found about a hundred lodges of Cheyennes still camped at Fort Laramie, uninvolved in the Grattan fight and patiently awaiting their apportionment, and he obliged them.[65] He then turned his attention to investigating the Grattan fight through the lens of an Indian Office bureaucrat, that is, finding someone other than himself or his superiors to blame and then shifting that blame. Investigations by military and congressional entities followed similar tracks and biases and would consume the attention of all in the coming months.

Before his September 2, 1854 departure for the East, Winship carried out yet another post inspection and did so with no apparent sense of irony when he reported that "[t]he oxen are old and are seldom worked on account of sore feet." However, the killing of Grattan now colored his observations, as it surely must have for the final writing and editing of the entire document. When Winship later submitted his report in person to his superiors, his observations now carried the weight of an eyewitness to war, testimony to the deeds of a fallen comrade and those of an unpunished foe. He also spoke of swift vengeance. In his report, Winship recommended that "the time has now fully arrived for teaching the barbarians a lesson. . . ." His superiors wasted no time in following this recommendation.

Chapter 2
Reluctant Executioner

The U.S. Army in late 1854, a small but scattered force, took the news of the loss of Lieutenant Grattan's command badly. It did not grieve so much as seek vengeance. In the months to come, army leaders would not hesitate to draw upon the nation's significant resources in talent and technology to send a punitive expedition to the Plains. This resolve for retribution permeated the highest levels of the federal government.

In 1854, Jefferson Davis, in half a dozen years the president of the Confederate States of America, served as secretary of war in the Democratic administration of President Franklin Pierce. As with all previous and subsequent secretaries, Davis found himself late in the year as the author of an annual report that contained some bad news.[1] "[T]he Indians," wrote Davis in December, "have repeatedly come into collision with our troops," and not all of these euphemistic "collisions" had occurred on the Plains. Besides the "massacre" of Grattan, which was quite fresh in his mind, he reported "disorders" (he did not use the word "wars") in Florida with the Seminole tribe, as well as in Texas, New Mexico, and the Pacific Northwest. Most had been exacerbated, in his opinion, by "the inefficiency of small posts." Consequently, and not surprisingly, the army needed to grow.

At this time, the authorized strength of the U.S. Army stood at about fourteen thousand officers and men, but actual strength was under a paltry eleven thousand. Obviously, concentrating a sizeable force from units flung across a continent at those locations where they were most critically needed posed a logistical challenge. As added emphasis, Davis made sure to state that the size of the American Indian population was one hundred thousand, with the "powerful and warlike" Sioux at Fort Laramie alone mustering between fifteen hundred and two thousand warriors. It would take no ordinary effort to punish them.

The task looked more daunting when he threw out this alarming statistic: The total force of the Department of the West, stationed in "the country between the Mississippi River and the Rocky Mountains, except the departments of Texas and New Mexico," amounted to a measly 1,855 officers and men. Understandably, efforts had begun to beef up these numbers through transfers. A recurrent theme for these months in late 1854 and early 1855 was one of a constant chess-piece maneuvering of desperately needed regulars across the military landscape. Already companies of the Second Infantry and Second Dragoons had been posted to the Department of the West, where they joined the thinly stretched Sixth Infantry.

Col. Newman S. Clarke, the top-ranking officer in the Sixth Infantry and Gen. David Twiggs's replacement as commander of the Department of the West, faced the problem of how to parcel out these men. Besides the eight stations on Captain Winship's inspection itinerary and his starting point of Jefferson Barracks, Missouri, Clarke's domain also included Fort Smith, Arkansas, and Forts Arbuckle, Gibson, and Washita in present-day Oklahoma. Fortunately, the military geography of the Great Plains had shifted in the 1840s and 1850s and had rendered these last four posts and the recently abandoned Fort Scott, Kansas, largely obsolete. In previous decades, a vertical line of posts had run north to south as a static line of defense on the "permanent Indian frontier." The movement of

Americans east to west and the formation of Nebraska Territory had swung the line of important forts ninety degrees, to correspond in the same coast-to-coast direction. This made Kearny, Laramie, Leavenworth, and Riley its preeminent points and left others the relics of a past strategy.[2] Therefore, Clarke, whose army service dated to the War of 1812, had some leeway in moving his troops around, plus a good idea where to position them. In fact, Fort Laramie had already seen its garrison grow to 171 in order to help see it safely through the winter. After reinforcements arrived, the garrison could finally leave the protection of the old adobe fort, where soldier and civilian had slept under arms for weeks.[3]

The news of Grattan had reached Clarke on September 7 via fast horseman and faster telegraph. Clarke passed the news along, and in the blink of an eye his superiors had decided on administering "a signal punishment."[4] With Winship's arrival at St. Louis on October 10, the commander now had at his disposal a living, breathing informant from Indian country. The captain's opinions carried the additional weight of coming from a West Point-trained, experienced veteran. A fellow northerner (from New York to Clarke's New Hampshire), the cavalryman had fought on the Mexican War battlefields of Palo Alto, Resaca de la Palma, and Churubusco. Winship's routine inspection report, therefore, easily transformed itself into an important intelligence document on the Plains Indians, one to be taken seriously. In particular, his survey focused on the strengths of the Lakota tribe and its "vast number of bands"—about three hundred Oglala lodges, three hundred fifty Brulé, and four hundred Miniconjou. With an estimated three warriors per tipi—a ratio his frontier informants insisted upon—Winship saw an opposing body of three thousand, one hundred and fifty men. All subsequent military moves sought to equal or surpass this perceived numerical advantage.[5]

Winship, a reputable but somewhat indiscreet narrator, may have revealed more about government policy and military prejudice of the day than useful intelligence. Opining alliteratively about past Indian policy, he argued that efforts at "purchasing a precarious peace" with government payments had been botched. First, he suggested, the Indians must feel the punishing power of the government, afterwards its "justice and magnanimity." The choice was clear to Winship. "Either the government must undertake to make these barbarians respect the lives and property of the immense number of our citizens who annually traverse the plains or the latter will be compelled to assume that task by punishing indiscriminately every Indian they meet. . . ." Winship obviously preferred the former, a "regular, legitimate, and vigorously conducted warfare . . . begun in season," in other words, to commence the summer of 1855. Furthermore, with the Grattan defeat, the authorities had the "tangible and notorious cause to justify an open rupture with the Indians."[6]

If Winship's observations sounded cold and cruel, they also smelled of sanctimony. As he outlined the various Plains intertribal rivalries "over the best buffalo region, perhaps, on the continent," he philosophized, "Is it not better then to allow them to destroy each other, than to preserve them only to be in the end, ourselves, their reluctant executioner?" His report moved up the military chain of command, a bald summation of the countless contradictions of nineteenth century Indian policy and humanitarian thought.[7]

Nor were the signals less mixed coming from the Office of Indian Affairs and the Department of Interior, beginning in the field with Agent Whitfield of the Upper Platte Agency. He blamed Grattan for breaking the peace and faulted the infantry posts in Indian country as incapable of restoring it. With no annuities as a bargaining chip, he jointly proclaimed with the besieged Lieutenant Fleming of Fort Laramie a prohibition of trading guns and ammunition to the Indians.[8]

Such interagency cooperation lasted for a while, especially while the Indians remained unpunished. Open bureaucratic bickering would come later, although the country's newspapers were not so reticent. The public had learned the troubling details about the incident nearly as soon as the authorities; the first bare mention of the Grattan fight appeared in a St. Louis newspaper on September 10. James Bordeaux's lengthy August 21 letter from the massacre site appeared in a St. Louis newspaper on September 13, together with Fleming's plaintive plea to pick up the Grattan dead (this embarrassing document in all likelihood supplied gleefully by Bordeaux). A well-timed editorial comment by former Superintendent of Indian Affairs David D. Mitchell, a Whig who had been bounced out of office by the Democrat, Pierce, faulted the "inexperienced, rash young officer" and the infantry's "petty little forts." All together, they showed Grattan in particular and the army in general in a most unflattering light.[9]

Similar criticism came from an unexpected source, the ranks of the army itself. Secretary Davis, in order to placate the U.S. Congress, turned over pertinent documents relating to the incident. Subsequently published, they showed that disagreements did not exist solely between civil and military authorities. After his arrival at Fort Laramie, Captain Winship had interviewed some of the principals and dashed off a special report, blaming the Indians for their wholesale resistance to the cow killer arrest. Regarding the events after Grattan entered the village, "there is much confusion, contradiction, and uncertainty, owing, doubtless, to the conflicting interests, prejudices, and predilections of the spectators of the same." Who fired first? "[I]t is impossible to ascertain which party struck the first blow. . . ." Winship, the good soldier, essentially dodged the issue of Grattan's blame. Maj. William Hoffman, who arrived on November 12 to relieve Lieutenant Fleming of the fort's command, did not. Within a week, he had concluded that "Lieutenant Grattan left this post with a desire to have a fight with the Indians," and "he appears to have ordered his men to fire." Amended statements by other first- and second-hand sources supported, contradicted, and/or waffled on these questions.

Col. Samuel Cooper, since his attendance at the Horse Creek treaty council promoted to adjutant general of the U.S. Army, disagreed with Hoffman's assessment of Grattan, which initiated an exchange of nasty letters between the two that lasted for months. Davis essentially settled the matter: He would brook no criticism of Grattan and offer no relief from culpability by the Indians. "[A]uthentic details have since proved that the massacre was the result of a deliberately formed plan, prompted by a knowledge of the weakness of the garrison at Fort Laramie, and by the temptation to plunder the large quantity of public and private stores. . . ."[10]

The military bureaucracy's quest to assign (and sidestep) blame would continue unabated through the next year, fueled by a steady stream of impertinent correspondence, much of it eventually seeing print. Although successful in drawing the nation's attention to a pressing problem, the Grattan debate probably did little to ease the immediate fears of the soldiers and civilians stationed at the Oregon Route forts. Those anxieties could only have increased after another reported Indian atrocity.

On November 13, 1854, fifteen Sioux raiders stopped the U.S. Mail party from Salt Lake City, twenty-two miles west of Fort Laramie. Three men, including the conductor Jamison, were killed, and C. A. Kinkead (or Kinkade), a fellow traveler, was wounded. Returning from California, Kinkead was also robbed of ten thousand dollars in gold coin.[11] Most interpreted, incorrectly it turned out, this depredation as a Sioux attempt

to close down the trail, although there was anecdotal evidence
to the contrary.

Brevet 2nd Lt. John T. Mercer, writing home in late
November from the safety of Jefferson Barracks, told of being
at Fort Leavenworth and attempting to join his Sixth Infantry
company already at Fort Kearny. Unfortunately for his travel
plans, "[W]hen I arrived it was reported that there were thirty
thousand Sioux Indians on the route." The ill-informed Mercer
and others seemed to have taken this outlandish statement at
face value; no escort from the fort could be scraped together.
Apparently, those in a position to appreciate it paid scant
heed to all that the following kernel of information contained:
"The day on which I arrived [at Fort Leavenworth], some immigrants came in from California and reported that they had passed
many warriors who said *they would not molest immigrants*
[emphasis added] but intended to kill every U.S. officer or
soldier they met. . . ."[12]

Lieutenant Mercer and presumably his colleagues, far from
being disinterested parties, focused on the second half of that
purported vow: "If I remain here this winter I may possibly
have the extreem [*sic*] felicity of being scalped by the Sioux in
the spring." Unfortunately, no one concentrated on the impli-
cations of the first half of the statement: The Platte Valley route
would remain open. Lakota anger and vengeance were directed
solely towards the government and its representatives. Sioux
motivations during the next trail season would never be clearly
articulated, much less understood fully, by contemporary white
observers.

No, the interests of young lieutenants such as Mercer lay
with the exciting details of the upcoming expedition. Stationed
as he was at departmental headquarters, his November take
on the situation revealed the scope of the planned response at
that early date. The expedition would "consist of the 2d Dragoons,

4 companies of my Regiment [the Sixth Infantry] and 2 batteries of Light Artillery; making in all about 2,000 men." They would face "at least 10,000 [Sioux] warriors and the probability is that there are many more." Mercer privately feared another army debacle, especially against foes that were "brave, well armed, well disciplined, and are equal to the whites man for man. . . . If they stand, they can easily kill every man in the expedition." But he would do his duty, no matter that the craven politicians decided "to offer up the expedition as a huge sacrifice in order to open the eyes of the stupid jackasses who sit nodding on their seats in Congress." Nevertheless, Mercer resigned to "go out and get scalped *pro bono publico*."[13]

Fortunately, for his peace of mind, Lieutenant Mercer's services were needed elsewhere the next summer. More highly desired were those of officers such as Henry Heth, commander of Fort Kearny when Captain Winship passed through during the fall of 1854. Winship described Lieutenant Heth as an excellent officer, who had "earned an enviable reputation for his energy and activity in exploring the Indian Country," a military man possessing "a profound knowledge of the Indian character, combined with the tact, skill, and judicious temerity of a partisan chief."[14] In Heth's autobiography, written decades later, he failed to return the compliment; he made no mention of Winship's visit or these or any other kind words by his champion. Actually, little of the winter of 1854–1855 made an impact on Heth, a veteran of more memorable clashes, such as the first day's battle at Gettysburg, Pennsylvania, in 1863. He wrote simply, "Nothing of interest happened during the winter."[15]

Much was happening back east, though, and it did not solely revolve around responsibility for starting this war. Early on, Jefferson Davis had made a more significant decision—who would prosecute this war. On October 26, 1854, scarcely two months after Grattan's demise, William Selby Harney, the

"Prince of Dragoons," was ordered to organize and lead the Sioux Expedition.[16]

Colonel and Brevet Brigadier General William Selby Harney arrived at Jefferson Barracks, Missouri, on April 1, 1855, and took charge of the Sioux Expedition. He immediately began his preparations for war, a job for which he was eminently suited. A veteran officer, Harney had led troops successfully in Florida and the Mexican War, and from his many years of accomplishments was "proud of his name and his honest titles to distinction." One of those titles was the brevet rank of brigadier general, and according to nineteenth-century military protocol, the rank that Harney, a colonel in the Second Dragoons, went by, and by which he was and will be referred.[17]

In addition to a reputation as an Indian fighter, Harney looked the part. A subordinate, noting Harney's "commanding presence" after their first meeting, admiringly pronounced him "the beau ideal of a dragoon officer." One awestruck civilian described him similarly: "His form was that of an ideal soldier, six feet four in height, as straight and erect as any Sioux chief that ever lived, brusque in manner, . . . harsh of speech. . . ." Harney's appearance alone justified the nicknames "prince of dragoons" and "white beard," but it would be his actions that summer that produced the nicknames "hornet" and "squaw killer."[18]

In September 1854, Harney was on furlough in Paris, France, a favorite location of his wife, and where the letter from Jefferson Davis that ordered him back to the States found him. He left France for the United States on December 24. In late March, 1855, Harney was in Washington, D.C., and formally took charge of the summer campaign. Supposedly, President Pierce told him in person, "General Harney, you have done so much that I will not order you to the frontier, but I do wish you would assume the command and whip the Indians for us." Of course, Harney could do nothing but comply! While in Washington he took the opportunity to go over the specifics of his orders and to begin gathering his considerable resources.[19]

Fortuitously, Congress had authorized the expansion of the U.S. Army, an action that pleased the Democrat, Davis, and the Whig, Scott. Two regiments of cavalry and two of infantry were added, which, on paper, helped increase the limit to nearly eighteen thousand officers and men. The legislation passed Congress on March 3, 1855, perfect timing for Harney's needs.[20]

Although Harney was known as a tough commander in the field, he possessed exceptional organizational skills in garrison. The next five months would consist of gathering intelligence about his enemy, planning his strategy, putting together an effective force of officers and men to implement that strategy, moving them and their materiel into place, and keeping his superiors informed. That Harney carried out all these tasks so effectively, served as a testament to his military ability. More so, it revealed his appreciation and deft handling of the transportation and communication networks of the mid-1850s. Without the railroad, steamboat, telegraph, and express mail, this expedition could never have been formed so quickly. Harney's foray into Sioux country would show the utility of big, temporary expeditions versus large, permanent garrisons. In this respect, the First Sioux War would turn out to be a very modern war with a very modern general.

✻ ✻ ✻

Harney's mandate was twofold: to protect the territorial frontiers and to operate against the hostile bands of the Sioux. Securing the trail for the upcoming season took immediate precedence as he prepared for the latter. He ordered companies D, E, H, and K, Second Dragoons, out on the Plains "when the grass shall have grown sufficiently to subsist the animals . . .

until active operations against the Indians are decided upon."
Each dragoon escort had to be at least a company in size. No
Grattan debacles would occur under Harney's watch.[21]

The makeup of the command was also taking shape, both
in men and animals. Besides the aforementioned mounted
troops, Harney had at his disposal hundreds of infantrymen,
including companies A, B, C, D, G, and I, Second Infantry,
the companies of the Sixth Infantry "not already in position,"
and Light Battery G, a company of Fourth Artillery. New recruits
would fill any gaps. Regarding a deficiency in horseflesh brought
to his attention by the dragoon commander, Harney replied,
"[I]f it can not be supplied by purchase at that post in due
season, you are directed to telegraph the fact, at once, and
horses will be purchased here."[22] The 1855 preparations for
war illustrated the rare occurrence when military necessity
outranked the customary frugality of the frontier army.[23]

Quality as well as quantity of his troops also concerned
Harney, sometimes at a surprisingly individual level. On April 18,
1855, he asked a battalion commander to "detail an intelligent
and soldierly man from your detachment, to report to these
Head Quarters as Orderly," preferably an American or "at least
a foreigner who speaks English perfectly. . . ."[24] Harney also
fielded complaints, such as the one from Lt. Col. Philip St.
George Cooke, the commander of the dragoon companies
and an old protégé of Stephen Kearny. It appeared that Col.
Edwin V. Sumner, the superintendent of the Cavalry Recruiting Service at Jefferson Barracks and nicknamed the "Bull of
the Woods," had sent Cooke urgently needed new recruits,
chosen, according to some rule, by having been at the station
the longest time. Evidently the cream had not slowly risen to
the top because, complained Cooke, "they . . . were the worst
men there." Desertions had depleted the ranks of the dragoons,
so Harney wasted no time in going over Sumner's head to try

to rectify this. Incidents of contentiousness, though, were common among such veteran, strong-willed cavalrymen.[25]

Little diverted Harney, though, on putting together his own team and calling on individual officers to join his staff. The first two who reported for duty were Captain Winship, as the expedition's assistant adjutant general, and Capt. Stewart Van Vliet, as its assistant quartermaster. Winship described himself as "the General's right hand man," but both were positions vital in keeping orders, requisitions, troops, and supplies moving about and accounted for. Harney left the details to these and his other staff officers, requiring only that they "have things ready when called for." To handle all the many particulars, Harney also needed a subsistence officer responsible for food for man and beast, an ordnance officer responsible for arms and ammunition, surgeons, a paymaster, and an engineer. His choice for engineer, 2nd Lt. Gouverneur Kemble "G. K." Warren, proved especially fortunate, if for no other reason than he became one of the expedition's ablest and more sensitive chroniclers.[26]

Lieutenant Warren came to Harney from the Pacific Railroad Surveys, a major undertaking of the army's engineers. Anticipating a transcontinental railroad, the Office of Pacific Railroad Explorations and Surveys sought to fill in the great gaps of knowledge about the West, a critical component before the federal government could make an informed decision on the route's location. The skills that Warren used in the office on "the railroad question" would transfer well to the field. They included "the critical examination of the reports, maps, profiles, and all original data submitted by the exploring parties," combined with the preparation of maps and reports based on these explorations. Warren excelled in his role of analyst, and he would prove equally adept as an observer. No less a high government official than Jefferson Davis knew of his "great intelligence, zeal, and energy." And so did Harney.[27]

To no surprise, Lt. Henry Heth, Sixth Infantry, the capable commander of Fort Kearny, also caught Harney's eye as a potential aide-de-camp. Agreeing essentially with Winship's earlier assessment, Harney observed, "The long experience of Lieut. Heth in the service on the plains renders him peculiarly fitted to fill the post." Heth relished the assignment, but reluctantly declined. The lieutenant fielded a better offer, a promotion to a captaincy in the newly formed Tenth Infantry regiment. But Harney did not lose his services because Heth's inexperienced Company E would ultimately join the Sioux Expedition and serve in a surprising capacity.[28]

Harney wasted no time before moving troops closer to the theater of war. On April 10, he sent four companies of Sixth Infantry at Jefferson Barracks to Forts Leavenworth and Riley, which also eased the overcrowding of quarters and the threat from disease. Aware again of seasonal constraints, Harney noted to New York headquarters, "These troops will be sent to their final destinations so soon as the animals of the baggage train can subsist on the plains." Their housing would consist of "thirty common and three wall tents." Harney took great interest in seeing that his men were adequately, if not abundantly, supplied for the campaign.[29]

His passion for the best military equipment and for detail continually came to the fore. On April 30, his first month on the job ending, he commented at length on the findings of a board of officers that had convened at St. Louis to examine cavalry bits. The officers' recommendation for change caused Harney great regret. "As a cavalry officer of many years standing, I can unhesitatingly say that we have had no bit which, all things considered, answers the purpose so well as that now in use. . . ."[30]

Later his attention turned to another bit of horse equipage—saddle trees. He followed up an earlier board of survey with a visit to Thornton Grimsley, the St. Louis manufacturer and a preferred army contractor after the Mexican War, and learned that the condemned saddle trees had been originally intended for the California market. Apparently the government contractor was "mortified" that his shoddy product had been deflected to dragoons rather than indiscriminating gold-seekers, and he was "anxious to replace them by others conforming to the established pattern. . . ."[31]

Apparently, this attention to excruciating detail did not distract Harney from larger concerns, namely the overall strategy for the campaign. By May, it was well formulated. The Sioux Campaign would be a year in duration and involve a two-pronged attack of Sioux country, one column launched from Fort Kearny on the Platte River, the other, surprisingly, from Fort Pierre on the Missouri. The latter fort was a privately owned fur trade post, but that status soon changed after successful negotiations with Pierre Chouteau, Jr. and Company, a St. Louis firm. The cost to the U.S. government was a staggering (for 1855) forty-five thousand dollars.[32]

Fort Pierre, Harney concluded, was destined to be his "principal depot" and the Second Infantry its initial garrison. This was so important to his plans that he urged his superiors to allow him the luxury of a quick trip up the river to satisfy himself about the fort's location and its doubtful condition.[33] General of the Army Winfield Scott turned him down, although Harney, who was no more reticent to move himself about than he was his troops, did get to fit in a ten-day excursion to the nearer Fort Leavenworth.[34] His reservations about the location of Fort Pierre eventually proved well-founded.

Harney had considerable experience with the Upper Missouri country to draw upon, although it had come three decades earlier. As a young lieutenant, he had accompanied the 1825 Atkinson-O'Fallon treaty-making expedition up the river and was eminently acquainted with the territory and with the

Missouri as a navigable stream. But the stream was no obstacle in his mind. Chasing Seminole Indians in the labyrinths of the Florida Everglades had taught Harney well the tricks of carrying out Indian wars "on water." In the last Seminole War, he had used a number of shallow-draft vessels to negotiate the unpredictable, twisting waterways. Little wonder, then, that he recommended the purchase of "a small, light draft steamer for service on the Upper Missouri."[35]

Although Harney readily hearkened back to past victories, he did little to encourage similar thinking by his superiors. If anything, he early and repeatedly attempted to lower their expectations. His correspondence to Scott and others overflowed with examples: For instance, the Missouri River has been "unusually low," which would slow steamboat travel. It has been a late, or "backward," spring, which would slow the overland travel. Indian agents have not been cooperating. He needed more cavalry. Whined Harney unconvincingly, "Had the time lost in Congress in passing the bill for an increased military been spared to the Expedition, it would doubtless have been ready to enter the field in season. Little can reasonably be expected from the Expedition this year."[36] As an experienced and cunning army commander, this tactic could insulate him from later political reversals, or so he may have hoped.

Chapter 3
Overland

Although General Harney may have lowered expectations with higher-ups, he did the opposite with subordinates. A "backward" spring or not, it was time to push overland to Indian country. On May 7, 1855, he ordered Maj. Albemarle Cady at Fort Leavenworth to "get your command in readiness to start on the prairies as soon as the grass will permit, which in all probability will be about the 10th [of May]. . . ." Cady's force consisted of four companies of the Sixth Infantry and the light artillery company. Cady's directive was later amended to wait until the arrival of a detachment of recruits on the steamboat *Arabia*.[1]

But Harney left nothing to chance. On May 12, he reported to General Scott that he had just returned from Fort Leavenworth, there "to make arrangements for hastening the departure of the troops which are to occupy Forts Kearny and Laramie" and presumed that they had left by now. He could not resist adding a cautionary note about the low stage of the Missouri River, critical to successful steamboat travel. He hoped "to get off the troops destined for Fort Pierre, by the first of June. . . ."[2] He followed up this report with a somewhat more reassuring May 19 telegram. "I will commence active operations so soon as I get the mounted force." When that would exactly be, he could not say.[3]

Therefore, June appeared to be the critical month for operations to begin in earnest, especially since delays—and maybe

Harney's absence from the frontier staging area—prevented the infantry companies from moving away from Fort Leavenworth until late May. Headquarters in St. Louis was more interested, though, in a revised schedule than excuses. Captain Winship, signing the correspondence from Harney to Cooke, the ranking officer stationed at Fort Leavenworth, stated rather mildly, "Indeed he [Harney] is somewhat surprised to hear that they have not already left; but, as they have not, only those destined for Fort Kearny will be required to move at once." Getting to specifics, the Sixth Infantry company assigned to Fort Laramie, along with several recruits, were to wait and escort the first government train for that post. The Fourth Artillery's Company G, "whose prairie battery has been telegraphed as unfit for service," was likewise to be detained until Harney received a full report. And lastly, Harney wanted Cooke to inform him when the freight trains planned on departing to Forts Kearny and Laramie.[4]

More troublesome than Light Company G, which had become lighter still with its broken-down cannon carriage, was the status of the mounted force. Although the remaining six companies of the regiment of Second Dragoons had been ordered to move to the Department of the West from Texas, where were they? And would they be available for the summer's campaign? Soon, Harney would learn the worst; the six companies were "feeble in numbers and badly mounted." He knew that without an adequate cavalry his chances of catching the Sioux were nil.[5]

Nevertheless, he sent word to Fort Riley to prepare for the arrival of the dragoon force, with more attention, perhaps, to its horses than its men. The commanding officer of the fledgling post received the mandate to provide for "an ample supply of hay." Regarding additional stables: "As the garrison [of Fort Riley] is expected soon to be reduced to one company, and

continue so until the arrival of the cavalry force which has
been ordered to the post, little, if anything, can at present be
accomplished by it [the garrison] alone, and hired labor must
be relied upon chiefly for continuing the public works."[6]

Similar careful instructions went further west to the commander of Fort Laramie, who was also expected to provide
winter accommodations for "four companies of Infantry, two
companies of cavalry, and stabling for the animals of the latter
and those of the Quarter Master's Department." Also, he was
to cut "a sufficiency of grass . . . to supply the animals during
the more severe part of the winter." Since timber along the
North Platte valley was a scarce commodity, Harney made a
novel suggestion for easing the housing shortage, that is "purchasing from the peaceably disposed Indians, the largest sized
lodges in use among them."[7] Three months later, Harney would
still be interested in housing soldiers in Indian tipis, but by
then would not have to pay for them.

Adding to these seemingly mundane concerns were the
usual petty squabbles among officers found in any army
command that consisted of Democrats, Whigs, southerners,
northerners, slaveholders, abolitionists, West Pointers, and
civilian appointees. To add to this mix, Harney had an apparent
penchant for new weaponry, and Cooke "surprised" and obviously exasperated him by failing to issue newly available Sharps
carbines to his troopers. "[Y]ou could not have forgotten that
. . . the forwarding of such supplies to troops under your
charge was . . . positive evidence that they were intended for
the use of the same." Moreover, Cooke had rebuffed 1st Lt.
George T. Balch, newly assigned to Harney's staff as its ordnance
officer, in the latter's attempt to introduce the innovative shoulder arm. In turn, Balch returned from Fort Leavenworth and
tattled on Cooke. Winship relayed Harney's disgust with the
latter when he wrote to Cooke: "[Harney] deplores this seeming

captiousness [faultfinding] all the more because of your rank and experience in the service, not to speak of the character and importance of the force which will probably be under your immediate orders. . . ."[8]

Besides Harney's censure here and a terse, stern, follow-up order to issue the Sharps, the breech-loading cavalry arm in question was difficult to ignore; its relative ease in reloading, without the need for a ramrod, stood in conspicuous contrast to the usual muzzle-loading, single-shot rifle, musket, or musketoon then in army service. Clearly, the Sioux warrior had nothing like this in his arsenal.[9]

The rivalries within the ranks, though, failed to distract all from the common enemy, the Sioux tribe. Useful intelligence began to dribble in from the Plains as the spring season progressed, although never enough "positive and reliable information" to please Harney.[10] A valuable source was, of all places, the newspaper, and the pages of such major organs as the *Missouri Republican* of St. Louis were scanned, although not necessarily believed. Harney even enclosed clippings—with comments— to accompany his reports.

In one example, he took Charles E. Galpin, an Upper Missouri trader and St. Louis native, to task when the latter spoke sympathetically of the Sioux. "[T]he opinion of Mr. Gulpin [*sic*] is to be taken with some caution, not only because of his long residence among and probable relationship with the Sioux, but because of his commercial connection with them . . . which would of course, be much damaged if not entirely destroyed by a war."[11] Harney countered Galpin with other correspondents who agreed with the general's preconceived notions about widespread Sioux hostility.

Some news especially rankled Harney. When he learned in April 1855 that the Office of Indian Affairs had included ammunition as part of the payment of that year's treaty annuities to the Sioux, he angrily advocated an embargo of this article from the list. Ever since the 1849 establishment of the Department of the Interior and its assignment to handle Indian affairs, such policy inconsistencies between the Interior and War departments habitually cropped up.[12]

The most trusted information was expected from Fort Laramie. Harney "confidently" looked to its experienced and forthright commander, Maj. William Hoffman, "for the earliest and most circumstantial information in regard to the movements, disposition, and designs of the Indians." Hoffman had never let him down. His reports from late 1854 provided some of the best details on the movements of the Sioux bands since the Grattan fight.[13] The situation had progressed to the point that civilians, unsure whether to risk the overland trip in 1855, received assurance from the military that four companies of dragoons would "patrol the route as far west as hostile Sioux may be presumed to make their appearance."[14]

The result in early June was a further refining of that summer's strategy that was spelled out to those above and below in the chain of command. Post commanders, such as Major Hoffman at Laramie, were to undertake no offensive operations, only those of a "purely defensive character." Harney did not want "to exasperate the hostile Indians, before a general and concerted movement against them can be combined."[15] To Lieutenant Colonel Cooke, the commander of the aforementioned four companies of dragoons on the Oregon Route plus three companies of the Sixth Infantry at Fort Kearny, he instructed: "[M]ove with your entire command . . . to overtake the trains freighted with government stores for Forts Kearny and Laramie should they have left before the communication reaches you; and then to escort them as far at least, as Ash Hollow, on the North Platte. . . ."[16]

A new strategic point in Indian country now had appeared in the general's reckoning.

"There are reports here of a large assemblage of Indians at Ash Hollow; and although these reports are probably exaggerated and possibly groundless, still the General wishes to be on the safe side. . . ." As with Hoffman, Cooke was to "avoid an engagement with the Indians, if possible. If they attempt to obstruct your progress, you will be obliged, of course, to give them battle, in which event you will doubtless give a good account of them. . . ."[17]

To Winfield Scott on June 2, the summer's strategy was put in the simplest and starkest of terms. A victory would be "no victory at all, in the eyes of the Indians, unless we destroy more of them than they do of us. . . .Savages must be crushed before they can be completely conquered." One staff officer shared this sentiment. "One decisive blow," Lieutenant Balch told his wife, "could do more good and insure peace in the future better than loads of glass beads and bales of blankets." That "decisive blow," as envisioned by Harney, must also include "[m]easures . . . to capture as well as to defeat the enemy." This last statement indicated that Harney would obviously target villages rather than war parties during his foray, a military tactic that one could trace back to the earliest days of the Republic.[18]

As usual, Harney took the opportunity to lower expectations and claimed, "little can reasonably be expected from the Expedition this year." He also raised the possibility of an unprecedented winter campaign on the Great Plains. "[T]here is reason to believe that winter will have set in before [the expedition] can penetrate far into the Sioux country. . . .A winter campaign near the base of the Rocky Mountains would doubtless be attended with no little risk and suffering to the troops."[19]

Later in the month, Harney prescribed geographic limits to Cooke's dragoon patrols. Routinely, Fort Kearny on the Platte, where "the several emigrant trails which leave the frontier settlements and intersect each other," would be the easternmost point of his range. Harney left the threat from eastern tribes (those other than the Sioux, particularly the Omaha, Oto, and Pawnee) to Cooke's best judgment. Almost prophetically, Ash Hollow to the west continued to draw the general's attention. "The government as well as the emigrant trains are much exposed at this place, more so indeed than at any other point between the frontiers and Fort Laramie." Ash Hollow was also considered the heart of the Brulé and Wazhazha Lakota, "the most deeply implicated in hostilities against the Whites." Harney directed that "Ash Hollow be made the rendezvous and point of rest of your returning detachments, escorts, etc."[20]

A month later on July 20, these instructions reached Cooke at Fort Kearny and provoked this response by diarist Capt. John B. S. Todd, Sixth Infantry: "This was a great disappointment to him, for his command had all their wagons packed and were in the saddle ready to leave when he received his orders." The observant captain believed this meant that there would be no campaign this fall.[21] Todd, who kept a virtual day-by-day accounting of the Sioux Expedition, had been in the field since May 28. An able diarist, he was greatly mistaken, though, when he concluded that this campaign faced derailment.

Captain Todd's matter-of-fact first entry in his diary, a Monday report, was short in length and shorter on drama. "Left the camp near Fort Leavenworth about 11 o'clock. . . . The command is composed of A, H, D, K companies, 6 infantry, and a detachment of recruits of about 100 men commanded by Lt. [William P.] Carlin destined for Fort Laramie." Todd commanded Company A, Sixth Infantry. The column arrived at Oak Grove, Kansas, to camp about 6 P.M. "The march was quite fatiguing, the day hot. . . . Distance, 15 miles."[22]

By 1855, overland journeys along the Oregon Route had become rather routine, even monotonous, especially for those with any measurable experience or for those traveling in large, safe military convoys. Brevet 2nd Lt. John P. Hawkins recalled that it took nine days to go from Fort Leavenworth to Fort Kearny, "The road . . . was as plainly marked as any road between two well settled towns in our country." Furthermore, the residents of Fort Kearny did not even use the term Oregon Trail, which was more a well-beaten road than a "trail."[23]

For organized travelers, such as an army column, just setting up camp became a drill of sorts. A dragoon officer of an earlier year detailed the process, one probably adhered to in 1855, especially by mounted troops: After a site was selected, the men dismounted, unsaddled their horses, and took them to grass, where they were picketed. Where their saddles lay was where the company lines of tents were pitched. Company wagons halted by these lines and were unloaded. Then the enlisted men took the appropriate tools and supplies and broke into three groups. Simultaneously, a third pitched tents, another third gathered fuel for the fires, and the last third started preparing the evening meal. The noise! Tent pins pounded in the ground, trees chopped up, pots and pans clanged together, horses neighing and mules braying, only the night's last bugle call inevitably brought silence within the camp.[24]

Day two with the overland force was more interesting but less encouraging. Todd noted it as a lost day, one devoted to rearranging and repacking wagons; one recruit died of cholera, and two became sick from the disease. Two of his company deserted.[25]

Nothing serious, though, deterred the column from its march to Fort Kearny. Usually beginning the march by 7 A.M., the men on horseback and foot traveled fifteen to twenty-five miles a day, give or take, before stopping in late afternoon. The army on the march did not observe the Sabbath, in contrast to the civilian freighting firm of Russell, Majors, and Waddell, which moved the government stores. Early on, Todd complimented himself on his marching stamina, which may sound surprising coming from an infantry officer, but, infantry or not, rank accorded him the privilege of riding. Soon tired and footsore, his point made, he took to his horse and left the trudging to the enlisted men.[26]

Of more interest was the wildlife now being encountered. On June 6, Todd saw his first antelope on the journey, but a brush with buffalo in the Blue River valley three days later made a far greater impact, especially in his reporting: "Very exciting sport this, especially when spiced with Indians."[27]

A mid-nineteenth century traveler's first encounter with the great American bison herds often evoked awe, wonder, excitement, and bloodlust, and in this regard, Todd, a self-proclaimed "novice on the plains," proved no exception. After spotting the beasts in the morning, "all was life and animation," and Todd teamed with lieutenants John Mercer and Robert E. Patterson to give chase. They soon experienced the old plains adage, "Where there's buffalo, there's Indians," after becoming aware of the presence of a sizeable party of Indians of unknown affiliation and intent shadowing them. Nothing came from this first brush with the natives, and the three returned unmolested to camp. Undeterred Todd set forth again in the afternoon, Lieutenant Carlin and a Mr. Scott having replaced Patterson.[28] It took a couple of hours for the party to work itself downwind and near the herd. Then commenced the shooting—an eerie foreshadowing to real war three months later—and Todd's breathless prose.

After discharging my long range rifle, we dashed at them, and then began the wildest, maddest, most exciting chase I ever was engaged

in, blind to everything but the prey; I followed up the herd with the
pertinacity of the Slough hound, firing to the right and to the left,
and on with my rifle and then with my revolver, now dashing with
fiery head long speed right into the midst of them, thousands on
either side, then holding up to breathe my horse and using my rifle,
and so I ran for an hour and a half, in a tornado of excitement such
as I have never experienced before. . . . [29]

Todd's wanton firing left four bison disabled and others wounded
but standing. He and his companions had ridden so far from
the column that they had to camp for the night before rejoining
the main body the next morning. His entry, though, revealed
more than another, all-too-common description of the era's
sporting life. Here was the first recorded use on the expedition of a significant new arm, the "long-range rifle."

In addition to the new Sharps breech-loading carbine,
described by its advocates as "light, handy, and efficient, easily
and rapidly loaded," the Sioux Expedition became a veritable
laboratory for the U.S. Army.[30] Chance had chosen the First
Sioux War and its participants to use and suffer from a new
technology in firearms. A suite of inventions and innovations
had come together to create a long-range shoulder arm, the
likes of which had not been seen before on the Plains.

Something as trifling as changing the shape of a lead bullet
produced remarkable results. Preceded by a measure of gun-
powder, round, lead balls, dropped alone down a gun barrel,
had been the ammunition of the U.S. Army since its beginnings. In 1849, Claude Minie, a French army officer, helped
revolutionize a new shape, the conoidal-cylindrical projectile.
It soon became known as the "minie ball." It was beautiful in
its logic. The ball was ever so slightly smaller in diameter than
the gun barrel and concave at its base. When fired, the force
of the blast pushed into the concavity and expanded the diameter

of the soft, lead projectile.[31] Modern ammunition was then combined with another, much older innovation.

The interior of the gun barrel had been physically grooved, or *rifled*, with barely perceptible spirals. As the ball passed, these spirals gave a twist to the projectile. This, in turn, caused the cone-shaped ball to spiral in the air, analogous to the aerodynamics of a modern football pass. When compared to the now obsolete round ball that had been shot from a smooth-bored musket, the result was a dramatic increase in accuracy and range. Increased range required rear sights that could be easily adjustable by hand for different distances. After this modification, and in the lingo of the day, the guns of the Sioux Expedition were said to have been "adapted to long ranges."[32]

Other developments helped speed along this process. Instead of a shot pouch and powder horn, the rifleman of 1855 had paper cartridges stored in their own box. A cartridge consisted of a minie ball and a pre-measured charge of powder, all enclosed in a paper wrapper, which, after being torn and poured down a barrel, itself served as the wadding for the charge. Cartridge boxes had forty slots in which the new ammunition snugly fit. Nor was the shooter encumbered by handling a single percussion cap, the technological successor to the gun-flint. Formerly a cap had to be individually placed on the gun's nipple. The hammer hit the cap, which created a spark that set off the powder charge. To improve this system, Edward Maynard had invented a strip of primers, the serious equivalent of the toy caps that children played with a century later. The percussion caps came embedded in strips that fed one after another onto the nipple, thereby replacing the need to delicately, if not frantically, grab a small cap box and even smaller cap during the heat of battle. Although all these innovations did not come overnight, those soldiers so equipped on the Sioux Expedition still had much to absorb.[33]

General Harney, again exhibiting his penchant for new technology, would order daily target practice—a rarity in the antebellum army regimen—combined with exercises in tactics. Some individuals would need no encouragement. Captain Todd, along with Lt. John Buford and Capt. Alfred Pleasonton, would continue to conduct their buffalo hunting with the new arm.[34] In a few years, on eastern battlefields, long-range rifles, minie balls, and the devastating effects of modern firepower would be anything but novel to these commanders.

On June 12, the overland force hit the Platte River, once described by Washington Irving as "the most beautiful and useless of rivers." Summed up Todd, his buffalo hunting adventures notwithstanding, "The march has been very trying and monotonous over an exceedingly uninteresting country, and we were very glad to see the river." The next day the men reached their initial destination, Fort Kearny, "a dreary looking place," which did nothing to ease anyone's weariness.[35]

Thousands of individuals had passed by Fort Kearny since its establishment in 1848, and Todd's 1855 description joined a history of unflattering comments. Of course, his was the critical eye of an army officer.

It is situated on a low level plain about 2 miles from the Platte and the same distance from the Sandhills and is an open work. Comg [Commanding] officers quarters and hospital on one side, a block of officers quarters on the right calculated for four and with the most miserable arrangements either for comfort or convenience being upstairs and down stairs for each two. On the third side is one block of Company quarters and on the fourth a guard house and sod store rooms. The quarters for the laundresses are built of adobes and sod; so are the stables. Take it altogether it is the most undesirable place I have ever seen in the army.[36]

Yet, Fort Kearny figured prominently that summer as a supply depot and probably would during the winter as a shelter for an enlarged garrison. Its commander, as had those at other posts, received word to lay up large stores of fuel and forage. Also, consistent with other orders, General Harney still desired "the most reliable information concerning the movements of every doubtful or hostile band or tribe of Indians. . . ." And with this came the usual restrictions against "hostile movements" by the troops. "This injunction is made," wrote Harney, "with the view to avoiding, as much as possible, all partial and disconnected operations. . . ."[37]

That no "disconnected operations" ever occurred speak well not only of compliant subordinates, but also of the relative ease and rapidity of communication. For instance, Fort Kearny had enjoyed an eagerly awaited monthly mail—"letters from home and piles of newspapers"—from Missouri for years, though one resident recalled, "What we read was always "news" to us, but in reality was "staleness."[38] Maybe that was true for 1913 when that reminiscence was published, but in 1855 the news was anything but stale.

On May 30, the column, barely away from Fort Leavenworth, had met the mail from Fort Laramie and learned from the carrier that the mail party that had left Fort Leavenworth on May 1 for Salt Lake had been "cut off" and that the Indians were "robbing the emigrants of their stock in the neighborhood of Ash Hollow. . . ." Accuracy of the news, not its freshness, may have been the element in short supply since these reports went unconfirmed. Interestingly Ash Hollow continued to emerge as a location of potential danger.[39]

A few days later the column met two military men on their way to Fort Leavenworth, who commented on this trail news; the two willingly took letters from their fellow officers back east. Soon thereafter the mail carrier to Salt Lake City appeared. Later this mail party, together with David A. Burr, the new surveyor general of Utah Territory, and two officers' wives, received a military escort of twenty men to Fort Laramie. On June 18, the escort met the downward mail at O'Fallon's Bluff, an overland trail landmark west of present North Platte, Nebraska. That mail party also boasted a military escort with no less a person than Major Hoffman among its members, the officer apparently anxious to welcome his wife, one of the two women heading west. Each escort then turned back.[40] The 1855 trail season bustled with military traffic, both in people and messages.

Harney was doing his duty in reporting this activity in a timely manner. On June 2, he relayed these facts: Four companies of Sixth Infantry (one of them Todd's) were en route to Fort Kearny. One of these would escort the supply train to Fort Laramie and the recruits sent to supplement the garrison. Two more companies of Sixth Infantry remained at Fort Riley. Two companies of Second Infantry were at Fort Leavenworth awaiting four more companies of their regiment, still east of the Mississippi. He had gathered stores sufficient for fifteen hundred men to subsist for a year. All that remained before he could "commence active operations" were more mounted troops besides the four dragoon companies sent on patrol, and Harney offered a partial solution. He sent Lieutenant Balch to inspect and repair the Fourth Artillery's "prairie battery," but "[s]hould it prove irreparable, I propose to incorporate the company, temporarily, with the mounted force of my command, as I shall be in great want of that species of troops."[41] Balch later reported the cannon carriages indeed irreparable, and the make-do transformation of this company from artillery to cavalry soon came to pass, although the change may have been mostly cosmetic.[42] Most of its horses arrived only just before its eventual departure from Fort Leavenworth for the Plains; the company trained only twice in "fighting on foot" before it indeed saw fighting.[43]

On June 14, Harney sent an update to the New York headquarters. The four companies of the Second Infantry had arrived in St. Louis the previous day. Company G, Fourth Artillery, would exchange their cannon for "the long ranged rifle and colts belt pistol." Minor communication problems had crept in between Harney and Cooke, but these were blamed on "blunders made by the telegraph lines," which had also "caused some embarrassment in the assignment of Medical Officers, which was intended to be made according to the rule and rank and importance of positions. . . ." To sum up: "With these exceptions, however, everything has gone on as favorably as could be expected, and indeed nothing but a most unusually backward season could have prevented nearly all of the troops now at my disposal from having got into position by this time."[44]

Still, Harney believed he lacked sufficient mounted troops, his anxiety exacerbated by the realization that the remainder of the regiment of Second Dragoons "cannot possibly reach Fort Riley before the first of August, and probably will not before a much later date. . . ." His solution was to push into the field any detachments of the new cavalry regiments "as fast as they can be organized."[45] But time ran out on Harney's cavalry reinforcements. They never arrived, and he would make do with substitutes. The time neared, though, to take to the field himself.

* * *

The Fourth of July was exceptionally dull at Fort Kearny. Complained Captain Todd, "Nothing to remind us of the day but a salute at noon, and that so awkwardly and lazily done as to admit of a gentle nap between the intervals."[46] Two days later three officers arrived from Fort Laramie with no real news to ease the boredom. The quiet was expected since "Col. Cook[e] with four companies of Dragoons was passing up and down the road." Fortunately the eastern mail arrived on July 9, bringing with it five letters from Todd's wife Kate, "the first I have had since the week preceding my departure from Fort Leavenworth." Periodically Todd shook himself from his lethargy with nearby buffalo hunts, although the same effect may have resulted if he had known that General Harney and staff had already departed St. Louis.[47] The local press noted this as the official commencement of, as it was termed, the "Sioux expedition."[48]

Now the pace picked up. On July 12, Harney boarded the steamboat *Cataract*, bound for Fort Leavenworth. Joining him were officers Timothy Andrews, George Balch, Henry Heth, Edward McKeever Hudson (a first lieutenant in the Fourth Artillery), Stewart Van Vliet, and Oscar Winship. From Fort Leavenworth on July 24, Harney ordered Major Cady to prepare his four infantry companies "to take the field at a moment's warning." Cady needed to gather two months' supply of subsistence stores, besides "proportionate" medical supplies, the latter the charge of Assistant Surgeon Aquila Ridgely, the lone medical officer with this command. Cady could expect the general in person by mid-August. This order reached Cady on July 31 by express and soon became common knowledge. Also, the overland force learned the latest from points west. On July 24, Cooke and two dragoon companies returned, having patrolled all the way to Fort Laramie. They brought news that "the Sioux are quarrelling among themselves, and are more likely to have a flare-up between their own bands than to unite against us." No matter because, belligerent or not, Harney left for Sioux country on August 4 with the intention "to attack any body of hostile Indians which I can overtake or may chance to encounter. . . ."[49]

Harney's grand strategy for the Sioux Expedition was set. I hope I shall be able to embrace the country lying between the White Earth river and the Black Hills, in which region I have but little doubt will be found those Indians who have determined to make a stand against our troops. . . .I propose to send a column of infantry from some point on the Platte between Ash Hollow and Fort Laramie, across to the White river to join a junction with another column of infantry from Fort Pierre. A small mounted force will be attached to these columns, whilst the main body of the cavalry, with three companies of infantry from Fort Laramie will be directed to penetrate the Black Hills in the direction of the North Fork of the Cheyenne. The infantry columns on the White river after having formed a junction will move in one body toward the South Fork of the Cheyenne, and concentrically toward the column in the Black Hills. . . .I hope to force the Indians to the alternative of giving battle, or of deserting their families just at the opening of winter, when the latter, of necessity would be obliged to surrender themselves or incur the risk of starving. [50]

For once, Harney allowed his superiors the opportunity to contemplate victory. He confidently requested "the terms upon which the hostile Sioux can have peace if they desire it, after having been well chastised."

Harney had over two weeks to mull over his strategy because he arrived at Fort Kearny on August 20, after an uneventful trip only marred by rainy weather. With him was the newly mounted Fourth Artillery company. Riding along was Captain Heth's newly formed Company E, Tenth Infantry, also transformed by Harney into a cavalry unit using "fine, good-sized" ponies purchased from the Sac and Fox tribes in eastern Kansas. Lieutenant Balch, also a member of this group, did little to calm any fears his wife may have had; writing home, he "anticipated meeting no Indians" during the trip between Leavenworth and Kearny, but beyond the latter "we are in the midst of the Indians and from there to Laramie we may expect surprises at any time." He expected no battle with the Indians before they reached Fort Laramie, but just in case, he carried his own

"Minie rifle." Hidden in plain sight in Harney's entourage was an anonymous correspondent to the *Missouri Republican*, probably a civilian gentleman, who reported their arrival at Fort Kearny and subsequent expedition events. They joined two companies of dragoons and five companies of infantry already present, the infantry having been reinforced by one more company from Fort Riley.[51]

On August 22, the command was unexpectedly surprised by the arrival of the party of G. K. Warren, the young lieutenant assigned to Harney's staff as its topographical engineer. And he came from an unexpected quarter, too—overland from Fort Pierre three hundred miles to the north. Completing his duties there, but too late to join Harney at Fort Leavenworth, Warren chose a more dangerous route through unexplored country to catch up with the general at Fort Kearny. Even the *New York Times* took note of the feat.[52] If anything, and judging from his actions that season, this decision reflected Warren's dedicated spirit rather than an impetuous nature.

Details of the trip also revealed his good judgment. It began at noon, August 8, with a party composed of experienced "mountain men," through territory considered "most likely to be infested with Indians."[53] These men were hired by Warren to get him, his assistants, and his scientific instruments through in one piece. Plus, here was more unknown land (at least to an army engineer) to map, unknown, perhaps, but far from uninhabited.

They took the necessary precautions. Two members of the party stood nighttime guard at any one time, two hours each. On August 14, near Turtle Butte, in present Tripp County, southeast South Dakota, Warren saw tracks of two Indians; this was somewhat expected since the day's journey had brought them to a well-known Indian trail near the Niobrara River. More interesting was the party's march through the famed

Sand Hills of Nebraska, which began in earnest on August 16, a geographic feature described as "generally very uneven, the rolls being quite steep and about 10 to 40 feet high." From the perspective of a road-builder, Warren's impression of this region as a possible route for a transcontinental railroad must have been negative.[54]

After arriving at Fort Kearny and reporting to Harney on August 22, to the latter's great delight since here was another source of Indian intelligence, Warren slept comfortably that night "in security without any guard."[55] He joined Captain Todd as a discreet, daily chronicler of the Sioux Expedition, somewhat less interested in hunting than Todd, equally lacking in any grandiose reflections on a war with Indians, and similarly invaluable in leaving moving accounts of the approaching, dramatic events in September.

* * *

Lieutenant Warren made it to Fort Kearny with little time to spare. After an unexplained delay of a day, Harney's expedition set forth from Fort Kearny on August 24, 1855.[56] He led about six hundred troops: The mounted force consisted of Companies E and K, Second Dragoons; Light Company G, Fourth Artillery; and Company E, Tenth Infantry. The men on foot came from Companies A, E, H, I, and K, Sixth Infantry. A detachment of "Ordnance men" followed Lieutenant Balch, as did a hospital steward and attendants for Dr. Ridgely; a party of civilians continued in the service of Warren. The lame and the halt were left to guard the fort. Figuratively, Harney left blind because he had no good idea where to find the Sioux. Warren suggested that the Brulés could be found in the Sand Hills, southeast of the Niobrara River, an area that encompassed several thousand square miles. Harney sought to improve his chances of a collision by ordering five companies of the Fort Pierre garrison to move west along the White River, "with a view of striking a decisive blow against any one of the hostile bands of Sioux which it may be found possible and expedient to attack."[57] And it was clear within the ranks why they fought, "to punish the Sioux for their various depredations committed for years against our people, but especially for the Massacre of Lt. Grattan and party in August 1854 and the party of the Great Salt Lake Mail in the following November."[58]

The only element Harney lacked, and he made sure to inform his superiors, was an auxiliary force of guides and hunters from "the friendly Indians." He mixed disappointment with blame for the Indian Office. "They have been led to believe that by going with the Expedition they will forfeit their annuities and claims."[59] Harney was prepared to hire twenty Sacs and Foxes and give them a dollar a day in wages (which was more than double an enlisted man's pay), a ration of food, and arms and ammunition. Furthermore, "I will allow as many others to accompany the Expedition as may desire so to do, and I will feed them when they cannot supply themselves, provided they will furnish the troops with meat when they get among the buffalo."[60] The offer was to no avail, as was a recruiting visit by Captain Heth to the Delaware, Pottawatomie, and Shawnee tribes in Kansas. Again, Harney suspected a "secret influence" exerted by the Indian Office and blamed the commissioner of Indian affairs. "Colonel Manypenny and his party (for he is recognized here as having a party) are and have been openly hostile to the measures of the Government relative to the Expedition placed under my command."[61] Harney made his point and remembered this affront, but he never got his Indian allies for the Sioux Expedition.

Between August 24 and September 2, though, all was routine. The men lived by the bugle calls. Reveille probably sounded at 4 A.M., with all horses and mules taken to fresh grazing. At five o'clock a fatigue party began striking the tents and loading the wagons of Harney and his staff. Likewise, the striking of the whole camp began at the sound of "The General." At 6:00, the animals were taken to water, after which civilian teamsters harnessed their draft animals with assistance from soldiers. "Boots and Saddles" came at 6:30 A.M. Sometime in all this flurry of activity, the men ate their breakfast.[62]

     During these nine days the average daily march was about eighteen miles, with eleven the shortest and twenty-three the longest. Todd and Warren noted the distances in their journals, usually with some minor variance. Engineer Warren had an advantage since he had an odometer in his possession.[63]

     For Corp. Eugene Bandel, a Sixth infantryman, the march on the plains was far from routine. A Prussian native who had immigrated to the United States in 1853, Bandel had failed to find work as a locksmith and joined the army the following year. He recounted to his parents back in the old country: "How strange it seemed to me on the very first evening after we left Kearny, when we stopped to make camp for the night, that not the least bit of wood could be seen for miles, although we were on the Platte river. But how much more surprised I was when the company received orders to gather up the dry dung of the buffalo, which lay about on the ground everywhere; and this, indeed, was our only fuel for months, for the general as well as for the private." An earlier military observer noted "a dozen men with horse-blankets soon collect a sufficient quantity for the use of a company for the night." Regarding the gathering this night, Bandel was an observer only; his rank of corporal kept him from this duty.[64]

     The ubiquitous buffalo also provided food for the companies' mess.[65] Lieutenant Balch, turning the tables on Lieutenant Warren, privately noted the latter's campground etiquette with some bemusement. "[Warren] lives in the most primitive style with some half dozen halfbreeds and voyageurs about him. His table furniture consists of three plates, a small butcher knife, and a tin cup. He whittles out a stick for a fork and has his table laid on the ground." Balch envied the hunting prowess and culinary arts of Warren's companions. "As long as we were in the buffalo country, his cart was constantly loaded with fresh meat, and his men cooked it in twenty different forms."[66]

Other than that, the expedition paused on the morning of August 31, the last day of the month, to be mustered for their pay, which gave Lt. Colonel Andrews, the rather invisible paymaster, something of importance to do during the expedition. The artillery company, cannon or no, argued for precedence in the line of march. Harney suffered from a mild bout of diarrhea, brought on, Lieutenant Warren feared, by the wild plums he had given the general; others suffered the same ailment, and Warren's act was overlooked.[67] Letter writers took the opportunity to send reports east by an express carrier just setting off. Lieutenant Balch advised his wife to look at the map that accompanied their copy of Capt. Howard Stansbury's report. "[Y]ou will see the whole road laid down from Leavenworth to Laramie, and you can trace my course exactly."[68] The anonymous newspaper correspondent, the luster already off the campaign, took advantage to vent his disgust at the country, the nearly dry Platte River, in particular, a "humbug." "From one hundred miles east of Fort Kearny to the foot of the Rocky Mountains, the land is entirely unproductive and uninhabited. It belongs to the Buffalo and the wild Indian, and should be given up to them entirely. No white man has any business here. . . ."[69]

And these incidents all came before a violent thunderstorm and its dangerously close lightning strikes; one horse was hit and killed.[70]

By this time, the command had reached the South Platte River, along which the overland trail continued on its south side. On September 2, the soldiers marched six miles along the South Platte before reaching a well-used river crossing. Here at the upper ford, the river was about a mile wide and not much more than the proverbial foot deep. After fording, the soldiers continued overland another eighteen fatiguing miles to the north fork of the Platte. The march took its toll. At a minimum, each enlisted man on foot carried a rifle, a cartridge box containing forty cartridges, a haversack with a day's rations, and a canteen. His heavy wool uniform only added to his burden and misery, although to the discerning eye, the dress of the soldiers looked different than earlier expeditions. The single-breasted, dark blue frock coat sported nine eagle buttons down the front. Piping around the collar and cuffs displayed the branch colors; in Bandel's case, the new "sky-blue." Adding to his burden, he could now wear brass shoulder scales on his coat, formerly the sole prerogative of the mounted troops. Maybe Bandel had been fortunate to substitute a more functional hat for his regulation "tar bucket" with pompom and eagle insignia. He needed to, because the day was extremely hot, as only a Nebraska September day can be; there was no water between the South and North Platte, and several horses gave out.[71]

"And so we reached Ash Hollow," wrote Corporal Bandel. The time was 4 P.M on Sunday.[72] On the next day Bandel's real work would commence because General Harney had found his Indians.

Chapter 4
Upriver

Although a glance at any map may indicate differently, 1,525 miles separated St. Louis, Missouri, and Fort Pierre, Nebraska Territory, or so the U.S. Army calculated. This distance was by river, specifically by Missouri River steamer. And it was by this route and by this conveyance that General Harney would send the other half of his great army into Sioux country.[1]

On June 7, 1855, at 5:45 P.M. the steamer *Clara* departed from St. Louis. On board was 2nd Lt. G. K. Warren, Topographical Engineers, en route initially for Fort Leavenworth, a stopover which knocked off over four hundred miles of the total journey. Also on their way west were over three hundred fifty troops of the Second U.S. Infantry, plus another ninety-six recruits. The regiment had been stationed previously at faraway Carlisle Barracks, in eastern Pennsylvania, and had ridden the rails to Alton, Illinois, on the Mississippi River. Only the day before, June 6, under the watchful eye of Harney himself, the troops boarded four awaiting government boats, *Arabia*, *Australia*, *Grey Cloud*, and *William Baird* at Alton. The *Grey Cloud* and *William Baird* may have been the general's pride, the shallow draft steamers that he had desired solely for the Sioux Expedition. Only the month before, he had dispatched Capt. Edmund A. Ogden, an assistant quartermaster and his purchasing agent, to Cincinnati, Ohio, and Pittsburgh, Pennsylvania, to scour the boatyards for steamboats; apparently the officer, whose other demands involved the continued building expansion of Fort Riley, Kansas, succeeded. The transports had to hold these Second infantrymen, their comrades already at Fort Leavenworth, and their quartermaster, subsistence, and ordnance stores, as well as the regimental band, all intended for Fort Pierre. All told, the gathering and rapid deployment of a large body of troops from an eastern station to a western staging area was a logistical triumph for General Harney and his staff, who left nothing to chance. They had used a flurry of telegrams to aid, abet, monitor, and prod along the force as it worked its way across the Midwest and now up the Missouri.[2]

Almost before the "armada" could lose sight of St. Louis, Harney's headquarters telegraphed ahead to the commanding officer of Fort Leavenworth of its departure. Another message ordered Maj. William R. Montgomery, commanding the two companies of Second Infantry already at the post, to gather enough clothing and camp equipment to outfit six companies for one year at Pierre.[3]

After the first full day's travel, Lieutenant Warren noted that his boat had made "a fine run," but was disappointed in not making "so much distance as was expected," due to "a considerable rise and much drift wood." Unlike his later diary entries on the Plains, Warren gave no consistent daily mileage on his progress.[4] That the experience would fail to inspire a journalist is not surprising. This was the heyday of Missouri River travel—cheap, commodious, and convenient—at least until the appearance of the superior railroad. Another Missouri River traveler of the era could not overcome the same writer's block when he commented on his "modern" steamboat trip aboard the *Cataract*. "Saving the occasional bursting of boilers, running foul of a snag, or some such casualty—which I have but seldom had an opportunity of witnessing—a trip of five hundred miles will scarcely furnish material for a paragraph."[5]

Unfortunately, the 1855 movement of troops upriver suffered one such "casualty." Only three days into the journey, near Glasgow, Missouri, the side-wheeler *Australia* struck a log snag and sank almost immediately, the water reaching a depth of one foot over its main deck. The men—and boys— of Company D and their baggage were taken off safely by *Arabia*, but not before virtually all of its public stores were lost. Among the losses were ninety-two boxes of ordnance stores, all of which Harney wasted no time in ordering replaced, as well as another boat, *Kate Sweeney*. Blame for the mishap was assigned immediately to the boat's pilot, who had only gotten his license, and to its owners, who had not only chosen the inexperienced helmsman, but also were rumored to have insured the boat and its cargo for more than their worth. No record has turned up whether the incident resulted in a government vs. contractor flap, but curiously, the *Australia* was later raised only to fall prey to an 1858 dockside fire at St. Louis.[6]

One of the survivors of the sinking was Augustus Meyers, age thirteen. With his mother's consent, Meyers, a native of New York City, had enlisted in 1854 for five years. He joined other boys in the one job the regular army offered poverty-struck boys of his age—he played in the band. His instrument was the flute, his musical and martial training at the depot for recruits on Governor's Island, New York. Eventually assigned to the Second Infantry, he had traveled with his comrades from Carlisle, Pennsylvania, to this unexpected stop in Missouri. The event definitely made an impact on Meyers, as evident by its prominence in his recollection. Over half a century later, he could still recall the dramatic cries of "Snag! Snag!" and the shrieks of the steam whistle. "We watched the final struggles of the boat filled with the fear that she might break in two. Then with a huge straining and a terrifying tremor she settled on the bed of the river." Meyers may have been inspired by later events; his reminiscence was published two years after the sinking of the ocean liner, *Titanic*.[7]

The stranded soon transferred to other boats in order to continue their cruise. Meyers, Warren, and the rest straggled to the Leavenworth landing on June 13 and 14, the remainder of this leg of the journey relatively uneventful.[8] The inhabitants of such river towns as Lexington, Kansas City, Westport, and Weston took no exceptional notice of the expedition. The people of these "jumping off places" were apparently jaded at the sight of large groups of passersby.

However, the contingent itself did little to stimulate public interest and wasted no time in proceeding upriver. On June 15, Warren's account again picked up the journey, and for the next month he recorded from the deck of the *Clara* the tortured nature of steamboat travel on the Upper Missouri. There was nothing routine involved. During this time of seasonal low water, the boats were forced to play an exhausting game of against-the-current leapfrog. Each, it seemed, took turns at running aground in the shallow stream, falling behind, working itself off, and inevitably passing an unlucky sister in similar straits. Even so, on those occasions when the boat was actually moving forward it made a respectable four to six miles per hour.[9]

Warren, the civil engineer, admired appreciatively the ingenuity of the steamboat crews to negotiate the "exceedingly crooked" river. For example, "It was found that a slight change which had been made in the loading of the *Clara* had vastly improved her steering, and she was now properly under the control of her pilots."[10] Other concerns, most of which were not faced by the wagon column following the Platte River, included strong head winds, sickness among the passengers, and the constant need for large quantities of wood as fuel. Considering the dearth of forests on the eastern edge of the

Great Plains, the latter required the most forethought and assistance by suppliers on the shore.[11]

The trip north passed several cultural and natural landmarks of present Kansas, Missouri, Iowa, and Nebraska. During a stop in Omaha, the army contracted with George Miller, a civilian doctor, to accompany the expedition and boost the ranks of its medical officers. Miller's services proved valuable in fighting an outbreak of scurvy among the enlisted men.[12] This portion of the journey, though, elicited little from Warren, who only noted the towns of St. Joseph, Missouri, and Council Bluffs, Iowa, and the mouths of such rivers as the Platte, Little Sioux, Big Sioux, and James. On June 28, pausing at Bon Homme Island, though, Warren's scientific and historical curiosity became aroused: "Examined one of the fortifications mentioned by Lewis and Clarke [sic] on B.H. Island and think along with most of the Gentlemen of the party that they were most likely formed by the water and wind."[13]

But few such intellectual distractions presented themselves. On July 1 and 2, and back to the daily grind, *Clara* had to be unloaded and lightened in order for it to draw no more than four feet of water. Of course, once across the sandbar, the boat had to be loaded again. Little wonder that two days later the men observed a "dull Fourth." One incident, though, did spice up the grueling journey. The *Kate Sweeney* crew had forgotten a passenger on an island, discovered their mistake, and sent back a relief party, which found the bewildered man near where he had been left; he was wearing a hat and nothing else when they retrieved him.[14]

The same day that this occurred, July 7, *Arabia* arrived at Fort Pierre, the first of the flotilla to reach its destination. Five days later *Grey Cloud* and *William Baird* followed. *Clara* and *Kate Sweeney* limped in later in the month after crawling over one punishing sandbar after another. Major Montgomery, the senior officer, took command of the post, but it was a skeleton garrison. As of July 20, only companies A and I were actually present. Most soldiers were guarding government stores scattered along the Missouri River for miles downstream, each pile of property a marker to the farthest point that the four boats, minus the successful *Arabia*, could reach loaded.[15]

* * *

Although Harney's instructions to the Second Infantry commander had mentioned "securing the public stores and getting the garrison under cover" as his first steps, the general was more concerned about securing intelligence about the Indians, while the command readied itself to go into the field "at a moment's warning." The initial confusion at Fort Pierre, though, reduced the likelihood that any of this might happen.[16]

Thomas W. Sweeny, a lieutenant with considerable experience in the Second Infantry and one of the first arrivals, wrote home of these first few days in garrison: "[T]aking into consideration the halt, lame and blind, with those we had to leave behind for the protection of our property, we could raise about one hundred fighting men to repel any attack the Indians might make upon us."[17]

The laggard *Genoa* and its passenger, the boy musician Meyers, would not reach Pierre until August 19. But the work could not wait for him, his Company D, or the guard detachments along the river.[18] Self-protection hurried the men along in their duties. Wrote Lieutenant Sweeny, "We have been very busy since our arrival, unloading the boats and getting the property inside the Fort, a rude picketing from 12 to 15 feet high, and about 300 feet square." Sweeny repeated stories that five thousand Indians were nearby, readying for an attack on the supplies, which, if successful, "certainly would break up this Expedition for this year by all events."[19] The Indian scare proved an outlandish rumor.

When Lieutenant Warren arrived on July 16, he found "every body busy, every thing in confusion." This state of confusion soon passed, especially when the young engineer began his assignment—examining the old fort and laying out a new one.[20] The "state" of Fort Pierre, though, became the more significant and immediate problem. What on earth had the government's $45,000 bought?

The fur-trading establishment of Pierre Chouteau and Company at the mouth of Bad River had been touted originally as perfectly suitable for a military post and supply depot. Its quarter century of operation indicated that its location at the mouth of Bad River had been a wise and strategic decision, at least to mercantile interests.[21]

But troubled voices rose among the ranks. Quartermaster David H. Vinton of the Department of the West, St. Louis, had reported bluntly to his Washington superior in March 1855 on the fort's faults: "Fort Pierre is unfitted for a depot of supplies for any considerable body of troops in its immediate vicinity." Vinton's reasons were daunting: The fort could accommodate the personnel "requisite for a depot," but not the animals of a mounted force. Not only were there insufficient facilities to handle animals and their feed, but forage in the area was inadequate. Vinton learned that a nearby island possessed the immediate area's only arable land (a parcel that General Harney made sure Lieutenant Warren included in the Fort Pierre military reservation). Other shortcomings: "Fuel for consumption . . . cannot be had at a less distance than twenty miles. The customary manner of procuring it in considerable quantities, is to send chopping parties above and raft it down to the place of deposit. . . ."[22]

Corn could be purchased for sixty cents a bushel, "but to carry it to the depot, a boat of extreme light draft must be

used." So Harney bought two boats. Others of Quartermaster
Vinton's words also came to pass, including "several boats will
be required to convey all the stores necessary to supply the
troops, cavalry as well as infantry, ordered there. . . ." Coming
as it did in the early days of strategic planning, his report in
some ways became Harney's job checklist for the Fort Pierre
wing of the Sioux Expedition.[23]

Fort Pierre's shortcomings did little, if anything, to derail
the negotiations. Even Vinton had to concede that "there is
no other place on the Missouri more eligible in view of the
communications to be kept up with Fort Laramie. . . ." The
property included "all the buildings within the enclosure,
around the fort, on the main-land [sic] and the island in the
vicinity." Among the structures were a formidable gate; blacksmith, carpenter, saddler, and tinsmith shops; stable; adobe
powder magazine; two blockhouses; icehouse; sawmill; stable;
and miscellaneous log houses and huts. The sale went through
on April 14, with the approval of Secretary of War Jefferson
Davis. After the soldiers arrived in July and could inspect the
premises for themselves, the buyer made some attempts to
get the seller to make repairs. Ongoing negotiations, though,
could not delay the onset of winter and the critical need for
more shelter.[24]

The army quartermasters had come up with a novel
solution, a mid-nineteenth century version of prefabricated
housing. "Portable cottages" for army use, the brainchild of
Capt. Parmenus T. Turnley of the Quartermaster Department,
were originally intended for units stationed in Texas and designed
for a more southerly, milder climate. In March 1855, a Cincinnati
contractor completed Turnley's order of thirty-seven structures,
an assortment of enlisted men's barracks, officers' quarters, storehouses, and hospital; and the unassembled pieces arrived in
St. Louis in early June. This schedule coincided perfectly with

Harney's schedule and with the needs of the Fort Pierre
garrison. The Quartermaster Department had already expressed
concern about lack of floor space at the post. Here it was in
the form of "knocked-down houses," ready for shipment and
assembly upriver.[25]

Turnley had advocated such housing for some time.
Although an advocate of new military innovations, Harney
had his qualms, but no time for a substitute. In May, Captain
Winship informed Turnley, who was in Cincinnati keeping an
eye on his progeny, that he need not send a sample cottage
for Harney's inspection. "[I]t is already determined by the War
Department to furnish them for Fort Pierre. . . ."[26] Turnley's
oversight of the project continued, and Harney subsequently
had him assigned as the assistant quartermaster for Fort Pierre.
In late July, as part of his surveying duties, G. K. Warren "laid
out the positions of Capt. Townley's [sic] new houses," although
it was some weeks before they could be erected. If the young
lieutenant had any reservations, he did not express them in
his diary, maybe because he had no intention of spending the
winter in Dakota. Others who did, vividly remembered the
cottages' thin pine board walls, the surfaces painted inside
and out in bright red, and the harsh winter of 1855–1856
which could not be kept out of the "cardboard houses." Lieutenant Sweeny was only half-kidding when he wrote, "I expect
we will all be frozen to death here next winter."[27]

The Fort Pierre garrison had more than food, feed, and
shelter to worry about. Its mission was to bring the war to the
Sioux, and operations must commence "at a moment's warning"
before this season had ended. On August 21 and in the field
himself, Harney sent such orders to Fort Pierre's commanding
officer. "[M]ove with five companies of the garrison of your
post . . . in the direction, and on the usual travelled route to
Fort Laramie, continuing thus your march, until you meet the

troops to be sent from the Platte. . . .With regard to the
Indian bands which you may chance to encounter, . . . they are
all more or less hostile, and could safely be treated as enemies.
The only exception to this remark would probably be found in
the band of Yanktons, who have ever been reported as friendly
to the Whites. . . ."[28]

With this exception, "attack them vigorously when the
opportunity for a decisive blow offers, secure if possible their
families, and capture their animals." Harney reiterated, though,
that the "main object of your movement . . . is to concentrate
the troops of the expedition as soon as possible," in other
words, join the two together.[29] Of course, these orders, issued
in August, needed to be carried hundreds of miles and resulted
in no immediate action.

Even though an express mail was now set up between
Fort Pierre and "civilization" (namely Sioux City, Iowa, on the
Missouri River), timely news still came to Harney through
indirect means. As of August 3, he still had no "official information" on the Second Infantry's arrival at the fort, but had learned
otherwise a week earlier, courtesy of the *St. Mary*, an American
Fur Company steamboat that had passed downriver by the
regiment and passed on its news at Fort Leavenworth. Harney's
order, though, did not reach the post until early September.[30]

Nevertheless, the second overland column, five of six
infantry companies present, set forth on September 16 on the
trail between Fort Pierre and Fort Laramie, its purpose, Harney
explained to his superiors, to "meet me on the White Earth
river, with a view of striking a decisive blow against any one of
the hostile bands of Sioux. . . ." Countered an anonymous correspondent from Fort Pierre, "The search for Sioux Indians
seems to be going on, and mayhap they will be found, if cold
and starvation don't overtake the troops and their animals."[31]
With another army command in the field, the second shoe of
the Sioux Expedition had dropped.

Chapter 5
Since Killing the Soldiers

After the Grattan fight, where did the Indians go and what did they do? These questions vexed U.S. Army officers, who had no way of knowing the outcome of the First Sioux War, and have largely been ignored by later scholars, who did know. The scholarly consensus was that the bulk of the Sioux left the North Platte valley and adjourned to their northern wintering grounds to hunt and reflect on the Fort Laramie disaster. Exactly where this might have been—near the Missouri River, within or about the Black Hills, or in the Powder River region—remained a guess for those few who gave it a thought.[1] In the defense of historians, the documentary evidence was rather slim. During the winter of 1854–1855, good evidence also remained elusive to the military.

Capt. Oscar Winship, arriving at Fort Laramie shortly after the Lakota exodus in August and himself departing for the East in early September 1854, found an Oglala camp of thirty lodges near the South Platte crossing (near present Big Springs, Nebraska). Big Road, the camp leader, and his people were friendly but understandably cool and reserved. Winship concluded that the Brulés had returned to the White River area and the Miniconjous, the bulk of whom had had no role in the massacre, remained farther north. He thought the traditional wintering grounds for each was: Oglala on both forks of the Platte; Brulé on the North Platte, Niobrara, and White rivers; and Miniconjou farther north on the Cheyenne River.[2]

Maj. William Hoffman, Fort Laramie's capable commanding officer that winter, reduced this vast haystack when he reported a thousand lodges of Brulés, Miniconjous, and other Lakota bands along the Niobrara in present northern Nebraska. Although he soon recanted this inflated estimate, he did refine the information forwarded to his superiors, much of it coming from Indian traders. The Brulés numbered two hundred lodges and the Wazhazhas of Conquering Bear, seventy-five, the latter group "made up of murderers and outlaws from other bands of Sioux." Their wintering place was thought to be within the Sand Hills bounded by the aforementioned Niobrara, North Platte, and White rivers. The Miniconjous, also considered hostile, had two hundred seventy-five lodges, and, with an estimated three warriors per lodge, constituted a formidable force in their own right. The two hundred thirty lodges of the Oglalas, though, were already distancing themselves, literally and figuratively, from their Brulé kinsmen.[3]

In November 1854, the Oglala chiefs sent a message to Hoffman to plead their case. They professed having taken no major part in the Grattan fight, blamed the Brulés for the entire affair, and endeavored to keep their young men from joining those bent on revenge. After the Grattan fight the Oglalas had moved to the forks of the Cheyenne River, where the Miniconjous had talked to them of war. To illustrate their desires for peace, the Oglalas had separated and moved west to the Powder River, where the tribe intended to winter and presumably avoid future hostilities. Hoffman cautiously endorsed such professions of peace. Oglala diplomatic efforts, independent of the Brulés, would continue throughout 1855.[4] More successful than not, they undoubtedly attested to the deft hand of Man Afraid of His Horses, the highest ranking Oglala leader.

The next month, Hoffman witnessed similar efforts by the Brulés, but he was less receptive. A deputation of Brulé leaders and warriors ventured to Bordeaux's nearby trading post to council. Hoffman refused their overtures of peace and did not meet with them, but accepted and passed on the written statements taken down by Seth Ward, a white trader. The Lakotas, Hoffman believed, were willing to surrender the murderers of the mail party; the wiping out of Lieutenant Grattan's command, though, was seen—wishfully by the Brulés— as "an act of self defence for which they will not be held accountable."[5]

Major Hoffman's casual brush-off did not reflect the careful deliberateness that must have preceded the Brulé offer. Their penned entreaty to Hoffman could only hint at the process.

"Before leaving the village we had a general council of all the Brulés after they had assembled. I (the Little Thunder) asked them what were their feelings towards the whites. The old chiefs answered that they had nothing to say." The old chiefs did indicate, though, that they depended on Big Partisan, Black White Bird, Eagle Body, Iron Shell, and Little Thunder "to do everything with the whites that was good for their nation." The five intended to go to Fort Laramie "to see our Father and see if he would not take pity on us as it was our wish to live and have peace if possible and whatever he told us to do we would listen to." However, the next day when they reached the site "where we had killed the soldiers our hearts entirely failed us. . . ."[6] Hence, the message was sent from the relative safety of Bordeaux's. Noticeably absent from the list was the name of Conquering Bear, dead from his wounds six days after receiving them, his body at rest on a scaffold along the Niobrara.[7]

One Indian name, however, stood out. Little Thunder had been conspicuous by his presence at the Grattan fight and continued to remain so. Even his physical presence commanded attention. He stood taller than nearly everyone, white or Indian, at an estimated six feet six inches. Such an imposing figure, and a reputation as a warmonger unfairly forced upon him in the ensuing months, seemed at odds with the words of peace he spoke.[8] Continued Little Thunder, "Again we hope you will take pity on us as we think it hard that our nation should suffer for what five has [sic] done."[9]

Unfortunately the deeds of the "five" were fresh, and Little Thunder's details of their killings that follow—a rare Indian account, hearsay as it is, of the November 13 attack on the U.S. Mail party—did nothing to erase the anger of the Americans, themselves now bent on revenge.

After the Bear died, Mr. Bourdeax's father-in-law [Big Partisan] left the village with five lodges and moved to the Sand Hills. A short time afterwards the Bear's family, about ten lodges, joined him. The Red Leaf, Big [Long] Chin, and their two brothers and nephew then started . . . to come to the Platte, and intended to go direct to the Fort, but previous to their starting Mr. B.'s father-in-law learned that they were going to war. . . .

They reached the Platte opposite the old mail station. They discovered a wagon coming down the road. The Big Chin commenced, called the Red Leaf a coward, and saying to him that the soldiers had killed his brother and wounded him; if he was brave, he would take pay for his wounds today. The Red Leaf said that he was no coward, but if he wanted to injure him and make him kill the whites, he would do so. . . .He would show that he was no coward. He then started and killed the first two. The Big Chin then killed the other. His two brothers and his nephew wounded Mr. Kinkhead [C. A. Kinkead].[10]

The lucky-to-be-alive Kinkead offered another version of the raid, and some details differed, for instance, the number of attackers (he gave ten to twenty). As a survivor's account, it must be remembered that the subject himself suffered a neck wound while a passenger in the mail carriage and took three or four arrow wounds, one of which knocked him off a mule while trying to escape. Upon seeing Kinkead rise (from the dead?), one raider merely waved his hand "as to tell him to go away" and rode off.[11] One can understand subsequent contradictory testimony.

Of more concern to Little Thunder than the actions of the few, though, was the welfare of the many. Since the killing of the blue-coated soldiers, his village of two hundred lodges had moved as far north as the Black Hills before moving back to its current location on the Niobrara River. Disturbing news came via some fellow Brulés who had spoken to traders on the Missouri River, who warned them, "the soldiers next summer would kill them all."[12] Little Thunder and his colleagues surely wanted to head off such a frightening possibility with their hasty trip to Fort Laramie. Unfortunately, this was an all too common example where whites confused individual and family acts of Indian vengeance with the intentions of an entire tribe, and their delegation met with little, if any success.[13]

Those Brulé hotheads who intended to winter near the Missouri did not help matters any. Their rhetoric spread throughout Indian country, only to be recorded by the whites. In the spring, they boldly said, "[T]hey intend commencing hostilities upon every white man they may meet with, and particularly the Emigrants."[14] All took such inflammatory statements seriously, especially when combined with a general sense that the other Sioux tribes living in the upper Missouri region felt likewise. When a roundup of "Nebraska" Indian troubles appeared in a New York newspaper that fall, it barely gave a mention to the Grattan fight at Fort Laramie in its litany.[15] Nebraska Territory had only been formed last spring, along with its Kansas neighbor. How would the Indian problem affect its development and more importantly the upcoming overland migration?

* * *

The emigration season of 1855 saw significant reductions in the number of overlanders. Sioux country and its Fort Laramie choke point could hardly be avoided when traveling the Platte Valley route. One indicator of lighter traffic is the number of historical accounts that have survived from that year, less than half of those from 1854, and many are by military, not emigrant, authors.[16] But some travelers would not be dissuaded under any circumstances.

William Keil of Bethel, Missouri, sorted through the rumors swirling about St. Joseph, Missouri, in spring 1855. If they could be believed, eight thousand Indians between Forts Kearny and Laramie awaited his party, but Keil merely retreated to a high hill, meditated momentarily, and decided to proceed.[17]

Of the seven thousand travelers whom the Sioux may have seen that year, Keil's party may have been the most befuddling. Or maybe the most befuddled. Keil, the strong-willed leader of a group of hymn-singing German American colonists, had left his northwest Missouri community with twenty-four wagons— and a hearse carrying the body of his deceased nineteen-year-old son, Willie. Keil intended to keep his promise to his son, made while Willie was still alive, that he would be a part of the new colony. "[F]ear is unknown to us," wrote William Keil from Fort Kearny on June 25, and this confidence born of faith and ignorance may have been all that was necessary to shepherd the flock unmolested.

Actually, Keil saw more soldiers than Indians on the Platte Valley route. Two days west of Ash Hollow, "supposed to be the worst place," his party came upon an Indian camp, presumably Lakota. "When they saw us, they took their ponies and other property, crossed the river, and camped on the other side. They did not come into our camp, neither did we go to them. The next morning we left and went our way, and so did the Indians. That was the last we saw of them."

Keil and his strange entourage later passed by graves of Grattan's command, stopped at Fort Laramie for the latest news, and continued on their way. When they came to the North Platte bridge near present Casper, Wyoming, they had seen only two Indians in the interim. Their journey passed relatively uneventfully, and they reached paradise or, in this case, Aurora, Oregon. William buried Willie with great ceremony, ending the transcontinental funeral procession.

The rumors of Indians on the warpath were largely overblown and never met expectations of those who feared a general uprising, but tales of occasional violent incidents, such as the November mail party murders, kept the flames fanned. In Salt Lake City on January 19, 1855, a returning mail carrier reported the trail unsafe for travel. A few days later Garland Hurt, a newly appointed Indian agent for Utah, arrived intact and dismissed the supposed dangers. At the other end of the trail, the U.S. Mail for January safely reached Independence, Missouri; no hostile Sioux were encountered.[18]

It was difficult to discount the Missouri newspapers, though. From the moment they learned of Grattan's demise and in the months thereafter, they bulged with yarns of Indian depredations and with recommendations for appropriate punishment. One is struck by the writers' stridency and irrelevance.[19] While plainsmen were saying all was (relatively) quiet in the West, one shrill contributor to the *Missouri Republican* offered this red herring: "[I]f those who had sympathy for the poor wronged Indians had seen the Indians and understood their motives, if they had had their houses burned, their wives taken captive by the Indians to live a life worse than death, and their infants tortured and burned at a stake, then this sympathy for such wretched red men might be changed to bitter hatred and a desire for revenge."[20]

Clearly, the people of the United States were at war—or, at least, the attentive readers of this St. Louis newspaper— even if all the Lakota people were not.

Early 1855 was marked by continued Lakota attempts to settle the difficulty, using traditional methods that showed their good faith. In early February, Little Thunder again offered the olive branch when he brought in seven mules stolen during the mail party raid. He was rebuffed anew by Major Hoffman, who again did not meet the chief in person. In the spring came assorted stories of Platte River Sioux returning stolen emigrant livestock, even Lakota herdsmen finding and helping gather stampeded cattle for their white owners.[21] But the efforts as good Samaritans were seen merely as isolated incidents, not as the sincere diplomatic advances of a political equal. They received less publicity and insufficient credit to counter the more notorious events of that spring.

February reports from Hoffman at Fort Laramie, which would have taken weeks to reach departmental headquarters in St. Louis, did little to relieve the tensions. The Brulés "are most eager to purchase powder and lead," wrote Hoffman, and "[t]he Minneconzhoo and Wah-sah-zhes [Miniconjou and Wazhazha] are on White river and are preparing for war." Conversely, though: "[The Brulés] are all, particularly the old men, very anxious to make peace and to have their trade opened, and they are looking for the arrival of the next mail with great impatience, hoping it will bring some favorable news for them."[22]

Such contradictions, if true, indicated the struggle that existed between peace and war factions within the Lakota tribes. Meanwhile, the Oglala continued to keep their distance.

Major Hoffman tried to track Indian movements, and his focus and that of others narrowed on the Brulés. "[T]he Brule camp of two or three hundred lodges, which was near Beauvais, has been broken up and moved over towards the Missouri. . . ." Of immediate interest were the small parties of young Brulé warriors who had left the village, prowled the North Platte area, and purportedly stolen trader livestock.[23]

In the late spring of 1855, though, seasonal emigrant and freight trains, and not resident, trader herds became targets for depredations. On June 22, Robert Gibson, a Missouri merchant and wagon master, met a party of sixteen apparently friendly Sioux near Deer Creek, a tributary of the North Platte west of Fort Laramie. While shaking the hands of one man, Gibson was shot fatally by another. The others in the train could give no motivation for the seemingly inexplicable killing. The same day an emigrant train on the north side of the river near Deer Creek suffered an attack, probably from the same bunch, who made off with several head of livestock. One raider caught up with a young woman, who had been away from the train milking a cow. The woman hit the man in the face with her milk pail, and he responded by lancing her twice in the shoulder with his spear. Fortunately, her wounds were not deep, and she recovered. Rumor had it that the Indians later sold the animals to another wagon train.[24] These sensational incidents in particular, especially given the lag until their news reached the authorities and the newspapers, perpetuated the war fever. Other Indian troubles distant from Fort Laramie only heightened the pitch.

In July 1855, a Sioux war party, composed primarily of Brulés, attacked a large Omaha tribal hunting party between the Elkhorn and Loup rivers in present Boone County, Nebraska, and killed its charismatic leader, Logan Fontenelle. His body was brought back for burial to the little Missouri River settlement of Bellevue, Nebraska Territory. Because he was the mixed-blood son of noted trader Lucien Fontanelle and a frontier celebrity of sorts, the killing received wide public notice.[25]

The Omaha and Pawnee tribes, longtime enemies of the Sioux, continued to be magnets for raids in eastern Nebraska Territory, which, in turn, unsettled the new and nearby white settlements. On July 29, fifteen Sioux encountered two men, named Demarest and Porter, of the Quincy Immigration Company near the village of Fontanelle, Washington County, and the Omaha villages. Again feigning friendship, the Sioux shook the hands of their victims before killing them. Porter's wife received a lance wound in the hip, survived, and crawled to town.[26] Although hundreds of army regulars now crisscrossed Nebraska Territory, only fledgling territorial militia existed to counter these threats. The Pawnee tribe was on its own; it had fought the Sioux at least twice during the summer of 1855. To complicate matters further, the Cheyennes also chose this summer to resume their customary raids on the Pawnee villages. An army officer at Fort Kearny watched helplessly as a large party of Cheyenne warriors passed by in early July.[27] Ironically, although he had taken the war to the heart of Sioux country, Harney left the Nebraska settlements feeling vulnerable, and Indian alarms became the order of the day. Complicating matters was an almost total inability to distinguish friend from foe, especially among the many Sioux tribes. Into this tumultuous setting came a new personality, a latecomer who tried to make this distinction and maybe help bring a peaceful resolution to the Sioux war.

* * *

Thomas S. Twiss succeeded as Indian agent for the Upper Platte Agency the ineffective John Whitfield, who had lasted only one turbulent year in the job. As the field representative of the office of Indian affairs, Twiss bore a determination and focus previously absent, and urgently needed. Maybe that came from his education at the United States Military Academy, brief service after graduation in the regular army, and a return to civilian life as an instructor and an engineer. He brought this interesting resume with him West.[28]

The appointment of Twiss, a native of South Carolina but at this time a resident of Troy, New York, came in March 1855, his official oath of office taken in St. Louis in May, and his departure for his post made from Westport (present Kansas City), Missouri, in June. No hostile Indians were encountered on the trip. An impending war did not prevent him from taking that year's annuity goods as stipulated by the Fort Laramie/Horse Creek Treaty of 1851. At times, war or no, the government could be surprising in its adherence to routine.[29]

Agent Twiss assumed his duties upon his arrival at Fort Laramie on August 10, 1855—which was a reasonable amount of time between appointment to and arrival at a distant western post—and immediately set to work. His initial reports to his superiors showed that he had wasted no time; he contacted Indian leaders, talked to all informed parties, and reached the following conclusions.

"It was soon made clear to my mind that some portions of the Sioux bands, the Brulés and Ogalallahs, had no share or part in the murders and robberies which had been committed during the last twelve months and were really desirous and anxious to preserve and continue their friendly and peaceful relations with the United States. . . ."[30]

After differentiating between friend and enemy for his own benefit, he needed to do likewise for the military force that he knew would eventually come. Twiss declared the North Platte as "the boundary between the hostile and friendly Sioux."[31]

On August 19, Twiss met with Big Partisan and the principal men of the Brulés, his intermediary and newly hired interpreter being frontiersman Antoine Janis. He convinced

them, and later the Oglalas of Man Afraid of His Horses at a
separate council location, to observe this directive. Efforts to
convince Little Thunder's group to do the same failed. Twiss
pleaded ignorance of their location—they were somewhere on
a hunting expedition—but Little Thunder's Lakota counterparts
at Fort Laramie attributed the absence to their continued
anger and obstinacy. Therefore, Twiss forbade ". . . these
murderers and robbers from crossing to the south side of
the Platte and required the friendly Brules to drive away from
amongst them all hostile Indians on pain of being declared
enemies. . . ."[32]

Twiss made much of these efforts of gathering up the
"peaceful" Indians, although the prospect of receiving treaty
payments may have helped. Man Afraid's band, for example,
had been expecting their annuities for three months and had
only come in from the headwaters of the Niobrara.[33] Ultimately
Twiss's tactic worked and created a clever cloak of safety for
the Indians near Fort Laramie. On September 3, 1855, the
energetic agent reported the progress that he and area Lakota
leaders had made.

No such halo surrounded Little Thunder's band, which on
that same day could have used it. Civil and military officials
identified its members as enemies of the United States; moreover their Lakota kinsmen wanted no part of them. By September they were camped alone, north of the Duck River (their
name for the North Platte), along one of its little tributaries.[34]
Technically the site was but a few miles away—a short march
for a man on foot—from the line of demarcation between
"friendly" and "hostile" Indians. The village was but a quarter
of its size earlier in the year; whether this was due to recent
political defections or natural dispersal is not known. Whatever
the reason, here the remaining villagers had accumulated and

dried the enormous amount of buffalo meat needed to get them through the upcoming winter.

The stream along which the Lakotas had set their tipis and set to this work was well known to them.[35] In their language they called it the "Minito Wakpala," or Blue Water.

Chapter 6
Blue Water Creek and the Day of Retribution

After William Harney and his army of six hundred reached the North Platte River on September 2, the soldiers made camp and the general made plans. The column survived the steep descent from the tableland into the deep gorge named Ash Hollow; as their reward, the soldiers enjoyed the amenities of this "oasis of the desert." The noted trail landmark situated adjacent to the North Platte river valley was known more for its good water than its ash trees, most of which had disappeared in years of emigrant campfires.[1]

Likewise camped, but six miles northwest, was a village of Brulé Lakotas, its location and makeup already known to Harney. Earlier on the trail, the expedition had met a passing train of civilian freighters who reported a minor fracas with some of the villagers. A party of young Lakota men had come into the freighters' camp at Ash Hollow, demanded some food, and insolently knocked over their coffee pot when rejected. This tale only confirmed to Harney, a sympathetic listener, that this was a hostile band. It consisted of some forty lodges of which thirty-three could be seen from the bluff heights at the mouth of Ash Hollow. Using a rule of thumb employed by frontiersmen, estimating ten residents per tipi, Harney would have known to expect a village of four hundred, of which about one hundred twenty would be males of fighting age.[2] Furthermore, the village leader was known to be Little Thunder; he and his followers were implicated in the Grattan Massacre and subsequent crimes. Harney must have blessed his good luck. Months of gathering Indian intelligence, largely a fruitless effort that had generated contradictory data, no longer mattered.

Harney decided to attack the next day, Monday, September 3. He then called his officers together, ostensibly for their opinions, although the meeting was more to unfold his set plans. First, he ordered Philip Cooke and his four companies of mounted troops—Companies E and K, Second Dragoons, Light Company G, Fourth Artillery, and Company E, Tenth Infantry—to move at 3 A.M., cross the North Platte River, and take up a position quietly to the north of the Indian village, the direction of any anticipated retreat. The infantry, technically under Maj. Albemarle Cady but in reality commanded by Harney, would leave an hour later, also cross the river, and commence the fight from the south. At the sound of gunfire, the mounted force would break cover and join the attack from the rear; if it was discovered prior to the signal, then it could commence without the infantry. Although Cooke concurred with the plan, this maneuver proved more difficult than it sounded.[3]

Cooke relayed the plan to his company commanders. He specifically asked Capt. Albion Howe, Fourth Artillery, if his newly mounted artillerymen were up to the task. This would be a circuitous ride through unknown territory in the middle of the night, a task challenging enough to the most experienced dragoon company. That was the easy part. More difficult would be the attack on the village, during which Howe's company and the Tenth Infantry company of Capt. Henry Heth would act as mounted infantrymen, that is, riding to a point on the battlefield, then dismounting to fire on foot. The dragoons under 1st Lt. Beverly H. Robertson (Company E) and Capt. William Steele (Company K) would remain in reserve until ordered to fight on horseback.[4] Apparently after hearing these instructions the company commanders replied in the affirmative.

For the infantry companies, preparations were easy. They refilled their cartridge boxes and were ready . . . for bed; they turned in at the usual hour after a hard day's march.[5] For all it was a short night of rest.

* * *

Before morning the Sioux were caught in a trap, such as, it is said, Indians never were caught in before.
William Chandless, *A Visit to Salt Lake*

The troops were roused in the wee hours before dawn as silently as possible. No loud talk was allowed, nor were fires, even those to light a pipe or cigar. These restrictions, though, did not apply to General Harney himself. Before he unleashed his men, he stood on the riverbank and unleashed his fury on the Indians. He gave a speech, one so memorable, so explicit, that William Chandless, an educated overland freighter whose wagon train camped with the army a few days later, heard about it and wrote it down. Nathan Augustus Monroe Dudley, a newly minted lieutenant, could recall its contents fifty-five years later! Using harsh language for which Harney was renowned, he thundered: "There are those damned red sons of bitches, who massacred the soldiers near Laramie last year, in time of peace. They killed your own kindred, your own flesh and blood. Now, by God, men, there we have them, and if you don't give it to them, you deserve to be ——. Don't spare one of those damned red sons of bitches."[6]

As Lieutenant Dudley attested with considerable understatement, "The old General was prolific in the use of profanity and utilized not a little of it to illustrate his earnestness. . . ." Chandless, an outsider, probably gave an astute assessment of the soldiers' state of mind when he wrote, "The soldiers . . .

hate the Indians because they bring them out on the plains to all sorts of privation and fruitless marching to and fro."[7]

Lieutenant Colonel Cooke and his mounted troops left camp at their appointed time to circle to the east around the sleeping village. The force succeeded in crossing the shallow, but shifting, sandy bottomed North Platte, making the difficult march, and passing unnoticed. As an officer recalled, it was all business. "There was no excitement, no noise or chinning, no transportation of wagons to create confusion or noise. . . . In columns of twos, occasionally doubled up at halts, we rapidly marched. . . ."[8] The horsemen eventually descended from the tableland north of the river into the valley of Blue Water Creek, the stream along which the Brulés camped. It was dawn on a clear day when the soldiers reached this point. They were surprised by what they saw.

Before daybreak at four o'clock, the other half of Harney's split command, the five infantry companies under Major Cady, left camp. They were led by Capt. John Todd (Company A), Capt. Samuel Woods (E), Lt. John McCleary (H); Capt. Henry W. Wharton (I), and Lt. Robert Patterson (K). The presence of Captain Woods seems surprising; exactly one month before to the day his entire family, consisting of his wife, two children, and servant, had died of cholera at Fort Riley. Conspicuous by their absences were Capt. Thomas Hendrickson, the commander of Company H, and Capt. Richard Garnett, the commander of Company K. Hendrickson had been ordered to remain at Fort Kearny to watch over its skeleton garrison, and Garnett, he with so much frontier experience among the Sioux, missed the expedition entirely because of recruiting duties in the East. Remaining at the Ash Hollow military camp were Capt. Stewart Van Vliet, assistant quartermaster, and Lt. Darius D. Clark, who had to stay and guard the supply train, which had cautiously formed a protective half circle. Lt. George Balch kept watch over his ordnance stores. Assistant Surgeon Aquila Ridgely waited until needed.[9] These four would not be eyewitnesses to the events that followed.

Harney and his staff left a half hour later and caught up with the column, and together they waited a while. Harney wanted ample time to elapse for the mounted force to get into position. Soon, though, his group crossed the North Platte en masse, headed north, and followed the west side of the Blue Water, a beautiful, clear, narrow but winding stream, its current running swiftly but only knee deep. A ridge of high buttes ran parallel to the west of the creek. The river valley itself was half a mile wide with many smaller hills to negotiate and "miry sloughs" to avoid, but the column moved "steadily and rapidly forward." Now three miles from the village and Captain Todd's company forming the advance guard, the soldiers witnessed a party of eight to ten Indian horsemen on a hill signalling . . . to whom? The soldiers to parley? The villagers to scatter? The answer came when the Brulé village came into view. Aware of the approaching infantry, which was marching "in beautiful style," the Indians had stirred, struck their tipis, and begun a rapid retreat up the valley. For some their morning meals still were cooking. To Harney's delight, they were moving "precisely in the direction from whence I expected the mounted troops."[10]

By the time the column passed opposite the village site, half a mile to the soldiers' left, all the tipis were gone. A testament to the skill of the Lakota women in breaking camp and to Plains Indian mobility in general, the "slowest" of the inhabitants were already a mile in advance of the footmen. Harney's delight turned to concern. What if the mounted force was not in position?[11]

Unbeknownst to the commanders and to Honore Tesson, a guide assigned to the mounted force, another, smaller village sat north about three miles from the Brulés. It consisted of eleven Oglala lodges, although a later observer thought it also sheltered some Miniconjou Lakota and Cheyennes. The surprising discovery of a second village along the Blue Water had extended Cooke's march to a total of ten to twelve miles through the sand hills and delayed his deployment. He succeeded, with Tesson's guidance, in concealing his command in a dry, sandy draw and the tall grass just half a mile north of the Oglalas. There he waited undiscovered for over two hours, having executed his maneuver flawlessly. Cooke himself was astonished by its success, "this most difficult and delicate of military operations. . . , that of a distantly combined night march and surprise." He only awaited the signal, the sound of the infantry's fire, before attacking the stirring village.[12]

Harney, unaware of Cooke's location, fretted further when Captain Winship returned from a short reconnoiter to the east and expressed his opinion that the rough ground must have delayed the mounted force. Harney concluded that his subordinate Cooke had failed to reach the objective and feared his mobile prey would escape. Therefore, the general sent out old Colin Campbell, a civilian guide who had been in the West since 1820, to initiate a parley with the Indians as a delaying tactic, although he would later phrase this episode more passively: "a parley ensued."[13]

Little Thunder, obviously aware of the danger he and his people faced, would only talk if Harney agreed to halt his troops, which was done. The chief rode out to the head of the column "at full speed" to meet him. Holding an open umbrella as a flag of truce, Little Thunder dismounted and offered his hand, but Harney refused to shake it. With Campbell as their interpreter, the two warriors talked for over half an hour. The tactic had done the trick. Little Thunder's followers had paused in mid-retreat. The conversation, though, proved to be a trifle one-sided. As with Lieutenant Grattan's "talk" with the Lakotas the previous year, the army only presented demands, ones that could not be met.[14]

Harney chastised his counterpart for Indian depredations, particularly the Grattan fight and the November murder of the mail party and warned that "the day of retribution had come." Here was the ultimatum: Deliver up the young men guilty of these deeds or suffer the consequences. Little Thunder professed peace but admitted his inability to keep his young warriors in check. Nor could he relinquish any of the purported murderers. Again Little Thunder offered his hand to Harney, who refused it, saying that "he could not take the hand of a man whom he expected to fight in a few minutes. . . ."[15]

As this sham neared its conclusion, the disposition of the dragoons was still unknown. Harney said, "You sent for me to come and fight you or have a talk, and now you are running away."[16]

Little Thunder replied "he did not want to fight," that "he was afraid to talk with so many soldiers." He did not deny that his band was involved in the Grattan fight and the murder of the mail party, but he could not fathom this concept of collective guilt. "[I]f we were bad, why would we be here? Why not have gone off like the other Indians?" Furthermore, added Little Thunder, "the agent [Thomas Twiss] had sent for him."[17]

Harney sidestepped this argument, and Lieutenant G. K. Warren heard his reply: "[T]heir Great Father [the president] had paid them to keep off this road and let his children pass. . . . [A]s for the Indian agent, he [Harney] did not mind what he said more than the barking of a prairie dog." Harney concluded that these were the Indians who "had fallen on 30 of our men at Laramie, hundreds at once, and wiped them out. . . . [N]one stood up to help them. Now he was ready to fight. . . . He had not come out here for nothing."[18]

A commotion broke out far to the north, and Harney suspected its cause. He broke off the talk and ordered Little Thunder to return to his people and to prepare for battle. Situated on all the prominent hills, Indians were watching the proceedings from across the creek a quarter to half a mile away. Mounting his horse, Little Thunder "took but a few minutes to regaining [sic] his position he occupied before the parley."[19]

Before this, Harney asked Todd if he was ready. Todd and his skirmishers were. After Little Thunder left his view, the general, not Major Cady, ordered the infantry to advance, Todd's company in front as skirmishers, McCleary's in support to the left, and the two remaining companies in reserve. No sooner had Little Thunder reached his people than Harney gave the order to fire. Wrote Todd, "The words were scarcely out of his mouth before the rattle of the rifles of my company was heard, and the 'Sioux Campaign' initiated in earnest."[20]

✳ ✳ ✳

I never saw a more beautiful thing in my life.
Correspondent, *Missouri Republican*, Sept. 27, 1855

As reported by the anonymous newspaper correspondent, an eyewitness to the beginnings of the fight, Harney's plan fell neatly into place. Two companies of infantry "advanced with spirit diagonally across the valley and stream, and charged up the heights on the opposite side," while firing their long-range rifles. Wrote an appreciative Corp. Eugene Bandel, "[T]heir arrows or the bullets from their poor flintlocks could not reach us." Those modern weapons that had so effectively brought down the mighty bison earlier in the summer drove the shaken Indians out of range and nearer to the cavalry.[21]

But Cooke had finally been spotted and not by the Indians on the high ground. Although the main body was some three-quarters of a mile away, a woman and two children, not waiting

for the parley's outcome, stumbled upon the soldiers; the trio
hurriedly retraced their steps and gave the alarm. Cooke paused,
though, still awaiting the signal or "some attempt of escape by
the enemy." To the contrary, some warriors "donned their war
bonnets," rode toward the soldiers, and uttered challenges.
Such bravery, a classic Lakota rear-guard action to distract an
enemy and protect dependents, impressed Cooke consider-
ably ("I could have destroyed them at a word"), but he did not
rise to the bait.[22]

Upon hearing the first volley, his command mounted and
rode forward in columns of four. An old dragoon remembered
John M. "Yankee" Sullivan, "the best bugler in the service,"
sounding the charge and "away we galloped." To the south,
"[w]hen the Infantry saw the Dragoons coming down in such
beautiful style, they gave a yell, which resounded far and wide."
Harney's infantrymen on the southern front adjusted the sights
on their rifles and continued to fire at distances up to half a
mile, far beyond anything the Indians had ever experienced.[23]
Recorded Todd that day in his diary, his literary skills honed
by describing past buffalo hunts:

"At first the Indians took it very coolly not dreaming that
we could reach them at the distance we were from them, but
very soon they were awakened from their apparent apathy by
the searching proximity of the leaden messengers sent among
them, and forthwith there was a wonderful display of fast riding,
accelerated as much as possible by the free use of raw hide
and spurs."[24]

As soon as the mounted force crossed the river, Cooke
gave Lt. Thomas J. Wright, his adjutant, an order to transmit
to Heth: Choose the nearest and most level route down the
valley, and take a position to block an enemy retreat, "the one
by they [the Indians] had ascended the bluff." Cooke reinforced
Heth's company, which only numbered about thirty recruits,

with ten dragoons from Robertson's Company E, this unit serving as Cooke's reserve during the charge.[25] The encirclement of the Indians was moving to its conclusion.

The cavalrymen brought to bear their eclectic mix of fire-arms and "a ruff and tumble fight ensued." As did Harney's infantrymen, the mounted artillerymen and mounted infantry-men also carried single-shot, long-range rifles. The dragoons, as the range closed, could use their breech-loading carbines and/or revolvers. The new arms, though, came with new prob-lems. The ring to which the carbine sling was attached proved defective, and many broke during the charge; subsequently several Sharpses were lost.[26] Whether individual dragoons paused and retrieved the guns in the tall grass or whether they lost them forever is not known.

❋ ❋ ❋

For a time they stood the attack bravely.
"Battle of Ash Hollow: The Recollections of
General Dudley," R. Eli Paul, ed.

Armed only with flintlock muzzleloaders, bows-and-arrows, and lances, the outgunned Oglalas retreated south of their little village to the bluffs on the valley's west side. The Brulés con-verged from the south and also sought refuge on the high bluffs, another classic Lakota, almost instinctual defensive move when trapped on the plains.[27]

But their respite proved short-lived as Captain Steele's company led the charge and Robertson's blocked yet another avenue of escape to the west. Even worse, a blistering fire continued to rain upon them, especially from Light Artillery Company G, which had arrived on the heights to Steele's left, halted, and was fighting "as skirmishers," on foot with rifle and revolver.[28] Caught in these pincers, the beleaguered Indians sought escape and took to their ponies.

Cokawin, the mother-in-law of Iron Shell and the only Lakota participant to leave a detailed oral history of September 3, described the confusing, one-sided events from a noncombatant's perspective. "When I saw that there was to be no peace, I started to run without a thing, not even my blanket. . . . The smoke and dust of the battle almost blinded me."[29]

Cokawin was no more fortunate than most survivors. One battlefield observer mentioned that the Indians lost "everything they had in the world. . . ."[30]

On her heels were all the soldiers. Major Cady, having only Captain Wharton's Company I, Sixth Infantry, remaining under his immediate charge, moved north up the valley "to a point where it came in from the west to catch the Indians in retreat." The distance, though, proved excessive for "an effective fire," even taking into consideration the increased range of the long-range rifles, and Cady's men stopped firing. Nevertheless, he continued his pursuit, and, before being easily distanced, the infantrymen killed one more Indian and captured four women.[31]

As the fleeing Lakotas passed for the last time by the other infantry companies: "[W]e poured a plunging fire upon them with our long range rifles, knocking them out of their saddles, right and left. The party was large and compact, and as their people fell, others replaced and carried them off."[32]

If this description of infantry firing appears wild, directed towards both sexes and all ages, it also seemed so at the time. Lieutenant Warren cautiously moved only so far as General Harney and fellow staff officers did, "none of which could get ahead of the Infantry during the fight without getting their fire." More frightening still was the narrow escape of Desomet, one of the mixed-blood army guides. He accompanied the dragoons but was mistaken on the battlefield by some of Todd's excitable, if not oblivious, infantrymen for an enemy, until he laid down his gun and an acquaintance vouched for him.[33]

But the fighting was shifting away from the infantry force, the riflemen ceased their firing, and the danger of friendly fire evaporated. Harney, his staff, and the exhausted footmen regrouped on the high hills to follow the movements of the mounted force. To urge them along, the infantrymen gave three cheers to their cavalry comrades.[34]

Although escape opportunities led to all northerly directions, the bulk of the survivors completed their descent of the bluffs, headed east-northeast, and crossed the creek near Heth's company. They sought safety "by the only avenue now open to them through the bluffs of the left bank of that stream."[35] However, the up-to-now flawless implementation of Harney's plan began to unravel.

First, Heth had picked a poor position—the "Bad Slough," as it later appeared on Lieutenant Warren's battlefield map— and was unable to maneuver easily and stem the flow of the villagers. Decades later, Heth selectively remembered the group as consisting of "two hundred bucks." Blue Water Creek now worked to the Indians advantage; its abrupt banks, three to four feet in height, and poor footing created intimidating obstacles to inexperienced riders. Heth's mounted infantrymen resorted to dismounting and shooting from long-range, before collecting themselves to give feeble chase. Heth found himself on an "unruly" horse with which to contend and did not join. He sent off Lieutenant Dudley to command the remnants of the company, who succeeded in finding a better crossing 150–200 yards north of the Bad Slough, possibly the same river crossing the dragoons used when they charged earlier. Steele's and Robertson's mounted troops, though, pursued immediately, as Cooke descended into the valley with his staff and orderlies and redeployed the two dragoon companies.[36]

Second, although the dragoons promptly complied with Cooke's wishes, Captain Howe's artillerymen, intended by Cooke to act as his reserve in the pursuit, did not. Lt. John Mendenhall, Fourth Artillery, assigned with sufficient men to hold the company's horses during the fighting on foot, "thought it strange we did not follow the Dragoons." So did everyone else on the battlefield.[37]

John Sullivan, chief bugler, Second Dragoons, sounded the calls "To Horse" and "Advance" no more than a hundred yards away! Serving as an orderly for Cooke, Bugler Patrick Walsh, Company K, Second Dragoons, arrived at Howe's position ten minutes after leaving Cooke with the directive to "move forward." But Cooke saw no response by the dawdlers and their commander and in despair galloped to Harney's hilltop perch and asked him if he had halted the company, which, of course, the aggressive general had not. Meanwhile Howe's men mounted up with some difficulty; they had become separated from their horses by over five hundred yards, and the animals became spooked by the confusion of men running to and fro and some carrying booty, such as buffalo robes. After this mess sorted itself out and the artillerymen descended into the valley, they made matters worse by aimlessly looking for an easy ford of Blue Water and, when they finally did so, stopped to leisurely water their horses. By the time Adjutant Wright, who had been dispatched by Cooke to move Howe along, found the company, it was "resting"—too late to accomplish much of anything.[38]

A contemporary referred to this "lapse" when he commented, "[B]ut for some error in the execution of the plan not a man could have escaped." Cursed an apoplectic Harney, Howe "is not worth the powder and lead it would take to kill him. . . . I shall put charges against this fellow." And so he did, two weeks later.[39]

Most of Howe's company eventually gave chase but were encumbered by prisoners, two wounded comrades, and some captured animals.[40] But Howe's participation was not vital.

The retreat had turned into a full-blown rout. Cokawin, the Indian woman, recalled: "As I looked around, I could see the soldiers galloping after groups of old men, women, and children who were running for their lives. Some were running across the valley, only to be met by soldiers and shot right down. It seemed as though there was no place to go. There were wounded horses every place; some of these were trying to get up, but could not. If I only could have run upon a wounded horse that could travel, I would have got on one with which to get away."[41]

The Indians split up in small groups and fled generally northeast. They were pursued over rugged country—the estimates ranged from three to twelve miles—by the cavalry "shooting and sabering everything that came in their way." The discrepancy of distances may be explained by the series of rearguard actions employed by the remaining Indian warriors to disrupt the dragoon pursuit.[42]

The Indians reached a range of hills where they dug in. The dragoons, who had fought the entire time on horseback, followed closely, but found it impossible to dislodge the Indians without suffering heavy casualties and withdrew. One dragoon stated that the actual fighting lasted four and a half hours; another remembered that his time on horseback since the first firing began lasted fifteen hours, in other words, from dawn until dusk.[43]

Tales of individual valor during the clash along Blue Water were noticeably absent. For the soldiers it may have been a guessing game at whom to shoot. "[I]n the pursuit, women, if recognized," commented Cooke unconvincingly, "were generally passed by my men." The difficulty in distinguishing men from women was an age-old soldier excuse in the Indian wars, and Blue Water was no exception, made more problematical by the increased range of the rifles. Cooke also accused Indian women of shooting at his men; for instance, before Lieutenant Dudley could convince two women to surrender, they took two potshots at him and missed.[44]

Such resistance was certainly not the case with the Lakota woman Cokawin. "I looked back to see if anyone was following me. Sure enough, there was a soldier just taking an aim to shoot me down. If I had not turned around that instant, he would have shot me right in the middle of the back, but by turning, the shot tore my stomach wide open just below the belt. . . .The bullet ripped me open for about six inches, a glancing shot. My bowels protruded from the gaping wound as I fell."[45]

Satisfied, the soldier went on; the woman struggled to save her life. "I saw a washout nearby and crawled toward that place. . . .I laid down in this hole and covered myself with the tumbleweeds that had collected in it. I tore off the wide calico sleeve of my dress and stuffed it in the wound to stop the bleeding. I lay there all the balance of the day."[46]

What few examples exist of individual glory achieved that day lie mostly on the Indian side. Shortly after the end of the parley between Harney and Little Thunder and the beginning of the infantry advance, Captain Todd, he of the purple prose, saw: "[A] warrior dashed out from the crowd, and approaching us, rode down the line at full speed parallel to it, and distant about 300 yards. Poor fellow! What hope of escape for him, what chance to come off scatheless from the Hundred Minnies levelled upon him, as furiously he dashed along this fiery gauntlet, his scalp lock and streamers trailing in the wind, now hanging close upon the neck of his horse and now proudly erect, shouting his cry of defiance, down they go, this daring fellow and his horse, now up again, then dips beyond the crest and disappears. How curious! Did he die? Quien Sabe!"[47]

Who knows, indeed, if this brave man lived or died? The same question arose among the troops about Little Thunder, whose actions that day after returning to his followers remain unknown (he lived). Iron Shell and Spotted Tail earned the admiration of their people for fighting heroically side-by-side. For Iron Shell, the older man, the son of a chief, and the second ranking leader of this village, this may have been a turnabout situation to which he was not accustomed. In 1843, it was he who had led a large Brulé force that surprised and overran a Pawnee village in eastern Nebraska, forcing its occupants into a desperate defense and leaving the site in ruins. For Spotted Tail, a warrior in his prime and destined to become the head chief of the Brulé tribe, the day's fighting only heightened an already impressive war record. He would survive Blue Water, purportedly suffering wounds in four places, two of them from pistol shots that passed through his body; he escaped on a dragoon's horse, presumably after wounding or killing the man. In a few months, Spotted Tail would perform an even braver feat.[48]

The bravery of the Indian men drew Lieutenant Warren's respect. "[W]hen cornered they defend themselves nobly." One example of desperate hand-to-hand combat was later told to D. C. Beam, one of the civilian teamsters back at Ash Hollow. One Indian man, "who was supposed dead, and had a death wound, raised up and shot a soldier. Then another soldier went to finish him with his sabre. As the soldier struck at him, the Indian threw up and received the blow on his gun, thus breaking the sabre at the hilt. An officer then thought to try his hand and rode up for that purpose, when the Indian grasped the broken sabre and with it nearly severed the leg of the officer's horse. The Indian was at last finished by a revolver ball."[49]

Similarly, and more believable, Cooke and his staff paused from their tactical preoccupations only long enough to kill "a straggling Indian who, from a hole, annoyed us with his arrows, which only wounded a horse. . . ." Little wonder, then, that the principled Warren felt nothing but disgust with the tales of valor he later heard from his comrades for "their [*sic*] were but few who killed anything but a flying foe."[50]

If one location on the battlefield came to symbolize the brutality and horror of war on civilians, it was the pocket of last resistance, "Hudson's Hole." Not joining in the flight north, a few remnants of the band had remained on the hilltop slopes and secreted themselves in some small limestone caves or overhangs; dense undergrowth hid the mouths of the caves. This drew the fire of the infantry and a detachment of fifteen mounted artillerymen under 1st Lt. Richard C. Drum, sent by Captain Howe. Two Fourth artillerymen lost their lives here, and their vengeful comrades kept up their barrage for fifteen minutes. First Lt. Edward Hudson, Fourth Artillery, was later credited, probably mistakenly, with leading the attack, his men resorting to leaning over the edge of the cave tops on their stomachs and shooting randomly into them. The soldiers ceased fire only after hearing a child's shrill cry. Within the shallow caves, scenes of smoke and confusion, they found two dead men and seven women and three children killed; the remaining women and children, some of whom were terribly wounded, were taken as prisoners. Drum placed this site on "the highest hill," a spot from which General Harney also chose to oversee the final scene of the dragoons chasing the straggling Indians to the north. This high point of the valley and low point of the Battle of Blue Water is now named Rattlesnake Butte.[51]

✻ ✻ ✻

This has been a busy and exciting day for us, but a bloody and disastrous one to the Sioux.
Journal of Capt. John B. S. Todd, ed. by Ray H. Mattison.

After the shooting had ceased, the fatalities were tabulated. Of a total of some three to four hundred Indians, eighty-six were killed, five were wounded, and about seventy women and children were captured. Soldier casualties were reported as being four killed, seven wounded, and one missing and presumed dead, all from the mounted forces, although the army surgeon suspected not all of the "slightly wounded" soldiers reported to him; some of these casualties would be credited later as the work of Spotted Tail of the Brulés. The wounded of both sides were moved to the banks of the North Platte, but not without great anguish. Lieutenant Warren, ever the dutiful engineer "endeavored to take a topographical sketch of the scene, but the calls of humanity prevented my doing much."[52]

Warren helped bring the wounded women and children from out of the rocks. "The sight . . . was heart rending, wounded women and children crying and moaning, horribly mangled by the bullets." His descriptions of the wounded Indians would almost equal the space in his diary entry for September 3 given for those of the fighting: "One young woman was wounded in the left shoulder, the ball going in above and coming out below her arm. I put her on my horse. Another handsome young squaw was badly wounded just above her left knee and the same ball wounded her baby in the right knee. . . .I had a litter made and put her and her child upon it." It had been this child whose scream had called a halt to the killing. "I found another girl of about 12 years lying with her head down in a ravine and apparently dead; observing her breath I had a man take her in his arms; she was shot through both feet. I found a little boy shot thro' the calves of his leg and thro' his hams. I took him in my arms. He had enough strength left to hold me round the neck. With this piteous load we proceeded down the Hill and placing them on the bank of the Blue water. I made a shelter to keep off the sun and bathed their wounds with the stream."[53]

Colin Campbell, his interpretive skills dormant since the Little Thunder parley, proved especially valuable in reassuring the captives. Eventually all the wounded were brought to Dr. Ridgely and his assistant. The bodies of the dead Indians were left to the scavengers.[54]

As the scattered troops regrouped, more details of the day's accomplishments came to light, and the military penchant for statistics asserted itself. Lieutenant Colonel Cooke refined Harney's total figures with the number of casualties his command inflicted: seventy-four Indians killed, five wounded, and forty-three women and children prisoners (there were no men prisoners taken).[55] But who could be certain of the exact number? Lieutenant Warren, who revisited the battlefield in the days to follow, noted: "The Indians were killed in places far apart, and in situations where the dead bodies could not easily be seen, so that it was almost impossible to make a correct estimate of the slain from observation after the fight. I passed very close to one body several times without discovering it till the fourth day after, when my attention was only attracted to it by a group of ravens."[56]

Added Corporal Bandel, "[A]s soon as an Indian fell from his horse dead or wounded, another sprang from his pony to save his scalp, threw the body over his own horse, and was off like the wind." In the retelling of the fight a few days later the number of Indians killed would mushroom to one hundred fifty, a precursor of later misinformation about Blue Water that would appear in print.[57]

Regarding soldier casualties, a Sergeant Healy of Company E, Second Dragoons, was wounded twice with a lance. Of the other soldier casualties, nine came from Captain Steele's Company K, Second Dragoons, the unit in the thickest of the pursuit. Cooke's mounted force also suffered eleven horses killed and wounded and two missing. Cady's infantry force reported no casualties.[58]

The names of the dead soldiers were Thomas Carrol and Robert Fitzpatrick, both of the Fourth Artillery, and Alexander Lyle (or Lyall) and Charles McDonald, both of the Second Dragoons.[59] As one officer observed, "The dragoons, you see, did the fighting."[60] Capt. William Gardner, far away with the Second Infantry at Fort Pierre, later expressed his doubts in a private letter home. "The Indians say very few of their warriors were killed, the mortality being confined for the most part to their women and children. Of the truth of this, I know nothing. It could not have been much of a fight for only four soldiers were killed, and one of them was shot by a squaw. That the Indians did not expect war is evident from the fact that they had not sent their families to a place of safety, which is always customary with them."[61]

Punishing the Sioux did not rely solely on a high number of casualties, but also the massive destruction of property before winter. The rout had forced the abandonment of nearly all the Indians' possessions, so much so that six to eight teams were "constantly engaged in bringing into camp everything of any value to the troops." This included "a good many horses" (at least fifty) and "buffalo meat enough to supply a whole company for some time," as well as food and three tipis for the prisoners. Even more was destroyed on the ground on the orders of Harney, at the direction of Cady, and through the labor of eighty men.[62] Lost were, "some as pretty tepees as I ever saw, new hides stretching over a circumference of eighteen feet, and running to an apex twenty feet high. Inside were bales of dried buffalo meat in skins piled three feet high all around next the outside."[63]

Massive quantities, a winter's supply of food and a season's accumulation of hides, were burned. Remembered an old soldier,

"The last operation was more disastrous to the Indians than the loss of over half their men."[64]

Saved, almost miraculously, was a wagonload of relics. Lieutenant Warren picked up bags, rattles, moccasins, knife sheaths, horse gear, a girl's doll, a man's hunting pouch, and more, all beautiful examples of Indian skill and art, and which the Smithsonian Institution now holds.[65] Also salvaged, and with a different motivation, were soldier clothing and equipment from Grattan's command, papers from the mail robbery, Indian ledger art depicting that incident, and two scalps supposedly from white females, "all of which," in Harney's judgment, "sufficiently characterize the people I have had to deal with."[66] Elsewhere, one dragoon remarked on soldier scavenging. "All our boys now have fancy Indian war dresses. . . ."[67] Unlike Warren's trove, these pieces, either as evidence of crimes or trophies of war, cannot be located.

* * *

I have never seen a finer military spirit displayed generally.
Harney, Report of Sept. 5, 1855

At day's end the overland force of the Sioux Expedition returned to its camp at Ash Hollow. There were wounded to care for, dead to bury, and reports to compose. For General Harney, the time had ended for lowering expectations; now began the trumpeting of his and his underlings' accomplishments. His report soon after the fight was liberal in its praise. Cady and Cooke "zealously and intelligently carried out orders." Heth, Robertson, Steele, and Todd were "in closest contact with the enemy." Patterson, Wharton, and Woods "rendered effective service as reserves and supports, taking an active share in the combat when circumstances would permit." Even the embarrassed Howe was mentioned; he "participated largely in the earlier part of the engagement, but, for reasons stated in his commanding officer's report, he took no active part in the pursuit."[68]

Virtually all of the officers were mentioned in this and other reports. Buford and Wright "did good service." Drum, Dudley, Hudson, Mendenhall, Lt. Thomas Hight, and Lt. Henry B. Livingston (the latter two serving with the Second Dragoons and mentioned virtually nowhere else in the events of September 3) "gave efficient aid to their company commanders." Lt. Marshall T. Polk, an aide-de-camp, and Captain Winship, "in conveying my orders to different portions of the command, discharged their duties with coolness, zeal, and energy." Dr. Ridgely was "indefatigable in his attentions to the suffering wounded, both of our own troops and of the enemy." Lieutenant Warren was "most actively engaged, previous to and during the combat, reconnoitering the country and the enemy." But Tesson, a civilian, received the greatest praise of all. Harney effused, "To his skill as a guide, and his knowledge of the character and habits of the enemy, I ascribe much of the success gained in the engagement." Even the officers in camp received attention, particularly quartermaster Van Vliet ("charged with the protection of the train—a service for which his experiences on the plains rendered him eminently qualified") and ordnance officer Balch. Such an opportunity for being associated with such a smashing victory could not be missed.[69]

So much had been accomplished with so little, or so Colonel Cooke observed: "[A]ll the mounted infantry and nearly all the dragoons were lately recruited, and unused to service, and the artillery company, but lately mounted, in part, and with a new arm. Under these circumstances they far exceeded my expectations, and in the night march, the surprise, in the action and the pursuit, and in all the fatigue of thirteen hours in the saddle, showed themselves good soldiers. . . ." Rewards should follow; in particular, the soldiers, "and with their excellent officers have won for themselves the gratitude of at least that portion of their countrymen whose lives and property have been exposed to the necessary transit of this great central wilderness."[70]

For the soldiers dead, their reward came that evening with a hasty burial—two each to a grave—just west of the mouth of Ash Hollow. Although their graves were later marked, no evidence of the interments exists today.[71]

Help also came to those still living. Warren continued his volunteer nursing of the Indian wounded, although he and the captives did not come into camp until 10 P.M. They endured this trek in the middle of a severe thunderstorm, a fitting capstone to a miserable day.[72]

The Lakota woman Cokawin, who had remained hidden during the day, also marked its end. "Just as the sun was sinking in the west, there was not a living soul on the bloody battle ground. I thought I had better follow along on the trail if possible. If there were others in hiding, I did not see them. All over the valley were dead horses and dead bodies. . . .I picked up a stick and used it for a cane and followed the trail the balance of the night."[73]

In a few days, General Harney and the Sioux Expedition, like Cokawin, would pick up and continue on the trail through Indian country.

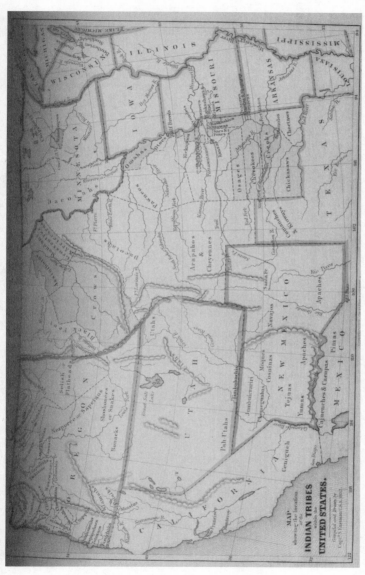

Location of Indian tribes within the United States. This was critical information when the map was drawn in 1852. Nebraska State Historical Society Photograph Collections.

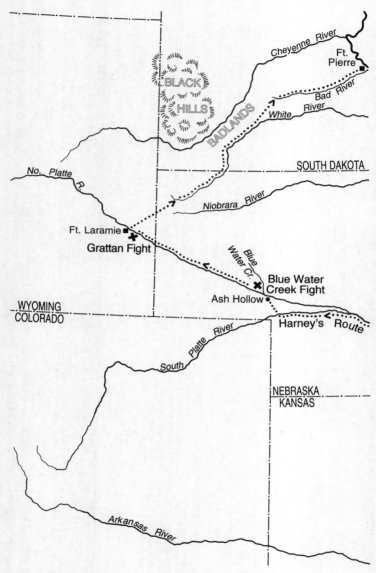

Map by Dell Darling.

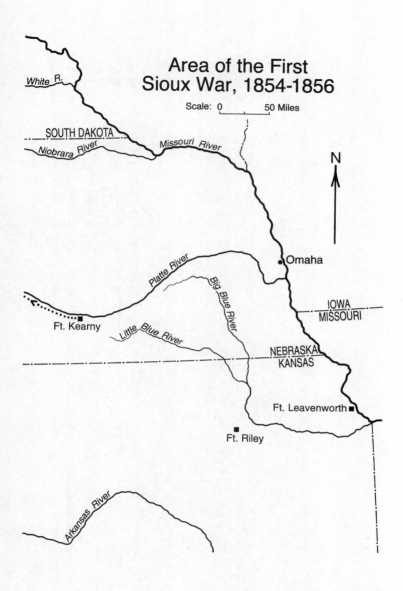

Area of the First Sioux War, 1854-1856

Scale: 0 ___ 50 Miles

N

White R.

SOUTH DAKOTA

Niobrara River

Missouri River

Platte River

Big Blue River

Omaha

IOWA
MISSOURI

Ft. Kearny

Little Blue River

NEBRASKA
KANSAS

Ft. Leavenworth

Ft. Riley

Arkansas River

The winding Blue Water, looking north. In 1929 the valley looked much as it did in 1855. Nebraska State Historical Society Photograph Collections.

Fort Laramie on the North Platte River, where the First Sioux War began in 1854. An engraving of Charles Preuss's 1842 drawing showed the adobe fur trade post that preceded later military structures. Courtesy Brent Carmack.

Fort Pierre on the Missouri River, where the First Sioux War ended in 1856. Drawing by Alfred Sully, 1857. Courtesy of the South Dakota State Historical Society, State Archives.

Oglala Lakota village camped along the North Platte River, a rare antebellum stereograph of a Plains Indian village by Albert Bierstadt, 1859. Nebraska State Historical Society Photograph Collections.

Fanciful 1890 engraving of the 1854 Grattan fight. Possibly the only fact depicted was the presence of a cannon at the scene. Nebraska State Historical Society Photograph Collections.

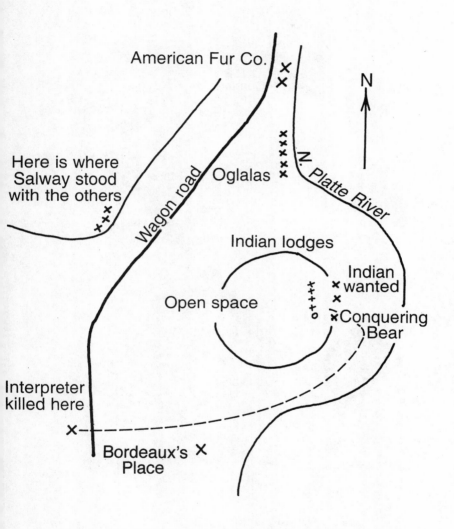

Frank Salway, an eyewitness to the Grattan fight, remembered several details decades later. Drawing by Dell Darling after Salway's 1906 sketch.

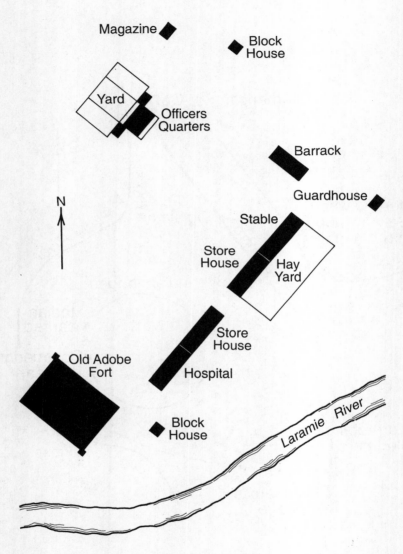

Fort Laramie layout, late summer, 1854. After the Grattan fight, Fort Laramie's remnant garrison retreated behind the walls of the old adobe post. Drawing by Dell Darling after Oscar Winship's 1854 sketch.

William Selby Harney, commander of the Sioux Expedition in 1855–56 and an imposing figure whether in uniform or not. Nebraska State Historical Society Photograph Collections.

GENERAL ORDERS,)
No. 1. 2.)

I. The following arrangements have been ordered by the War Department with a view to the operations about to be undertaken against the hostile Sioux, and for the purpose of protecting from Indian hostilities the frontiers of Kansas and Nebraska, and the emigrant routes leading from the Missouri river to the West.

1. Brevet Brigadier General William S. Harney, Colonel 2d Dragoons, is assigned to the command above indicated according to his brevet rank of Brigadier General.

2. The following named military posts and troops, besides such as may hereafter be added, will constitute Brevet Brigadier General Harney's command, viz:

Military Posts—Forts Riley, Kearney, Laramie, and the Post to be established on the Upper Missouri.

Troops.—The four companies of the 2d Dragoons, (D, H, E & K,) now at Fort Leavenworth.

The light battery (Company G.) of the 4th Artillery, now at Fort Leavenworth.

Six companies of the 2d Infantry—four, (A, D, G & I,) now at Carlisle Barracks,—and two (B & C,) now at Fort Riley.

The 6th Infantry.

3. The Commanders of the posts and troops just enumerated, will, immediately on the receipt hereof, report by letter to Brevet Brigadier General Harney, at Saint Louis.

4. The preparations for the campaign will immediately be commenced, by establishing the principal depôts, and collecting the necessary supplies. With this object in view the forces will be disposed as follows:

The battery of artillery, and four companies (one in addition to the present garrison) of the 6th Infantry, at Fort Laramie.

Four Companies (three in addition to its present garrison) of the 6th Infantry, at Fort Kearney.

The Head-Quarters (under the Lieutenant Colonel) and two companies of the 6th Infantry, at Fort Riley, relieving the companies of the 2d Infantry, now at that place.

The first General Orders of the Sioux Expedition, with an original signature of Irwin McDowell. Courtesy Jerome A. Greene.

The Head-Quarters, and six companies of the 2d Infantry, (four from Carlisle Barracks, and two from Fort Riley,) at the Post to be established by them on the Upper Missouri, between the White-earth and the Cheyenne rivers.

Until active operations are about to commence, the four companies of Dragoons will be employed in giving protection to the frontiers, emigrants, &c.

As soon as practicable, eight companies of the.....Cavalry, will be added to Brevet Brigadier General Harney's command; and when this is done, the cavalry force will be distributed as follows:—Two companies at Fort Laramie; four at the post on the Upper Missouri, and six, in reserve, at Fort Riley.

5. The movements necessary to place the troops in the positions above indicated will be commenced by their respective commanders, at such times as shall be indicated to them by the commander of the expedition, and be carried out as he shall direct.

6. Brevet Brigadier General Harney will make his reports to the Head-Quarters of the army direct.

7. Three of the companies of the 7th Infantry, from Fort Gibson, will be employed on the plains during the Summer, either in the neighborhood of Fort Atkinson, or of the Big Timbers.

II. The General commanding the department of the West will give such orders for the movement of the companies of the 7th Infantry to the Upper Arkansas, and their return, and cause such arrangements to be made for their supply, as shall be necessary.

BY COMMAND OF BREVET LIEUTENANT GENERAL SCOTT.

Irvin McDowell

Assistant Adjutant General.

This artist's misleading rendering of the decidedly one-sided 1855 Blue Water fight appeared in an 1878 authorized biography of General Harney. Nebraska State Historical Society Photograph Collections

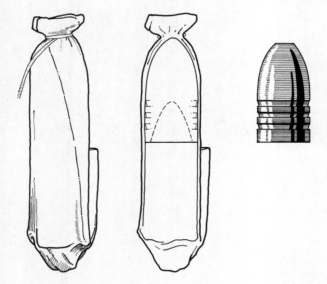

Paper cartridge, a cross-section, and a lead projectile. The newly developed Minie ball (right), fired from a rifled arm, gave a tremendous technological and firepower advantage to the U.S. Army in the Blue Water Creek fight. Drawing by Dell Darling.

G. K. Warren, official engineer and unofficial diarist of the Sioux Expedition, later earned great fame as a Civil War general at Gettysburg. Courtesy of the author.

Mike Henry, boy musician who served under Harney and participated in the fight at Blue Water Creek. Courtesy of the author.

Sin-Tig-a-leo-ka
Spotted Tail

Spotted Tail, Brulé Lakota warrior, whose bravery at Blue Water Creek foreshadowed his later accomplishments as a famed Indian leader. Nebraska State Historical Society Photograph Collections.

Over a half-century later, Retired General N. A. M. Dudley recalled his exploits as a young army lieutenant at Blue Water Creek. He proudly sent this portrait and his reminiscence of the fight to the Nebraska State Historical Society, Lincoln, where both are held today. Nebraska State Historical Society Photograph Collections.

Visitors to the site in 1929, with the Blue Water Creek battlefield to their backs. The distant bluffs to the south are those to which Little Thunder's people retreated. Nebraska State Historical Society Photograph Collections.

Historian LeRoy Hafen (second from left) and party stood on the meager sod remnants of the army's Fort Grattan in 1931. Nebraska State Historical Society Photograph Collections.

Chapter 7
Arms Raised, Palms Forward, Peace

After the Blue Water fight, General Harney's command took five days to regroup before resuming the war. On September 4, 1855, Harney moved the camp from Ash Hollow to the mouth of Blue Water, only to move it back to the mouth of the hollow on September 6. One puzzled officer attributed the decision to Harney's fear that Indian corpses had tainted the creek. Lieutenant Warren duly noted these campground changes on his "sketch" of the battlefield. Harney also became concerned about marking the graves of the dead soldiers. He put the otherwise underutilized Lieutenant Balch to the task, and he eventually came up with three red cedar headboards with inscriptions burned into the wood. The graves now numbered three since another dragoon had died from his wounds. Meanwhile, mounted troops left camp almost daily to return to the scene to look for "plunder" and returned Indians. They found much evidence of the former and little of the latter. Rather, wrote Warren, "The Ravens, Bussards and Wolves had begun their work with the dead, and already little but the bones of some of them were left."[1]

Since the surviving Indians obviously had left the immediate area, Harney sent out expressmen with appropriate alarms. Informing Fort Laramie to the west of the previous day's engagement, he also warned Major Hoffman, its commanding officer: "[B]e especially on your guard against hostile parties of Sioux who may be disposed to molest the various detachments of troops engaged in the labors of building and supplying your post." The general also sent a circular to unwary overlanders that hostilities had commenced and they traveled at their own peril.[2]

To reduce the immediate risk, Harney assigned Captain Heth and his Company E, Tenth Infantry, to escort two wagon trains heading west on September 7. Thinking longer range, the general decided to throw up a fortification at the mouth of Ash Hollow, "a point of support for the public and emigrant trains and the monthly mail," and leave a company of men as a garrison. Again drawing on his engineering expertise, Warren laid out the fort, made from the only material at hand, cut sod. It would be one hundred feet square, six feet high, and three feet thick at its base, and the infantrymen-turned-sodbusters followed the Warren template. "Fort Grattan," as it was immediately named, was a miserable hovel, the sketch by Warren more resembling a corral than a fortress. No one except Harney thought the effort worthwhile. Finished the evening of September 8, its main use would become that of serving as a more substantial hospital for the Indian and soldier wounded.[3]

This may have come as some relief to Warren, who remained concerned about the Indian wounded and their welfare. "The wounded baby died this morning [Sept. 4]; its mother does nothing but cry and moan, and as my tent is near the hospital tents, it distresses me greatly."[4]

One cannot tell if the occasional discovery of additional Indian survivors, one of whom was the Lakota woman, Cokawin, helped console him. Cokawin recalled her surrender to the soldiers, an uncommonly brave deed.

"As I nearly reached the camp, I could dimly see the sentinels walking their beat back and forth by the camp. It was like facing death, so I began to sing a death chant. In Indian life there are songs for everything, but to sing your own death chant is an awful thing. The sentry who met me presented arms and spoke. As I could not understand what he said, all I could do was to raise my arms with my palms forward. This, you know, is the Sioux sign of peace."[5] Cokawin entered the camp unmolested and joined the other captives.

On September 9, about the time his order reached the Fort Pierre garrison to march west from the Missouri River and meet him, Harney broke camp, left Ash Hollow and Blue Water, and set out for Fort Laramie; the Sioux Expedition resumed. He left Captain Wharton, Company I of the Sixth Infantry, a dozen wounded prisoners, one of the wounded soldiers, and all the buffalo robes and meat that had not been destroyed in the field. Surgeon Ridgely left a trained enlisted man and some medical supplies. Warren left ten dollars with Wharton to spend on the wounded. Harney took the Indian prisoners who could travel, along with lodges to shelter them, and through no choice of his own, the many orphaned Indian dogs of Little Thunder's camp. Although thus encumbered, no one within the procession could presume that the Blue Water fight would be the Sioux Expedition's last.[6]

For the next week, the soldiers marched northwest along the north bank (where the grazing was better) of the North Platte River, and the diarists of the expedition resumed their overland accounts. Twenty miles were covered the first day, eighteen the next, as they progressed along the "emigrant road" to Fort Laramie. By and large the first days of the estimated one hundred-forty mile journey proved relatively uneventful, so the soldiers could enjoy the scenery. On September 11, for example: "[F]or the first time saw the court house and chimney rocks, which are on the south side of the river. On our side saw a number of fantastic objects, such as chimneys, spires, tables &c cut from the hills by the rains and torrents. With these exceptions the march has been totally devoid of interest."[7]

However, reminders of the events of September 3 and earlier punctuated their reveries. On September 12, two Indian sisters, the older about twelve years of age and badly wounded in the shoulder, were found along the banks of the North Platte, starving and nearly naked. Dr. Ridgely attended to them, and they joined the troupe. Later on the march, the soldiers found the bodies of two more Indians, their ponies grazing casually nearby. Concluded Corporal Bandel, "They must have fled to that point and there perished of their wounds." On September 15, the command crossed to the south side and passed Bordeaux's trading post and the site of the Grattan fight. One officer could see from a distance "the pyramid of masonry which Col. Hoffman . . . has had erected over the remains of the 29 men who fell there." Later, the command camped near the mouth of Laramie River. The aforementioned Hoffman, the fort's commander, rode out to greet his comrades, giving a hearty welcome especially to his fellow Sixth Infantry officers. The next day, Harney's headquarters and the infantry camp moved within a quarter mile of Fort Laramie, while the mounted force moved up the Laramie several miles to look for sufficient grazing. It had taken thirteen months for Grattan's avengers to come in force, a span of time that seems excessively long today but reasonably short in an era and locale dependent on horsepower, footspeed, and deference to the Great Plains environment.[8]

Not surprisingly, the news of the Blue Water disaster and the many soldiers in Sioux country preceded this arrival and created great consternation amongst the Lakotas, their leaders, and their agent. Thomas Twiss had spent the time since September 7, when he learned about Blue Water from Harney's expressman, meeting with the chiefs and headmen of the Oglalas and Brulés. During his spell at Fort Laramie, Harney did little to fritter away his advantage, either with the Indians or with

Indian affairs. On September 18, Harney requested an "official interview" of Agent Twiss, whom he credited with gathering the three hundred lodges of Brulés and Oglalas camped peacefully, if not fretfully, on the Laramie thirty-five miles away. The meeting's purpose was to rubberstamp a circular that Harney had already written and was preparing to send out. In essence, it compelled traders to congregate near Forts Laramie and Pierre and prohibited their sale of ammunition to the Indians. As justification for this restriction of commerce, he stated, "In the camp which I destroyed on the Blue Water, . . . a large quantity of powder was found, which I am informed was purchased on the Missouri." The commanding officers of these two posts would henceforth supervise the Indian trade, traditionally the bailiwick of the Interior department.[9] Here were the makings of another bureaucratic wrangle between War and Interior, one that would play out over the ensuing months with Twiss and Harney as stand-ins for the two departments.[10]

After making his demands known to Twiss, Harney had him bring in Man Afraid of His Horses, Big Partisan, and other leaders on September 22 to expand on them. Harney's one-sided discourse with this group, as reported to his superiors, repeated the gist of his earlier parley with Little Thunder. "I told them that the only conditions on which they could expect peace were the prompt delivery of the murderers of the Mail party in Nov. last, the restoration of all stolen animals, and a pledge on their part to keep the road through their country open and safe for travel." Interestingly, as the names of the mail party murderers were given, the father of one was present in the delegation, a man named Grease.[11]

Unlike Little Thunder, the Lakota delegation tentatively agreed to these demands, although they needed to take them back to the village for discussion, a process estimated to take three days. Harney baited the proposal with an offer to release promptly the Lakota captives, but there was more: "I also told them that they must remain South of the Platte and take no part in the affairs that might happen North of that river. I am not prepared to say that I have any great confidence in these [their] promises, but I consider it but just to give them an opportunity to prove their desire for peace by their acts. Besides this will allow me to move towards Fort Pierre thru the hostile Sioux Country, in accordance with my original intentions." There would be consequences if this tentative peace agreement at this summit did not hold: "Should the Indians fail to comply with these conditions the delay will at least allow me to mature my plans and bring more troops into the field next Spring."[12]

Similar to the Blue Water parley, Harney was playing for time, both with the Sioux and with Washington. "[N]o positive instructions have been given me as to the course I should pursue with these Indians in the event of their making propositions for peace."[13]

Settling a war, it seemed, required just as much planning as preparing for one.

Other tribes, both allies and rivals of the Lakota, took the opportunity to declare their peaceful intentions. Some members of the Crow tribe, who "loved the white man and hated the Sioux," had come to the fort on September 21 to ask Harney what they could do to help. Harney bluntly replied that "if they wanted to fight the Sioux, they might do as they pleased," a suggestion that surely would have made Twiss, an advocate for tribal harmony, shudder if he had heard it. The next day, before the Lakota appearance, some Arapahos also made a call. They, too, were told to keep south of the Platte. Harney added this gratuitous threat to members of a tribe known for its longtime friendship with the United States, "[I]f they behaved, we would not make war on them."[14] One tribe noticeable by its absence was the Northern Cheyenne, whose leaders did not take the opportunity to declare their loyalty to one side or the other.

Some minor raiding—horse thefts and the like—still sporadically occurred, but nothing that the military and Lakota leadership wanted to make an issue of. The rumor mill, though, found hostile Indians aplenty. According to the correspondent to the *Missouri Republican*, now with a Fort Laramie dateline: "The Indians say 'come on.' They are on White Earth [White River] in large numbers and have sent messages to Gen. Harney to 'come on with his young men—that they were ready, and wanted his horses—that he had better not come further into their country, or he would cry.'"[15]

And that response, the penetration of Sioux country, is just what General Harney intended to do, but first he had some unfinished business with Capt. Albion Howe.

On the Blue Water battlefield, Harney had promised to court-martial Howe, sealed it with an outburst of profanity, and wasted no time after arriving at Fort Laramie beginning the process. The formal charge was disobedience of orders. Informally, Howe's inaction was blamed for allowing many Indians to escape Harney's sprung trap. "[B]ut for some error in the execution of the plan not a man could have escaped," wrote a contemporary. Beginning on September 18, the court, composed of fellow officers, defendant Howe, and Lieutenant Edward Hudson as judge advocate, took testimony.[16]

Lieutenant Colonel Cooke began the testimony for the prosecution. For the next few days, the proceedings granted the witnesses an opportunity to replay the battle, in particular, the mounted charge and pursuit. It also provided the opening, in keeping with military courtesy and politeness, for fellow officers to skewer Howe in the most innocuous and oblique of terms. John Mendenhall, a young lieutenant in Howe's company, spoke volumes when he volunteered the aside, "I thought it strange we did not follow the Dragoons."[17]

The military tribunal served as mere sideshow, especially since Howe escaped conviction and punishment on a technicality. The important actions came in the deployment of troops in anticipation of the Sioux Expedition's next phase. A flurry of orders ensued: Lieutenant Dudley would go as far as Fort Kearny to collect thirty straggling recruits of Company E, Tenth Infantry. After doing so and returning west, he would briefly relieve Captain Wharton at Fort Grattan, who would abandon the post and move his Company I, Sixth Infantry, and all wounded east to Fort Kearny. Capt. Lawrence P. Graham, in charge of Companies D and H, Second Dragoons, and part of the Fort Laramie garrison prior to Harney's arrival, would march to Fort Grattan accompanied by a wagon, load the Indian tipis and tipi poles left there, and return quickly "after breaking up Fort Grattan." Graham's squadron would join Harney's command at Fort Laramie or catch up with the general on the trail if he had already departed. Lieutenant Colonel Cooke would return with a detachment of men and his Second Dragoon staff to Fort Riley, join the remaining assemblage of the regiment gathered there, and sit out the winter. Any wagon trains encountered by the detachments would be provided a protective escort.[18] In the opposite direction, either Captain Heth, Dudley's commander, and his Company E, or Maj. Marshall Saxe Howe (Albion's brother) and one of the dragoon companies would take thirty days' rations and escort the Salt Lake bound train of Livingston and Kincaid at least as far as Devil's Gate.[19] Harney, who masterminded all this, could see these chess pieces as he moved them about. But what about his other army in the field which he could not see?

Without really knowing where the Fort Pierre column of Second infantrymen was, on September 20, Harney counter-

manded ("hastily," criticized Captain Gardner) his orders of
August 21. Issued only four days after the force's mid-Septem-
ber departure from its Missouri River post, the new directive,
as well as news about Blue Water, would not reach this field
commander until October. By that time, the column had traveled
one hundred fifty miles from Fort Pierre before having to
retrace its steps. This miscommunication notwithstanding,
improved connections looked promising because now Harney
could take advantage of a relatively unknown, yet strategic trail
between Fort Pierre and Fort Laramie, which today has been
nearly forgotten.[20]

Fur traders had blazed the trail between the two posts
long before they fell into government hands.[21] But this was
somewhat familiar country to the U.S. Army. In 1849, Captain
Van Vliet, Harney's assistant quartermaster, had been a member
of a small military detachment that had successfully traversed
the 323-mile route. Prior to the Fort Laramie arrival of the
Sioux Expedition, an army supply train had ventured on this
trail in the late summer and early fall of 1855, proving that
wagons could make the trip, especially if no Indians were
encountered. That the trail passed through Sioux country of
the White and Bad rivers made the next step irresistible to
Harney. That he had Warren, an engineer, to map it, was a
bonus.[22] This then was the route Harney took when he left
Fort Laramie on September 29 on his hunt for Miniconjous
and more Brulés, accompanied by "enough troops to whip the
Indians whenever he meets them."[23] He could leave knowing
his rear was relatively safe.

On September 25, some of the Indian leaders came in
with Twiss to formally agree to the general's demands, and they
literally smoked a pipe of peace. His subsequent instructions
to Hoffman presumed their compliance: "[Y]ou can permit the
Ogalalas and Brules bands of Sioux to establish a camp in the

vicinity of Fort Laramie should they comply with their promises to deliver the murderers of the Mail party and restore stolen property. . . ." The accused, if surrendered, would be confined at Fort Laramie until they could be transported to Fort Leavenworth. Harney considered these Lakota men, though, captives, not criminals, and representatives of their people, not pariahs. He astutely added, "Should any of their friends desire to accompany them you can permit from ten to twenty to do so." And, as he had done during months leading up to Blue Water, Harney encouraged Hoffman to continue to gather useful intelligence on the Indians, their conduct, and intentions.[24] But unlike before, no sense of urgency permeated this request.

Agent Twiss promised to do the same, gather intelligence, for his superiors, but he put into words what Harney was not yet prepared to do. "The Sioux war is near its termination. If I am not totally mistaken in my judgment, all of the Sioux bands to the north will submit to General Harney and sue for peace; they have no desire nor wish to fight or prolong the war. The affair on the Little [sic] Blue Water, on the 3rd of September, was a thunder clap to them and has opened their ears and given them to understand truths which they did not believe before that chastisement."[25] But, just in case things turned out differently, Twiss planned to stay in Indian country for the winter.

The September 29 departure of the command saw the loss of Heth's mounted company—the company would winter in Indian tipis at the North Platte bridge, near present Casper, Wyoming—and the gain of two companies of Sixth Infantry—formerly part of Major Hoffman's Fort Laramie garrison. The civilian contingent of "mountain men," composed of hunters, scouts, and "spies," now swelled to about twenty-five. Their job was to find Harney more Indians, either on the trail or on a possible side trip around the Black Hills. No one knew if another collision would occur on this next excursion overland.[26]

Actually, the men astutely saw more imminent danger from the elements than from the Indians and supplemented their issued supplies with more blankets and heavier clothing. Others looked with envy on the Indian lodges versus their canvas tents. The rumor circulated that Harney intended to take enough tipis—ones surely expropriated from Little Thunder's village—for his and his staff's use. To add insult to injury, he would also retain some women prisoners to pitch and strike them![27]

By October 1, the soldiers reached the Niobrara River. Two days later, they paused at a White River camp on the future site of Fort Robinson, Nebraska. The site made impressions on both Captain Todd and Lieutenant Warren. Todd happily wrote: "We encamped on a pretty tongue of land lying at the base of, and surrounded to the West and North by, high hills covered with pine, while down the river the view is beautiful. The hill on the eastern side of the camp is 800 or a 1,000 feet high, presenting a singularly castellated appearance, with its towers and domes. (The day is delightful.)"[28]

To Warren the pine-ridged landscape was no less striking, but to be remembered more as the site of a soldier burial. Joseph M. Lake, a dragoon who died of illness on the march, was buried near "a remarkable bluff," probably Todd's high hill.[29] This somber event provided the impetus to name that impressive landmark, Soldier Cliff, a place name that continues today, although wrongly assumed by many to refer to soldiers of 1874 who founded Camp Robinson.

The next morning, October 4, the camp awoke to three or four inches of snow on the ground and the reality of a winter campaign on the northern Plains. Grass was scarce for the six hundred animals in the column. Some adjustments were immediately made, even though the snow disappeared before day's end. Todd, for one, took the opportunity after a short day's march to pitch his Indian lodge; he "found it comfortable although small." For the teamsters it meant extra care for their mules, even helping them to their feet before the morning harnessing.[30]

The personalities and interests of officers Todd and Warren manifested themselves in the diary entries during this, as yet, uneventful journey. On October 7, Todd detected an upcoming break in the boredom because the troops were nearing the "Mauvaisse Terre," or Badlands of present-day South Dakota. Warren's entry for the same day concentrated on the road and his thoughts about how to improve it for future wagon traffic. Scenery rather than duty, though, won out.[31]

Not since describing buffalo hunting or Indian fighting had Todd so exercised his vocabulary. "For the last three days we have been passing along the edge of the Mauvaise Terre, . . . and some good geological specimens have been picked up by various persons of the command. . . .[T]he towering masses and deep ravines of the Bad Lands stare us fully in the face, and tomorrow we shall be among them. Many of us are anticipating great pleasure from our promised explorations and the new wonders that will be opened up to us."[32]

For a time fossil hunting became a soldier craze. Recorded Todd: "This morning every one who could be spared and felt any curiosity started out with the hope of adding something new to the collections already made." Todd himself left the road with a dozen budding paleontologists. "Everywhere, all over and through, these hills and ravines, were strewed the remains of turtle, petrified, of all sizes, shattered and perfect, some not larger than the crown of a hat, others of huge proportions— one very fine specimen now in the possession of Genl. H., I pointed out to Capt. Van V[liet]; it consists of two petrified turtles. . . ." Lieutenant Balch, especially proud of his collection of "fossils and petrifications," intended on sending his to "Prof. Bailey for the cabinet of the Military Academy."[33]

The general, though, had other things on his mind and had reached the conclusion that all he was going to stumble across this fall would be dead turtles, not live Indians. He made more moves. On October 10, he sent Light Company G, Fourth Artillery, and Companies C and G, Sixth Infantry, back to Fort Laramie to seek winter quarters, while the remainder of the command set forth on the last push to Fort Pierre.[34]

Harney and his staff left the command on October 19 and reached the fort that day, preceding his troops. The bulk of his command became delayed by a furious storm of freezing rain and snow, an appetizer of the months to come. Since leaving the North Platte, the Sioux Expedition had marched through "hostile Brule country," yet hardly encountered any Indians, belligerent or otherwise.[35] There would be no replays of Blue Water this season, nor, it turned out, the next. The combination of harsh weather, a tired command, and a vanished foe would keep the troops close to home this winter. So would Lakota overtures of peace.[36]

Twiss was right. The war was essentially over.

❊ ❊ ❊

Captain Heth, stationed on the North Platte, remembered the winter of 1855–1856 as the most severe he had ever endured in the West. Private Meyers, stationed at Fort Pierre and who experienced much the same, cursed Captain Turnley's "cardboard" houses. When the snow, cold, and wind inevitably arrived on the northern Great Plains, his comrades took steps to improve their shelter. They dug trenches around the houses and banked the earth. After a storm blew away some roofs, the men tied down the flimsy affairs with ropes. Firewood was lacking, water had to be carted or sledded from a great distance, and forage for the animals disappeared.[37] The elements proved to be the greatest concern of the expedition's commander.

Ever since his first look at Fort Pierre, itself an unhappy experience, General Harney had focused his mind on keeping his nine hundred men—four companies of dragoons and ten of infantry—and livestock intact through a rigorous Dakota winter. He may have understated his dismay when he reported that the fort and its buildings were "in a more dilapidated condition than I had been led to expect." For some officers— specifically Lieutenant Balch (Ordnance Department), Captain Van Vliet (Quartermaster Department), and Lieutenant Warren (Topographical Engineers)—this was moot; they were escaping to the States, said Balch, "as fast as possible before the snow sets in," ostensibly to prepare for next year. The recent widower, Major Woods, left for Fort Riley to take care of long-delayed personal business. Captain Winship was relieved from duty on Harney's staff and replaced by Capt. Alfred Pleasonton as his assistant adjutant general and ordered to St. Louis, thus ending this officer's involvement in the war. Not long after passing through the city on his way to Troy, New York, Winship died of natural causes in his hometown on December 13, 1855.[38]

For the benefit of the vast majority who had to stay, Harney took immediate steps. In November the dragoons, the Sixth infantrymen, and all but two companies of Second Infantry were dispersed from "the bleak plains of Fort Pierre to the shelter of the woods" in the river bottoms, housed in recently purchased Indian lodges or hastily built log huts. Capt. William Gardner was put in command of "Cantonment Miller," composed of three companies of Second Infantry and located on the east bank of the Missouri River over seven miles above the fort. The move must have especially rankled Gardner who presciently wrote his mother earlier: "I predict there will be a good deal of wrangling here this winter about quarters, and, as the officers are of different corps and quite unacquainted with each other, there may be broken heads before spring. I had just got myself comfortable, and the idea of being reduced to one room is any thing but agreeable. . . .I never felt more like deserting in my life."[39]

But at least Gardner seemed to make the best of a bad situation. One of his "men," the boy musician Meyers, had a regular Huck Finn winter. Meyers fraternized with a small village of Yankton Sioux who were wintering near Fort Pierre. He learned a smattering of their language, ate and lounged in their lodges, traded a few trifles, and came away impressed by these "most interesting people."[40]

Such a scene of domesticity did not repeat itself everywhere. Maj. Marshall Howe, his dragoon squadron dispersed south and from whom Harney had heard nothing, prompted the general to venture out in late December to inspect Howe's camp. "To know every thing satisfactorily a commander must see every thing with his own eyes," wrote Harney. To show how safe Harney felt, he made the 230-mile, overland trip with only two officers and eleven men.

Harney found conditions deplorable: the camp was on the open plain, men were frostbitten, and most of the horses had died. The immediate result was an enraged general, an extended effort to set things right, and the court-martial of another Howe brother. The longer-term consequence was that Harney found the future site for Fort Pierre's eventual replacement, Fort Randall.[41] His reasoning involved more than current conditions. "In this country the troops select and command the few positions where the Indians can congregate and from which they can act. Let these be occupied, and the Indians must cease to disturb the country. . . .The affair at Blue Water has sufficiently proven they cannot escape us."[42]

The Indians were never far from Harney's thoughts that winter. From Fort Laramie came word that the Sioux were delivering several stolen animals. More importantly Big Chin, Red Leaf, and Spotted Tail had surrendered to the post commander on October 28. This brave, potentially suicidal act by men implicated in the mail party murders to offer themselves as hostages for their people was treated rather casually. Harney's only acknowledgment was an order to take the trio under guard to Fort Leavenworth. He had bigger fish to fry. That same month he had begun distributing a circular to "the principal chiefs of the different Bands of the Sioux Indians." It ordered them to Fort Pierre for a talk, where Harney intended to "make all the demands that will satisfy for their offences [sic] which have brought on this war. . . ."[43]

The Sioux Expedition was not far from the public's thoughts either, and the fall and winter of 1855–1856 gave the American public and government representatives time to digest the reports from the Indian war and the Nebraska frontier. The *New York Times* of September 25, 1855, had blared the news of a "Great Battle Between the United States Troops and Indians," which hurriedly reprinted the account from St. Louis's *Missouri Republican*. Subsequent updates and summaries usually came filtered through this organ and other western newspapers. Sometimes the news could be traced to official sources. On October 6 readers of the *Times* benefited from a telegraphic dispatch from Washington, where its correspondent already had access to Harney's Blue Water battlefield report of September 5.[44] Debate erupted immediately. Commented "Aquiday," no friend of the War department, to the *New York Times* and written from Washington:

The lamentable butcheries of Indians by Harney's command on the Plains have excited the most painful feelings. The so-called battle was simply a massacre, but whether those Indians were really the same who have cut off emigrant trains with so many circumstances of savage cruelty, or whether it is possible to distinguish between the innocent and the guilty in retaliating these outrages, are points on which we have no reliable information. It is, however, my impression that if the business of protecting immigrant trains had been entrusted to the Secretary of the Interior, he would not have dispatched Harney's expedition. . . .I trust the time has passed forever when Americans can look upon these holiday campaigns against Indians with exultation.[45]

A few weeks later "Aquiday" let loose another barrage, and Blue Water became a means to recount past political arguments.

"The Indian massacre by Harney's command proves the justice of the objections raised in Congress to the increase of the army. This miserable and treacherous butchery was perpetrated, perhaps, by way of vindicating the necessity of the new regiments. It is not unlikely that some further outrages will be committed in order to convince Congress of the expediency of very large appropriations to meet the contingencies of Indian wars."[46]

Such news and comment were the wonders of modern communication. But meanwhile, on the frontier, Harney had to wait one hundred days and see if his circular would succeed in getting its subjects to Fort Pierre by March.

* * *

Thomas Twiss, an ex-officer, could not abide by treaty councils called for and conducted by army officers, and he feebly tried to block Harney's diplomatic efforts. In February 1856, after Harney learned that Twiss had instructed Oglala and Brulé leaders not to go to Fort Pierre, the general instructed the commanding officer of Fort Laramie to essentially put him under house arrest and hustle the delegation on.

But Twiss's opposition only reflected that of his superiors in the Indian Office. In January 1856, Alfred Cumming, the superintendent of Indian affairs, returned to St. Louis from a season-long excursion on the upper Missouri, capped by a fall meeting with Harney at Fort Pierre. Cumming's February report of his 1855 activities focused on his productive encounters with the tribes and stepped lightly around the year's War Department successes. He could not resist, though, making oblique criticisms of Harney.

For instance, on July 1, 1855, Cumming's upriver boat passed the abandoned site of the Arikara Indian village (in present North Dakota) attacked by Col. Henry Leavenworth in 1823. Leavenworth's punitive expedition was largely seen at the time as a failure since the Arikaras escaped virtually unscathed, although their earthlodge village was wrecked. Surely referring to Harney, Cumming wrote: "The conduct of Colonel L. was much censured at the time, but the shape of the country plainly shows that it was an act of mercy on his part to the poor wretches, as he could easily have occupied a position which would have entirely cut off their retreat, and they must all have perished in their dirt lodges or been slain in any effort to escape by land or water; they have ever since continued to live at peace with the whites."[47]

Since Harney was never known as being merciful, Cumming piously continued in the same vein: "The occasional exhibition of the military strength of the government seems to be indispensably necessary to insure the respect of the Indians; but I believe that a magnanimous and merciful course is more productive of permanent benefit than wholesale and indiscriminate butchery."

This would be Cumming's closest to making a backhanded acknowledgement of the apparent success of the Sioux Expedition. Twiss's delays and Cumming's barbs had no effect on the schedule of the treaty council. By late February some seventy to hundred Lakota leaders, minus the Oglalas, were camped near the headquarters of the Sioux Expedition.[48]

The Fort Pierre treaty council of 1856 had none of the pomp and majesty of the Horse Creek proceedings of five years before. It was short on ceremony and long on business, lasting only from March 1 to March 5. Nevertheless, it had its moments. Harney, the sole speaker on day one, wielded a velvet-covered fist. On one hand he warned, "We will have blood for blood;" on the other, he turned revisionist and hinted at what worse could have happened to the Indians at Blue Water, "They might have suffered a great deal more, but I left a door open for them to escape." On day two, resolute Little Thunder, the first to speak and the one who had suffered the most, spoke for all, "I don't wish to fight you."[49] Such was the magnanimity of the victors and the pragmatism of the losers.

Harney had his authority and instructions from President Pierce in hand. Basically, there were only a few conditions: The Sioux must surrender the murderers, return stolen property, and keep away from the emigrant road. In return, the United States would restore their annuities, return the Blue Water prisoners, and protect the Sioux from the whites. This last provision, although the most amorphous and puzzling, received little discussion about its implementation. And the result after three more days of talking? "[T]he different delegations of the Sioux . . . have agreed and consented to each and all of the conditions the President and the General have thought proper to impose upon them." The council ended with a flourish. Six months after meeting at Blue Water, Harney now offered Little Thunder his hand, pledging "I will always be your friend hereafter." The crowd applauded.[50]

Harney also gave the Sioux permission to trade again and alerted Major Hoffman at Fort Laramie of this. Hoffman and Captain Wharton of Fort Kearny were also instructed to turn over to Little Thunder all the Blue Water women and children prisoners they held. Chief Iron Shell, a council delegate, made a point of asking for his wife, who was at Fort Kearny. Still up in the air was the fate of two Lakota individuals, "the man who killed the cow," otherwise known as High Forehead, and an unnamed "man who killed Gibson." They were yet to be "delivered up by the nation," the capture of whom was strictly, in the eyes of the army, now "an affair of their own. . . ." The army, it seemed, would make no overt effort to get them.[51] This apparent turnabout later proved effective.

One Lakota leader who made a favorable impression was Bear's Rib, Little Thunder's counterpart and head chief of the Hunkpapa Lakota. His extended remarks during the council included this vague reference: "My brother [Harney], if you will look around this fort, you will see some dry bones, which show my nation how to behave well towards some whites." The person keeping the minutes had to include this aside to explain the "dry bones" term: "meaning the bones of an Indian he [Bear's Rib] had killed for misbehaving towards the traders." In the early 1850s, the story went, a Sioux Indian man had killed a cow owned by a Fort Pierre trader and not paid damages. The trader had turned to Bear's Rib to punish the offender. Bear's Rib immediately left the fort, found the culprit, and shot him dead.[52] This was the type of leader with whom Harney and the government could work. There would be no Grattan disasters on his watch.

On May 20, a Sioux delegation returned to Fort Pierre and brought all the stolen property and the last two prisoners, High Forehead (the cow killer) and the murderer of Gibson. Harney, citing mitigating circumstances in their crimes and to great fanfare, set both men free. Politically, their punishment no longer mattered. Diplomatically, this closed "all our difficulties and grievances with the Sioux." The March proceedings at Fort Pierre and an April follow-up with the Oglalas, though, had already convinced Secretary of War Davis in Washington,

who proclaimed on May 31, 1856, that the war had been brought
"to a successful termination."[53]

* * *

Only a few loose ends remained, including several
hundred soldiers garrisoning faraway posts. At Fort Pierre in
early April, the frozen Missouri broke up, and soon the "spring
rise" commenced. On May 17, the steamer *Grey Cloud*, loaded
with much-needed corn and potatoes, made an initial landing
near Fort Pierre.[54] Future suppliers would have to travel no
farther up the Missouri than thirty miles above the mouth of
the Niobrara River. After spending the better part of June in
the area, Harney designated this the location of Fort Pierre's
successor post. All but a modest guardian force moved downriver to build Fort Randall in July. In a final act of frugality
the soldiers would knock down Turnley's portable cottages for
their immediate reuse.[55]

At the same time, General Harney was making his own
preparations for departure. Harney received orders in mid-July
to "close the operations of the Sioux Expedition"—by now a
fait accompli. He wasted no time in leaving and on July 22
reported from Fort Leavenworth, Kansas, that he and Captain
Pleasonton were wrapping up some paperwork there. By August,
the general was in Washington, D.C., receiving his next assignment.[56] More interest was probably being paid in the nation's
capital to the current presidential campaign than a past Indian
campaign.

The new season on the Plains brought a new, larger crop
of emigrants and another set of Indian problems. In 1856, the
tribe that caused trouble was the Cheyenne, and even while
he wound down, Harney was forecasting the need to chastise
these Indians. Throughout the Sioux troubles, the Cheyenne
tribe had been nearby, somewhat passive, but not disinterested
witnesses to the events that had swirled about Fort Laramie.

They had not participated in the demise of Grattan and Conquering Bear or the vengeance of the Brulés and therefore had largely avoided being tarnished by other native misdeeds, but not completely. In 1854, agent John Whitfield had called them the "sauciest" Indians he had met, and Captain Winship's report of the same year had lumped Cheyenne warriors with their Lakota counterparts as potential, if not inevitable, military foes. Less than a year after Blue Water, this indeed came to pass.[57]

The Cheyenne troubles of 1856–1857 followed a now all-too-familiar pattern. Near a North Platte site, a relatively minor fracas between soldiers, Indians, and livestock escalated into acts of violence, retaliatory raids, and calls for a punitive expedition, which followed a year after the initial incident. This time Col. Edwin Sumner, another old cavalryman, led a sizeable, mounted force onto the Plains. The season's climax of the Cheyenne Expedition came at the Battle of Solomon Fork in Kansas. The Cheyennes encountered there on June 29, 1857, made a brave stand, but were soon routed.[58] On the surface, the greatest distinction between Blue Water and Solomon Fork was the lack of noncombatant deaths, due primarily because of the absence of a sleeping Cheyenne village at this battlefield. The first major battle between the United States and the Cheyenne tribe resulted in another beaten Indian foe and another precarious peace. Together with the Sioux Expedition, they defined the successful military expedition.

Chapter 8
Memory and Legacy

One hundred and fifty years have passed since the First Sioux War and the fight at Blue Water Creek, an event for which a contemporary exclaimed, "I do not suppose the Indians in this country ever had such a perfect clearing out. . . ." This individual thought the memory among the Sioux could not wane. "They will have cause to remember General Harney."[1] And in their way, the Lakota made efforts to keep the memory from being extinguished. Lakota keepers dutifully recorded happenings on their winter counts, the pictographic record of a year's significant events, if not to the tribe, then at least to the chronicler. Several of these calendars on hide or paper survive, a few kept by Brulé Lakotas. Many events and the symbols denoting them have lost the stories that accompanied them and have become objects of scholarly scrutiny and puzzlement. Such is not necessarily the case for the time corresponding to the years 1854–1856. For instance, the interpretation that accompanied one Brulé winter count symbol mentioned Little Thunder by name and the "others taken prisoner at Ash Hollow."[2]

On the other end of the cultural spectrum, the surviving overlander narratives for the emigration season of 1856, hardly with the war ended, gave no special notice to the events of the previous year.[3] In 1857, Helen McCowen Carpenter's wagon train reached Ash Hollow on June 23, and from an ex-soldier she recorded an account of the fight.

"In this engagement the Indians were routed. Those who took refuge in a cave in the bluffs were followed by the soldiers who tried every means to induce them to come out. Being unsuccessful, volley after volley was poured into the cave, with the result that not one Indian came out alive. There were in all, 18 men, women, and children. . . ."[4]

As with all subsequent passersby, Carpenter did not visit the battlefield itself, but gathered her images of the fight from others or from the few visual reminders along the road at Ash Hollow. "We passed the graves of five soldiers who were killed in Sept. 1855. . . .Tomb stones were made of cedar, brought from the bluff hewn into shape, then painted white, with black lettering." Obviously moved, Carpenter solemnly added to one headboard a bit of romantic poetry ("He sleeps his last sleep, he has fought his last battle. . . ."). She may have offered this sign of respect to counter those of a more practical "Dr. J. Noble," who had passed the graves earlier and had painted an advertisement for his medical services on each cedar slab.[5]

Capt. John W. Phelps, U.S. Army, also traveled through Ash Hollow in 1857, and his interests were more military, specifically the ruins of a fortification. "A little enclosure made of sods, close upon the bank of the river about a hundred paces from me, occupied for a while after the affair at Ash Hollow, or Blue Water as it is called, by two companies of Infantry, but long since wholly deserted, bears the name of Fort Grattan— in its loneliness and abandonment a fit symbol of the fate of him from whom it was named. . . ."[6]

Captain Phelps and another American army were on their way to Utah to battle Mormon rebels, not Sioux warriors. In 1855, Capt. John Todd had reflected the general consensus of the Americans. "Never for years has there been such an utter rout and disorganization of a band of Indians. Whether it will have the effect to exasperate or intimidate them remains to be seen."[7]

In the short-term, relations were good, or at least quiet, between the United States and the Lakota nation. Nothing shook the unsteady peace during the interim, not even the failure of the U.S. Senate to ratify Harney's treaty. Maybe the tribe was still in shock from Blue Water or in a state of diplomatic confusion. Was the treaty of 1856 in effect? Or the treaty of 1851? Whatever the reason, the short-term significance of the outcome of the First Sioux War was a perceived armistice. Besides, with Cheyennes, Latter-day Saints, Missouri border ruffians, and Kansas Free-soilers, the U.S. government had other distractions.

Coincidentally, General Harney initially headed the military excursion to Utah Territory to punish the Latter-day Saints for various misdeeds and to exert federal authority over another recalcitrant populace. The Utah Expedition brought even greater numbers of soldiers to the Platte valley in 1857–1858 to keep the vital lines of transportation and communication open to the West Coast. The soldiers (without Harney, who was replaced as their leader) would follow the well-beaten path, nee military road, to Fort Laramie and points further west.[8]

By the 1858 travel season, the events of the previous years had become jumbled, at least to some overlanders. Thaddeus Kenderdine, another literate teamster in the vein of William Chandless, reached Ash Hollow and garbled its history. "Near this spot a battle was fought a year before between the Cheyennes and the Americans under General Harney."[9]

As with Helen Carpenter, Kenderdine had the benefit of an "eye-witness" account. "The Cheyennes were entirely routed, with the loss of 200 of their number and all their tents and baggage, which were burned in a huge bonfire by the victors. The squaws were taken prisoner and distributed among our gallant soldiers, but were afterwards given up to their lawful owners."

In spite of factual inaccuracies, the consequences of the battle, no matter who was involved, resonated with all over-landers. They felt safer. Continued Kenderdine: "The severe castigation which the Cheyennes received here has humbled them greatly, and they are far less mischievous now than formerly. Old Harney is held in great detestation among them, and the mere mention of his name will bring a scowl on the face of a Cheyenne brave."

For army veterans of the First Sioux War, its aftermath brought little relief, as the aforementioned campaigns attest. Corp. Eugene Bandel survived the winter of 1855–1856 at Fort Pierre and for the next two years saw service in "Bleeding Kansas," that ugly prelude to the Civil War. The Utah Expedition brought him and his Sixth Infantry company in 1858 again to Ash Hollow, this time uneventfully as his correspondence to his parents in Germany indicates. His experiences in the ranks did not dissuade him from undertaking a later civilian career as a master mechanic for the U.S. Army. It was on one such job at Vancouver Barracks, Washington, in 1888, whereat Bandel fell from a tower to his death. His remains lie in a military cemetery there.[10]

Musician Augustus Meyers, another participant, also exhi-bited no ill effects from his stint in the West. Meyers witnessed the abandonment of the detestable Fort Pierre in 1856 and the establishment of Fort Randall on the Missouri River. He also saw police duty in Kansas Territory before his enlistment expired. After a brief interlude as a civilian, he reenlisted and rejoined his old Second Infantry mates in time for the Civil War. New assignments took Meyers to the East, where he served in the Army of the Potomac in Virginia. He survived his second enlistment to enter civilian life again and after a long

and prosperous business career, which he attributed to his
Civil War training as an army clerk, he wrote his memoirs.
Ten Years in the Ranks, U.S. Army (1914), possibly a minor if
overlooked classic, was really two books in one, divided neatly
into two episodes, service on the frontier in the 1850s, and in
Virginia in the 1860s. Before it was published, Meyers, a New
York City resident, returned to his old Fort Pierre haunts to
look around. But time had spared neither him nor the fort.
He needed help from the locals of Pierre, South Dakota, to
find the site.[11]

By the time of Meyers's visit, the twentieth century was
well underway. Most of those senior to the boy musician, and
whose lives and careers had remained intertwined with the
northern Plains, had long since perished. The fates of others
were a mystery, such as "The man who killed the cow." The
Miniconjou man High Forehead (or Straight Foretop) who
had helped spark a war gained a reprieve in 1856 and dropped
from sight. Or did he? Curiously, another Miniconjou man by
the similar name of High Foretop was accused in 1874 of
murdering a white employee of the Red Cloud Agency. That
action brought the U.S. Army from Fort Laramie to Soldier
Creek in northwest Nebraska, where they established Camp
(later Fort) Robinson. At the site where Captain Todd and
Lieutenant Warren had witnessed the burial of dragoon Joseph
Lake in 1855, the army set up camp and stayed until 1948.[12]

Cokawin, the Brulé who had survived Blue Water, lived
for many years, long enough to pass on her story to Susan
Bordeaux, the mixed-blood daughter of Fort Laramie trader
James Bordeaux. Susan described her as a "fine-looking, stately
Indian woman." When recounting her story, Cokawin showed
Susan her scars from that day.[13]

Spotted Tail, who had shown such valor at Blue Water and
at his later surrender, survived his captivity at Fort Leavenworth.

A model prisoner, he soon received a pardon, apparently from President Pierce himself, and returned to his Brulés in summer 1856. He assumed a leadership role, one he never relinquished. Later observers concluded that his prison stint taught him the futility of resisting the United States. It might have, militarily, but Spotted Tail remained diplomatically an astute antagonist to relentless government efforts to weaken his people and his own authority. In 1870, he headed a Brulé delegation to council with President Ulysses S. Grant. Upon meeting in Washington a delegation of Cherokee Indians from Indian Territory, in appearance more white than red, he dismissed the lot as not "real Indians." The same could never be said of Chief Spotted Tail.[14]

His Rosebud Reservation colleague, Iron Shell, lived until 1896, long enough for him and his descendants to pass on valuable information on the life and culture of his people to interested scholars. Iron Shell fought again in the 1860s Sioux wars against the whites and survived to sign the Fort Laramie Treaty of 1868, the peace accords that ended the wars. Maybe he passed on this trait of survival to his son Hollow Horn Bear. The infant had purportedly been found on the Blue Water battlefield and was later returned safely to the tribe. The son cast a commanding figure. He became a noted leader in his own right and his portrait served as the model for a fourteen-cent U.S. postage stamp issued in 1922.[15]

And what of Little Thunder after his dramatic handshake with Harney? The elusive survivor of Blue Water continued to be rather elusive in the historical record after the 1856 Fort Pierre council. Apparently his influence and the number of his followers during the ensuing decades remained some-what modest, and later historians killed him off in 1865 and 1879.[16] The latter year seems more likely since in 1873, Maj. Nathan A. M. Dudley encountered under odd circumstances his old adversary near Sidney Barracks, in present Sidney,

Nebraska. Little Thunder's band of Brulés was spotted north of the post, hunting wild horses, and the chase nearly brought all into town. Post commander Dudley sent six men and an interpreter to ascertain the Indians' intentions, and they found thirty-five lodges moving south to meet another forty lodges to hunt buffalo on the Republican River. The meeting prompted Dudley to recall the past . . . incorrectly. "Little Thunder is the Brule chief that General Harney fought near Ash Hollow on the third day of December [*sic*], 1855. I know him well."[17]

Some things had not changed, particularly the army's opinion of Little Thunder's leadership skills. "I think him to be a good old Indian, meaning well, but he says his young men are very hard to control now as they do not get enough to eat on the reservation." The party then went into camp east of town, no trouble occurred, and the chief passed gently from the scene.

The same could not be said of Bear's Rib, the head chief of the Hunkpapas, who continued to advocate peace with the whites. This position became increasingly difficult to sustain within this, the tribe of Sitting Bull and the other northern Lakota tribes, and in 1862 Bear's Rib was assassinated by another Lakota, dead at about age fifty. Some said it was for signing Harney's 1856 treaty and being too friendly with the whites.[18]

Faring better was an opponent of Harney's treaty, Thomas Twiss, the government agent during the First Sioux War. He remained in charge of the Upper Platte Agency through the remainder of the Pierce and all of the Buchanan administrations. His years immediately after Blue Water were ones of good service to the Indians, all things considered, and his tactic of separating "friendly" from "hostile" Indians became something of the norm in later conflicts. In 1857, Twiss moved the agency away from Fort Laramie and its distractions to the relative isolation of Deer Creek. He took an Oglala wife, with whom he had a large family, and took to wearing Indian clothing. Acquaintances remembered an Old Testament-like figure with long white hair and beard, carrying a six-foot-long staff. Abraham Lincoln's election as president in 1860 drastically changed his status, and he and his brood drifted to eastern Nebraska by the end of the decade. After his death a few years later, his widow returned the family to her people. The surname, sometimes in the variation "Twist," survives among residents of the Pine Ridge Reservation.[19]

Another former West Pointer also took his leave from the army and stayed in the West. John B. S. Todd, the excitable diarist of the Sioux Expedition, resigned his commission in 1856 to become the post sutler at Fort Randall. A prosperous businessman and a successful politician in early Dakota Territory, Todd was not hurt by the fact that his cousin was Mary Todd Lincoln.[20]

Most of Twiss's and Todd's fellow West Pointers who remained in the military saw warfare on a greater and grander scale than anything their frontier service ever afforded them. Three veterans of Blue Water became major players in the greatest Civil War battle of all—Gettysburg. Henry Heth, a Virginian who defected to the Confederacy and was a general by July 1, 1863, led a division of men and made the first major contact with Union forces. Gen. John Buford, ever the cavalryman and the Union loyalist, delayed Heth with his own division.[21] Both men commanded thousands of men compared to the few dozen in 1855.

A later biographer rather surprisingly saw a connection between the tactics employed at Blue Water and those at Gettysburg. General Buford, it was claimed, drew on the experience of Blue Water to look beyond the saber charge as the cavalry's sole purpose and to combine horses as vehicles for heavily-armed infantrymen. At Gettysburg, Buford deployed such troops rapidly and dismounted them before the enemy, against whom they effectively discharged their long-range firearms. Heth failed to embrace the concept, and "eight years later Buford used this formula to keep his former comrade halted and confused at a crucial moment in history."[22] This conclusion came not from a biographer of either general, but of another alumnus of the Sioux Expedition, Philip St. George Cooke. The commander of Harney's cavalry (and also a Union general) was something of an author himself—he even wrote a book entitled *Cooke's Cavalry Tactics*—but he apparently never himself ascribed such significance to Blue Water.[23]

For another veteran of the Sioux Expedition at Gettysburg, old talents served his country well. On July 2, 1863, Gen. G. K. Warren, the chief engineer of the Army of the Potomac, drew on his topographical acumen to identify, then shore up the weaknesses at the strategic Big and Little Round Tops. By all accounts, his prompt decisions on the Union's left front saved the (second) day. Today a visitor can see his bronze, full-scale statue on the Little Round Top prominence, gazing west across the battlefield, binoculars in hand.[24]

A romantic might say that Warren should look in no other direction. In 1856 and 1857 Warren returned to Sioux country, where the diminutive officer was known as "Little Chief." He made further explorations in Nebraska Territory on behalf of the Topographical Engineers, filling in the blank spaces of a vast region. His work, embodied in his valuable reports and maps, and those of other army explorers, helped pave the way for the transcontinental railroad to become a reality a decade later. This was an engineering achievement in which he must have taken some pride.[25]

But like Buford and Heth, Warren's military career would be defined overwhelmingly by what he did or did not do in the Civil War. Most writers would find their frontier service incidental, if mentioned at all, although twists of fate, the stuff that biographers crave, certainly abound. Gen. Richard B. Garnett of the Confederate Army, the captain who had sent Lieutenant Fleming from Fort Laramie to the Miniconjou village in 1853, achieved everlasting glory on the third day of Gettysburg. As a brigade commander, he would die gallantly and mysteriously in Pickett's charge, his body never identified. He would never know his son William, the product of his liaison with an Oglala woman. "Billy" Garnett lived well into the twentieth century, a noted interpreter, historian, and cultural intermediary. This surname, too, appears prominently today on the Pine Ridge Reservation, as it does amongst one of the first families of Virginia.[26]

And almost laughably, Gen. Albion P. Howe, the officer whom Harney would have gladly shot at Blue Water for his dawdling, ended his Civil War service in court. He sat not as a defendant but as one of the judges of the military tribunal for the Lincoln assassination conspirators.[27]

Although finally receiving his promotion to brigadier general in 1858, William S. Harney played no great role in the Civil War. At its commencement he commanded the Department of the West, and from his St. Louis headquarters almost lost the state of Missouri to the secessionists. His political bungling prompted his superiors, particularly President Lincoln, to freeze him out from any future commands, before his forced retirement in 1863. Though a native Tennessean, Jacksonian Democrat, and slave owner, Harney remained loyal to the Union through the war.[28]

If Harney had no opportunity to burnish his war record in the Civil War, one last, fleeting chance to do so in the West presented itself in 1862. In Minnesota the Dakota, or Eastern Sioux, rose up against their white neighbors, and a full-scale insurrection ensued. Desperate, then vengeful, Minnesotans called on Lincoln to send the greatest living Indian fighter to their aid, but the president refused, and the settlers had to settle for a substitute general. Harney could only observe from afar as the next round of Sioux wars erupted.[29]

In 1864, the conflict with the Lakota that he had only delayed became a full-scale war, far surpassing in size and scope the one in 1855. The next year the new government of President Andrew Johnson, a fellow Tennessean, called on the old soldier, now sixty-five years old, to go amongst the Sioux, not as a warrior, but as a diplomat. For the next three years, Harney made trips to Indian country, now criss-crossed with telegraph lines and the beginnings of a transcontinental railroad. Occasionally he encountered old adversaries—Iron Shell, Red Leaf, and Spotted Tail. The response was, on the surface, quite surprising, and accounts from the time indicate that Lakota leaders greeted "White Beard" with great respect and deference, if not overt friendship. Some Lakota leaders still brandished their chief's certificates from the Fort Pierre council.[30]

The work brought its own sort of compensation. A Fort Laramie army officer recorded this remarkable scene of Indian-white relations, quite a contrast to the 1850s. "General Harney and a party of us went to a dog feast yesterday. . . . It was very good, tasted like lean, cold pork. Our dessert was almonds, raisins, champagne . . . cigars with toasts and songs in English, French, and Indian. We ate in a large lodge, the ground covered with robes and rag carpet, a white table cloth pegged on the ground, in the centre, twenty-four guests sitting. . . . Coming home the four mules drawing our ambulance ran away with us, doing but little damage except to our harness and to General Harney's temper."[31]

Endeavors such as this as a peace commissioner helped culminate in the drafting and signing of the significant Fort Laramie Treaty of 1868, and unlike his 1856 effort, the U.S. Senate approved this agreement.[32]

But while the second act of Harney's government service played itself out, something happened to remind the world about the first. On the morning of November 25, 1864, Col. John M. Chivington and his Colorado Volunteers attacked a Cheyenne village camped along a stream called Sand Creek. Chivington split his mounted command and hit the villagers, barely roused from their sleep, at several points. Many Cheyenne warriors bravely staged a rearguard action, while their dependents fled, but resistance, although stubborn at times, essentially turned into a rout. The Cheyennes suffered terrible casualties.[33]

The similarities to Blue Water in 1855, "when Harney made peace with his guns," did not escape notice, and, in fact, was even termed by westerners as the "Harney and Chivington style of warfare." Gen. Samuel R. Curtis, Chivington's superior, had little use for either Indian fighter. He grumbled, "[S]ince General Harney's attack of the Sioux many years ago at Ash Hollow, the popular cry of settlers and soldiers on the frontier favors an indiscriminate slaughter. . . ." But the controversy that arose from Chivington's actions overshadowed any of Harney's. The Sand Creek Massacre became a political issue that soiled the victors and even threatened to embroil the old general. In 1865, the Plains still aflame with war, Harney applauded Chivington's actions and saw his impolitic praise printed in a Denver newspaper. Concerning Indians on the warpath, he would "give them a little more of Sand Creek."[34] But this was not the last time an Indian fight prompted a Harney quote or a Blue Water retrospective.

The next came in 1876 during the Great Sioux War and after Lt. Col. George A. Custer's unexpected demise at the Little Bighorn. This disaster has been debated ever since, although rarely using potentially relevant precedents, such as Blue Water: Another U.S. Army commander surprised yet another Indian village, situated so that once again an attack by a split command seemed a good idea.[35] What could have gone wrong? Samuel Walsh, an old dragoon, totally avoided the question and a few days after the world learned of the Sioux victory only offered to the press his memories of Blue Water.[36] Warrior-turned-diplomat Harney did likewise, giving an updated account of the fight and ascribing some blame for the war's start to Lieutenant Grattan. He also looked beyond the battlefield and gave the public this gentle reminder, "If they had carried out the treaty I made with the Sioux, there would have been no war."[37] Throughout his life, General Harney remained proud of his Indian fighting and peacemaking accomplishments and through a compliant biographer attempted to solidify his place in history.

As with so many high-ranking military men after the Civil War, a worshipful, probably authorized biography appeared on William Harney's life and career in 1878. Naturally a chapter was devoted to the Sioux Expedition, characterized by its lack of fealty to the facts and a highly imaginative engraving depicting the battle.[38] But after Custer's death had been avenged and the dust had settled on this latest Sioux war, critics of the government's military policy held court. One of the more interesting was George Manypenny, writing a quarter century after his tenure as commissioner of Indian affairs. Consistent with his earlier views, Manypenny voiced his opinion to a new generation, which was that the Indians at Blue Water were, "an innocent band of Sioux, who were in nowise involved in the sad affair with Lieutenant Grattan's command. . . .It is the common practice of our troops, when out on expeditions, to kill Indians whenever found, without care to know whether they be guilty or innocent."[39]

It took another century before a modern biographer thankfully fleshed out the real story on General Harney, as well as put back in what the hagiographer had left out—or never knew. What does one make of Harney, the efficient, profane, and proud leader of the Sioux Expedition, the central figure of the First Sioux War, after one learns that he beat a female household slave named Hannah to death in 1834? The crime brought shame to the young officer, but, it seems, had no material effect on his career. Although indicted in St. Louis for murder, he was acquitted the next year in a jury trial. It does give a shading to his actions previously missing, especially that awful temper.[40]

It should come as no surprise that such a military leader destroyed an Indian village and pauperized a tribe, even if no formal instructional manual, as such, existed among the frontier army.[41] The longer term significance of the First Sioux War is that, no matter the commander, his personality, or the decade, the destruction of Indian villages continued to prove an effective military tactic. It remained the goal and the practice, not the exception, even after the Lakota nation was broken. In 1890, Big Foot's Miniconjou village was annihilated on Wounded Knee Creek, another small but significant stream coursing through Indian country and Lakota history. The aftermath of this "battle" prompted memories of previous conflicts, but too much time had separated the two events. Too many of its major participants were gone, and others looking back could see no farther than the 1860s and 1870s. In the next few decades, when all knew there would be no more Sioux wars, a few living relics of the antebellum frontier army would be tracked down and their eyewitness accounts recorded. Some Lakotas and mixed bloods would pass down their families' experiences as well. Even the occasional, glory-hunting fraud would adopt Blue Water as a personal exploit; there was no one to dispute fraudulent claims.[42]

But the twentieth century was still young when living memory, accurate or otherwise, died out, and determining the legacy of Blue Water Creek and the First Sioux War would be left to the historians. Knowing how the story came out, writers would focus on the Mormon cow, the brash Grattan, the unfortunate Little Thunder, and the incorrigible Harney just long enough to get to the heroes and villains who followed. Blue Water became, almost inevitably, mere prologue. The bulk of their penned efforts, as predicted by the historian Francis Parkman in the epigraph that began this book, would be devoted to later, greater events.

The First Sioux War is the foundation for understanding the entire history of conflict between the United States and the Lakota people. It foreshadowed so much that followed. When Wounded Knee occurred during the last Sioux "war," the template of Blue Water was largely forgotten, even though the narrative of the great struggle now had its beginning (Blue Water), its middle (Little Bighorn), and its end.

Appendix
Participant Accounts of the First Sioux War

A goal of this book has been to gather, use, and make known the robust mix of contemporary sources available on the First Sioux War. These sources include participant accounts by soldiers, civilians, enlisted men, and officers, versions of the Blue Water fight by men on horse and on foot, official reports and private musings, writings from August 1854, September 1855, and March 1856, and reminiscences half a century later. The rare Indian statement or remembrance stands in stark contrast and ranks in equal importance. The list to follow is itself complemented by a host of secondary, analytical sources, many of which can be found in the notes and bibliography. These sources are the "stuff" of history and beckon others to further examine the First Sioux War.

Obridge Allen, overland traveler: (1) Statement of Mr. O. Allen, regarding the engagement which took place near Fort Laramie on the 19th of August 1854, between a party of United States troops under the command of Brevet Second Lieutenant John L. Grattan, Sixth Infantry, and a body of Sioux Indians, "Letter from the Secretary of War, Transmitting Information Relating to an Engagement between the United States Troops and the Sioux Indians near Fort Laramie," *House of Representatives Reports*, 33rd U.S. Cong., 2nd sess., 1854–55, No. 63, Serial 788; and (2) Statement of Mr. Obridge Allen, *Ibid.* Neither statement is dated, but the first was given to Captain

Winship at Fort Laramie, probably in late August; the second accompanied a report by Major Hoffman, Fort Laramie, Nov. 19, 1854. Only a few statements included in this report are from eyewitnesses to the Grattan fight, such as Allen, and no statements were included that came from Indians (see Big Partisan, Little Thunder, and Man Afraid of His Horses). This report was reprinted in George E. Fay, ed., *Military Engagements between United States Troops and Plains Indians: Documentary Inquiry by the U.S. Congress, Part Ia: 1854–1867*. Occasional Publications in Anthropology, Ethnology Series, No. 26. Greeley: Museum of Anthropology, University of Northern Colorado, 1972. Accounts of the Grattan fight.

American Horse, Oglala youth: Addison E. Sheldon's notes of his interview of American Horse, July 30, 1903. Addison E. Sheldon Collection, Nebraska State Historical Society Archives, Lincoln. Reminiscence of the Grattan fight.

Jim Baker, civilian scout: *New York World*, from Denver. *Omaha Daily Bee*, Nov. 25, 1887. Reminiscence of scouting for Harney at Ash Hollow.

George T. Balch, first lieutenant, Ordnance Department: (1) Balch Papers, Bancroft Library, University of California, Berkeley. Letters to his wife Harriet during the Sioux Expedition. (2) Letters Received, Records of the Office of the Chief of Ordnance, Record Group 156, National Archives, Washington, D.C., which includes a letter from Balch, Camp on Blue Water River, to Maj. George D. Ramsay, Commanding St. Louis Arsenal, Sept. 5, 1855. (3) A related document is attached to a letter from Harney, Fort Pierre, to Thomas, New York, Dec. 11, 1855, "Report of a Board of Officers made in compliance with Orders No. 10, Head Quarters, Sioux Expedition, on the subject of the armament of the troops of the Expedition," Fort Pierre, Oct. 23, 1855, Letters Received, Office of the Adjutant General, RG 94, NA. Private and official correspondence of the ordnance officer on the Sioux Expedition

Eugene Bandel, corporal, Sixth Infantry: *Frontier Life in the Army, 1854–1861*, ed. Ralph P. Bieber. Glendale, Calif.: The Arthur H. Clark Co., 1932. Enlisted man's letters home based on his diary of the Sioux Expedition.

D. C. Beam, teamster: "Reminiscences of Early Days in Nebraska," *Transactions and Reports of the Nebraska State Historical Society* 3 (1892): 292–315. Reminiscence of a former dragoon assigned to the wagon train of the Sioux Expedition.

Big Partisan, Brulé leader: Statement of Big Partisan, Letters Received, Department of the West, Records of the U.S. Army Continental Commands, 1821–1920, Record Group 393, National Archives, Washington, D.C. Account of the Grattan fight.

Black Horse, Indian artist and descendant: Paul L. Hedren, fwd., and Carroll Friswold, intro., *The Massacre of Lieutenant Grattan and His Command by Indians*. Glendale, Calif.: The Arthur H. Clark Co., 1983. Five color drawings of the Grattan fight; drawn in the 1920s by an Indian artist living on the Pine Ridge Reservation and based on the descriptions of his Oglala grandfather, an eyewitness.

James Bordeaux, trader: (1) Letter from "Sarpy's Point, Nebraska Territory, 8 miles east of Fort Laramie, per Samuel Smith," Aug. 23, 1854, which appeared in the *Missouri Republican*, Sept. 13, 1854, and in Albert Watkins, ed., "Notes on the Early History of the Nebraska Country," *Publications of the Nebraska State Historical Society* 20 (1922): 259–60; (2) "Statement of James Bordeau," *House of Representatives Report No. 63*, Serial 788; and (3) "Statement of Mr. Bordeau, a trader living at the place where the affair occurred," *ibid.* The first of the two statements was given to Captain Winship; the second accompanied Major Hoffman's report of Nov. 19, 1854.

William J. Bordeaux, a descendant, later authored *Custer's Conqueror* (Smith and Co., Publishers, n.d.), which included a reminiscence of the Grattan fight (pp.12–13) by Tripe, his Lakota grandaunt. Accounts of the Grattan fight.

Albemarle Cady, major, Sixth Infantry: Cady, Camp on Blue Water Creek, to Capt. Oscar F. Winship, Sept. 4, 1855, Letters Received, Records of the Office of Adjutant General, Record Group 94, National Archives, Washington, D.C. Official report by the nominal commander of the infantry force at Blue Water.

William P. Carlin, first lieutenant, Sixth Infantry: (1) "Battle of Ash Hollow," in George W. Kingsbury, *History of Dakota Territory 1*. Chicago: The S. J. Clarke Publishing Co., 1915: 62–63; (2) Robert L. Girardi and Nathaniel Cheairs Hughes, Jr., eds., *The Memoirs of Brigadier General William Passmore Carlin, U.S.A.* Lincoln: University of Nebraska Press, 1999. Reminiscences of an officer on the Sioux Expedition.

William Chandless, teamster: *A Visit to Salt Lake: Being a Journey across the Plains and a Residence in the Mormon Settlements at Utah*. London: Smith, Elder, and Co., 1857. Overland account by a very literate Englishman, whose freight train arrived at Ash Hollow three days after the fight.

Julia Clifford, daughter of army interpreter: Letter from Julia Clifford, daughter of Lucien Auguste (Grattan's interpreter), Martin, S. Dak., to Lulu Brown, Stockville, Nebr., Febr. 16, 1926, selections printed in Bayard H. Paine, *Pioneers, Indians and Buffaloes*. Curtis, Nebr.: The Curtis Enterprise, 1935: 36–37, 75–76. Family story of the Grattan fight.

Cokawin, Brulé survivor: Susan Bordeaux Bettelyoun and Josephine Waggoner, *With My Own Eyes: A Lakota Woman Tells Her People's History*, ed. Emily Levine. Lincoln: University of Nebraska Press, 1998:57–58, 62–65. Reminiscence of a Brulé woman, the mother-in-law of Brulé chief Iron Shell, recorded by the mixed-blood daughter of Fort Laramie trader James Bordeaux; the only detailed eyewitness account by a Lakota of the Blue Water fight that has survived.

Philip St. George Cooke, lieutenant colonel, Second Dragoons: "Report of September 5, 1855," *Senate Executive Documents*, 34th U.S. Cong., 3rd sess., 1856–57, No. 58, Serial No. 881. Official report by the commander of the mounted force at Blue Water.

Samuel Cooper, lieutenant colonel and assistant adjutant general: "Recollections of Incidents and Characters during Fifty Years of Military Service," Samuel Cooper Papers, Southern Historical Collection, University of North Carolina, Chapel Hill. Account based on a diary of the Horse Creek treaty council, 1851.

Lewis B. Dougherty, civilian sutler: (1) Letter from Fort Laramie, Aug. 29, 1854, to John Dougherty, his father, which appeared in the *Liberty* (Mo.) *Weekly Tribune*, Oct. 6, 1854; (2) Ethel Massie Withers, ed. "Experiences of Lewis Bissell Dougherty on the Oregon Trail, Part II." *Missouri Historical Review* 24 (July 1930): 552–54; 555–56. Reminiscence by a Fort Laramie sutler of the Grattan and Blue Water fights.

Richard C. Drum, first lieutenant, Fourth Artillery: "Reminiscences of the Indian Fight at Ash Hollow, 1855," *Collections of the Nebraska State Historical Society* 16 (1911): 143–51. Reminiscence of an artillery officer whose company served as mounted troops during the Sioux Expedition.

Nathan A. M. Dudley, first lieutenant, Tenth Infantry: R. Eli Paul, ed., "Battle of Ash Hollow: The Recollections of General N. A. M. Dudley," *Nebraska History* 62 (Fall 1981): 373–99. Reminiscence of an infantry officer whose company served as mounted troops during the Sioux Expedition.

Fort Pierre Council Minutes: "Minutes of a council held at Fort Pierre, Nebraska Territory, on the 1st day of

172 APPENDIX

March, 1856, by Brevet Brigadier General William S. Harney, United States army, commanding the Sioux expedition, with the delegations from nine of the bands of the Sioux," *House Executive Documents*, 34th U.S. Cong., 1st sess., No. 130, 1855–56, Serial 859. Official account of the Harney treaty council at Fort Pierre.

William M. Gardner, captain, Second Infantry: Gardner Papers, Southern Historical Collection, University of North Carolina, Chapel Hill. Letter from Fort Pierre after the arrival of the Sioux Expedition, Oct. 18, 1855.

William S. Harney, colonel and brevet brigadier general, Second Dragoons: (1) "Report of General Harney, Commander of the Sioux Expedition, September 5, 1855," *Senate Executive Documents*, 34th U.S. Cong., 1st and 2nd sess., 1855–56, No. 1, Serial 811. (2) "Ash Hollow: General Harney's Description of the Fight," *Chicago Inter-Ocean*, Aug. 4, 1876, reprinting an interview in the *St. Louis Republican*. Official report and reminiscence by the commander of the Sioux Expedition of the Blue Water fight.

John P. Hawkins, brevet second lieutenant, Sixth Infantry: John Parker Hawkins, *Memoranda Concerning Some Branches of the Hawkins Family and Connections*. Indianapolis: Privately printed, 1913. Reminiscence of an officer stationed at Fort Kearny in 1854.

Henry Heth, captain, Tenth Infantry: *The Memoirs of Henry Heth*, ed. James L. Morrison, Jr. Westport, Conn.: Greenwood Press, 1974. Autobiography of an infantry officer whose company served as mounted troops during the Sioux Expedition.

Albion P. Howe, captain, Fourth Artillery: "Proceedings of a General Court Martial Convened at Fort Laramie, N.T., Sept. 18th, 1855," Court Martial File #HH551, Court Martial Case Files, 1809–1894, Records of the Judge Advocate General, Record Group 153, National Archives, Washington, D.C.

Testimony relating to the actions at Blue Water of an artillery officer whose company served as mounted troops; witnesses included Philip St. George Cooke, Richard C. Drum, Henry Heth, John Mendenhall, William Steele, John M. Sullivan, Patrick Walsh, and Thomas J. Wright. This record group also contains files on seven enlisted men and one civilian teamster whose cases were heard at this same general court martial: Franklin Buck (teamster), Zader Habick, Jeremiah McQuin, Wm. A. Musselman, George Pike, Jr., Joseph Smith, Daniel P. Walling, and Christian Warolf.

Marshall S. Howe, major, Second Dragoons: "Proceedings of a General Court Martial Convened at the Dragoon Encampment near the mouth of the Big Sioux river, Minnesota Territory, June 26th, 1856," Court Martial File #HH661, Court Martial Case Files, 1809–1894, Records of the Judge Advocate General, Record Group 153, National Archives, Washington, D.C. Testimony relating to the actions of a dragoon officer commanding a winter camp of the Sioux Expedition; among the witnesses were: Albemarle Cady, William S. Harney, Thomas Hight, Henry B. Livingston, Thomas C. Madison, Alfred Pleasonton, A. H. Plummer, Parmenus T. Turnley, Stewart Van Vliet, and Patrick Walsh,

William Knowles, civilian accompanying the troops: *Sioux City Journal*, May 20, 1923. Reminiscence of a sixteen-year-old, supposed "mascot" of Harney's troops who witnessed the Blue Water fight; an embarrassing fraud.

Little Thunder, Brulé leader: Statement of Little Thunder, Letters Received, Department of the West, Records of the U.S. Army Continental Commands, 1821–1920, Record Group 393, National Archives, Washington, D.C. Account of the Grattan fight and aftermath.

Man Afraid of His Horses, Oglala leader: Statement of Man Afraid of His Horses, Letters Received, Department of the West, Records of the U.S. Army Continental Commands, 1821–1920, Record Group 393, National Archives, Washington, D.C. Significant portions were published in Lloyd E. McCann, "The Grattan Massacre," *Nebraska History* 37 (Mar. 1954): 1–25. Account of the Grattan fight.

John T. Mercer, brevet second lieutenant, Sixth Infantry: Mercer letter, U.S. Army Officers' and Soldiers' Miscellany Papers, William R. Perkins Library, Duke University, Durham, N.C. Letter to a family member from Jefferson Barracks, Mo., Nov. 23, 1854.

Augustus Meyers, enlisted man, Second Infantry: *Ten Years in the Ranks, U.S. Army*. New York: The Stirling Press, 1914. Autobiography of a boy musician, who at the age of thirteen went up the Missouri River to garrison Fort Pierre in 1855 and wintered there.

George L. Miller, contract surgeon: (1) "The Fort Pierre Expedition," *Transactions and Reports of the Nebraska State Historical Society* 3 (1892):110–19. (2) "The Military Camp on the Big Sioux River in 1855," *Ibid.*: 119–24. See also Miller, "Personal and Other Notes of the Early Days," *Transactions and Reports of the Nebraska State Historical* Society 4 (1892): 194–98. Reminiscence of an early Omaha, Nebraska Territory, doctor who went to Fort Pierre as part of the Sioux Expedition.

Missouri Republican (St. Louis), anonymous battlefield correspondent who "went out as a volunteer aid[e] to the Doctor": Letter sent from "Mineto, or Blue Creek, Near Ash Hollow, 150 miles from Fort Laramie, September 5, 1855." This and portions of other letters by this correspondent are reprinted in Watkins, "Notes," 278–81. Other Missouri newspapers carried news of the First Sioux War and are cited extensively in Carolyn Minnette McClellan, "The Sioux Expedition, 1854–1856," Master's thesis, Washington University, St. Louis, Mo., 1945. Account of the Blue Water fight.

John Y. Nelson, civilian hunter and trader: Harrington O'Reilly, *Fifty Years on the Trail: A True Story of Western Life*. New York: Frederick Warne & Co., 1889. Reminiscence by a frontiersman who knew Spotted Tail and saw the Indian prisoners at Fort Kearny after the Blue Water fight; to be used with care since Nelson, a member of William F. "Buffalo Bill" Cody's Wild West troupe, was known as one of the biggest liars in the West.

Dick Parr, civilian friend of Harney: Louise L. Parr, "Sketch of the Life of Dick Parr," *Annals of Wyoming* 9 (July 1932): 649–65. Daughter's account of her father's western adventures; a supposed "protege" of Harney's who as a boy accompanied the general on the Sioux Expedition; simply outlandish fiction.

Aquila T. Ridgely, assistant surgeon: Letters Received, Records of the Office of the Surgeon General, Record Group 112, National Archives, Washington, D.C. Other assistant surgeons whose reports are represented include: William Alexander Hammond, Thomas G. Madison, and David L. Magruder. The official correspondence of Ridgely, the medical officer for the overland force of the Sioux Expedition, includes a Sept. 17, 1855, account of the Blue Water fight.

Rocky Bear, Oglala youth: "Rocky Bear's Story," from the *Cheyenne* (Wyo.) *Leader*, which appeared in the *Sheridan Enterprise*, Oct. 1, 1907. Reminiscence of the Grattan fight.

Frank (Francis) Salway, trader: (1) Addison E. Sheldon's notes of an interview of Salway, July 31, 1903, Addison E. Sheldon Collection, Nebraska State Historical Society Archives, Lincoln; (2) Interview of Salway, Tablet 27, Eli S. Ricker Collection, Nebraska State Historical Society Archives, Lincoln. Other interviews by Ricker that briefly touch on the First Sioux War include ones of American Horse, an Oglala man, and Clarence Three Stars, who said that the "Indian who killed the cow" was his grandfather. Significant portions of the Salway interview, including a sketch of the Grattan site, were published in McCann, "Grattan Massacre." Reminiscences of the Grattan fight and aftermath.

Leodegar Schnyder, ordnance sergeant: *Omaha Daily Herald*, Oct. 16, 1879, "from a letter to the *N.Y. Times*." Reminiscence by a Fort Laramie soldier of the Grattan fight.

Sioux Expedition Letters Sent, 1855–56: Department of the West, Records of the U.S. Army Continental Commands, 1821–1920, Record Group 393, National Archives, Washington, D.C. Official correspondence in the form of a letterbook kept during the expedition, a virtual day-by-day account of military activities; available as a microfilm publication from the National Archives. Related correspondence can be found in Letters Received, Department of the West, 1853–1861, RG 393, NA. The library of the Fort Laramie National Historic Site has transcribed selected correspondence relating to the Sioux Expedition from the following: Letters Sent, Fort Laramie, Records of the United States Army Commands, RG 98, NA; and Letters Received, Records of the Office of Adjutant General, RG 94, NA.

Jake Smith, soldier: Robert McReynolds, *Thirty Years on the Frontier*. Colorado Springs: El Paso Publishing Co., 1906. Account by a "soldier with General Harney" (pp. 213–17) of the Blue Water fight; a tall tale told by a phony.

Robert J. Spotswood, civilian with the supply train: Edwin A. Bemis, "Wagonmaster," *The Westerners, Denver Posse*, *Brand Book* 8 (1952): 141–56. Reminiscence of a boy on the Plains; fanciful version of the Blue Water fight.

Samuel H. Starr, first lieutenant, Second Dragoons: William K. Bixby Collection, Missouri Historical Society, St. Louis. Letters to his wife Eliza during the Sioux Expedition.

John M. Sullivan, chief bugler, Second Dragoons: *Liberty* (Mo.) *Weekly Tribune*, Sept. 28, 1855, and *Missouri Statesman* (Columbia, Mo.), Oct. 5, 1855. Letter sent by a dragoon from "Camp on the Blue Water," dateline Sept. 5, 1855; reprinted from the *Leavenworth* (Kans.) *Herald*, Sept. 22. Account of the Blue Water fight.

Thomas W. Sweeny, first lieutenant, Second Infantry: Richard Joseph Coyer, ed., "'This Wild Region of the Far West': Lieutenant Sweeny's Letters from Fort Pierre, 1855–1856," *Nebraska History* 63 (Summer 1982): 232–54. Letters to his wife Ellen during the Sioux Expedition.

John B. S. Todd, captain, Sixth Infantry: "The Harney Expedition Against the Sioux: The Journal of Capt. John B. S. Todd," ed. Ray H. Mattison, *Nebraska History* 43 (June 1962): 89–130. Day-by-day overland account by an infantry officer on the Sioux Expedition; manuscript collection held by the Minnesota Historical Society, contains a map of Blue Water battlefield copied from the Warren original.

Parmenus T. Turnley, assistant quartermaster: *Reminiscences of Parmenus Taylor Turnley: From the Cradle to Three-Score and Ten*. Chicago: Donahue & Henneberry, 1892. Reminiscence of the establishment and garrisoning of Fort Pierre during the Sioux Expedition.

Thomas S. Twiss, Indian agent: Letters Received, Upper Platte Agency, Records of the Office of Indian Affairs, Record Group 75, National Archives, Washington, D.C. Select letters appeared in *Senate Executive Documents*, U.S. Cong., 1st sess., 1855–56, No. 1, Serial 810. Official correspondence from the Indian agent at Fort Laramie, 1855–56.

Two Strikes, Brulé man: William J. Bordeaux, *Custer's Conqueror*. Smith and Co., Publishers, n.d., 14–15. Account of the Blue Water fight.

Stewart Van Vliet, captain and assistant quartermaster general: (1) Van Vliet, "Camp on Blue Water," to Thomas S. Jesup, quartermaster general, Sept. 3, 1855, Consolidated Correspondence File, 1794–1915, Special File "Sioux Expedition, 1855," Records of the Office of Quartermaster General, Record Group 92, National Archives, Washington, D.C. Other official correspondence relating to the Sioux Expedition can be found in the letters received of this record group. (2) Letter to J. Sterling Morton, July 10, 1896, J. Sterling Morton Collection, Nebraska State Historical Society Archives, Lincoln. Account of the Blue Water fight by a member of Harney's staff and a later brief mention of the Sioux Expedition.

William Vaux, army chaplain: Report from Fort Laramie, Oct. 1, 1854, which appeared in *The Spirit of Missions* 22 (1855): 40–41. Account of the Grattan fight.

Samuel Walsh, enlisted man: "Ash Hollow Memories" and "Ash Hollow, Gen. Harney's Battle with the Sioux Twenty Years Ago: Its Effect on the Indians," *Omaha Daily Herald*, July 15, 1876. Reminiscence of a former soldier living in Sarpy County, Nebraska; doubtlessly prompted by news of the June 25 Custer battle.

Gouverneur K. Warren, second lieutenant, Topographical Engineers: (1) "Explorations in the Dacota Country, in the Year 1855." Includes as Appendix C, "Report of September 4, 1855, and Sketch of Battle Ground at Blue Water Creek," *Senate Executive Documents*, 34th U.S. Cong., 1st and 2nd sess., 1855–56, No. 76, Serial 811. Official report by an engineer officer and his map of the battlefield. Related correspondence can be found in Letters Received, Office of the Chief Engineer, Records of the Topographical Bureau, Record Group 77, National Archives, Washington, D.C.; available as a microfilm publication from the National Archives. (2) *Preliminary Report of Explorations in Nebraska and Dakota, in the Years 1855–'56–'57.*

Washington Government Printing Office, 1875. Reprinted as *Explorer on the Northern Plains: Lieutenant Gouverneur K. Warren's Preliminary Report of Explorations in Nebraska and Dakota, in the Years 1855–'56–'57*. Engineers Historical Studies No. 2, ed. Frank N. Schubert. Washington: Government Printing Office, 1981. (3) James A. Hanson, *Little Chief's Gatherings: The Smithsonian Institution's G. K. Warren 1855–1856 Plains Indian Collection and The New York State Library's 1855–1857 Warren Expeditions Journals*. Chadron, Nebr.: The Fur Press, 1996. Includes a day-by-day account by an engineer officer on the Sioux Expedition, his field sketches of the battlefield, and the descriptions of the artifact collection he made after the destruction of Little Thunder's village.

John W. Whitfield, Indian agent: Letters Received, Upper Platte Agency, Records of the Office of Indian Affairs, Record Group 75, National Archives, Washington, D.C. Select letters appeared in *House Executive Documents*, U.S. Cong., 2nd sess., 1854–55, No. 1, Serial 777. Official correspondence from the Indian agent at Fort Laramie, 1854.

Oscar F. Winship, captain and assistant adjutant general: (1) "Report of an Inspection of Forts Ripley, Ridgely, Snelling, Laramie, Kearney, Riley, Leavenworth, and Atkinson," Letters Received, Office of the Adjutant General, 1822–1860, Main Series, Record Group 94, *National Archives Microfilm Publication No. 567*, roll 508, National Archives, Washington, D.C.; (2) Report of Captain Winship, Sept. 1, 1854, "Letter from the Secretary of War, Transmitting Information Relating to an Engagement between the United States Troops and the Sioux Indians near Fort Laramie," *House of Representatives Reports*, 33rd U.S. Cong., 2nd sess., 1854–55, No. 63, Serial 788. Winship reported on the condition of the forts in the Dept. of the West, as well as investigating the Grattan fight; later served as Harney's adjutant on the Sioux Expedition.

Notes

Preface

1. James T. King, "Forgotten Pageant: The Indian Wars in Western Nebraska," in *The Nebraska Indian Wars Reader, 1865–1877*, ed. R. Eli Paul (Lincoln: University of Nebraska Press, 1998), 2.

2. Robert Harvey, "The Battle Ground of Ash Hollow," *Collections of the Nebraska State Historical Society* 16 (1911): 158. Harvey walked the area several times over many years. Robert Harvey, "Report of Committee on Marking Historic Sites," in *Annual Report of the Nebraska State Historical Society for the Year Ending December 31, 1909* (1909): 22–28. The location of Harvey's "sentinel of the valley," a landmark for the fight, is the Southwest corner of Section 28, Township 17 North, Range 42 North.

Chapter 1. Origins

1. Unless otherwise noted, the account in the following paragraphs of Oscar F. Winship's tour follows his "Report of an Inspection of Forts Ripley, Ridgely, Snelling, Laramie, Kearney, Riley, Leavenworth, and Atkinson," Letters Received, Office of the Adjutant General, 1822–1860, Main Series, Record Group 94, *National Archives Microfilm Publication No. 567*, roll 508, National Archives (NA), Washington, D.C. (Henceforth, this particular document will be cited as "Winship report." Other documents from this National Archives record group will be "LR, AGO, RG 94, NA.") Winship's handwritten, 133-page report also included a copy of his orders, a map of his western travels, and layout plans of most of the forts and their reservations. The quotes about the nature of Winship's inspection trip came from the *Kansas Weekly Herald* (Leavenworth), Oct. 6, 1854, which noted his return.

2. Michael L. Tate, *The Frontier Army in the Settlement of the West* (Norman: University of Oklahoma Press, 1999).

3. The seizure of these guns at Fort Atkinson is discussed in Leo E. Oliva, "Fort Atkinson on the Santa Fe Trail, 1850–1854," *Kansas Historical Quarterly* 40 (Summer 1974): 227.

4. Here, Winship was preaching to the choir. As early as 1849, his superior, Twiggs, was voicing the necessity to recall troops for the winter. Merrill J. Mattes, *The Great Platte River Road: The Covered Wagon Mainline Via Fort Kearny to Fort Laramie* (Lincoln: Nebraska State Historical Society, 1969), 487.

5. Oliva, "Fort Atkinson," 229–30. For lists of goods purchased for distribution on the Arkansas River, see pp. 231–32.

6. The subject of the Cherokee Trail has received considerable study recently. See Jack E. Fletcher and Patricia K. A. Fletcher, "The Cherokee Trail," *Overland Journal* 13 (No. 2, 1995): 21–33; Patricia K. A. Fletcher, Jack Earl Fletcher, and Lee Whiteley, *Cherokee Trail Diaries* (Sequim, Wash.: Fletcher Family Foundation, 1999); and Lee Whiteley, *The Cherokee Trail: Bent's Old Fort to Fort Bridger* (Denver: The Denver Posse of the Westerners, 1999).

7. Lee Whiteley, "The Trappers Trail: 'The Road to Fort Laramie's Back Door'," *Overland Journal* 16 (Winter 1998–99): 3–5.

8. Fort Laramie has been the subject of intense scholarly study. Historical overviews of value include: LeRoy R. Hafen and Francis Marion Young, *Fort Laramie and the Pageant of the West, 1834–1890* (Glendale, Calif.: The Arthur H. Clark Co., 1938); David Lavender, *Fort Laramie and the Changing Frontier* (Washington: National Park Service, 1983); and Remi Nadeau, *Fort Laramie and the Sioux Indians* (Englewood Cliffs, N.J.: Prentiss-Hall, 1967). Its continuing importance to Sioux-white relations, decades later, is demonstrated by Paul L. Hedren, *Fort Laramie in 1876: Chronicle of a Frontier Post at War* (Lincoln: University of Nebraska Press, 1988).

9. The best analysis of this question—and summarized here—is Kingsley M. Bray, "The Oglala Lakota and the Establishment of Fort Laramie," *Museum of the Fur Trade Quarterly* 36 (Winter 2000): 2–18.

10. For historical narratives of the Oglala and Brulé western migrations, see George E. Hyde, *Red Cloud's Folk: A History of the Oglala Sioux Indians* (Norman: University of Oklahoma Press, 1957), and

his companion volume, *Spotted Tail's Folk: A History of the Brulé Sioux* (Norman: University of Oklahoma, 1974). Unfortunately, no comparable work exists for the Miniconjou Lakota. The Sioux population figures come from estimates based on historical sources. Kingsley Bray, "Teton Sioux Population History, 1655–1881," *Nebraska History* 75 (Summer 1994): 171, 174.

11. For the 1845 Kearny "dragoon march," and its significance, see William H. Goetzmann, *Army Exploration in the American West, 1803–1863* (New Haven: Yale University Press, 1959), 111–16, and Frank N. Schubert, ed., "March to South Pass: Lieutenant William B. Franklin's Journal of the Kearny Expedition of 1845," *Engineer Historical Studies*, Number 1 (Washington: U.S. Government Printing Office, 1980).

12. Mattes, *Great Platte River Road*, 484.

13. Here, an officer in the First Dragoons, Cooke provided an eyewitness account of Kearny's expedition. Philip St. George Cooke, *Scenes and Adventures in the Army, or Romance of Military Life* (Philadelphia: Lindsay & Blakiston, 1859), 282–395; Otis E. Young, *The West of Philip St. George Cooke, 1809–1895* (Glendale, Calif.: The Arthur H. Clark Co., 1955), 153–71.

14. This debate is discussed in Arthur P. Wade, "Forts and Mounted Rifles Along the Oregon Trail, 1846–1853," *Kansas Quarterly* 10 (Summer 1978): 4, 12–14.

15. These examples of the growing role of the federal government in the late 1840s and early 1850s are presented in John D. Unruh, Jr., *The Plains Across: The Overland Emigrants and the Trans-Mississippi West, 1840–60* (Urbana: University of Illinois Press, 1979), chap. 6. Details of the Loring expedition can be found in Raymond W. Settle, ed., *The March of the Mounted Riflemen: First United States Military Expedition to Travel the Full Length of the Oregon Trail from Fort Leavenworth to Fort Vancouver, May to October, 1849* (Glendale, Calif.: The Arthur H. Clark Company, 1940). For a description of Fort Laramie in 1849, see Mattes, *Great Platte River Road*, chap. 15.

16. Francis Parkman, Jr., *The Oregon Trail* (New York: Penguin Books, 1985 repr. of 1849 edition), 161. Estimates for numbers and changing demographics of travelers can be found in Merrill J. Mattes, *Platte River Road Narratives: A Descriptive Bibliography of Travel Over the Great Central Overland Route to Oregon, California, Utah,*

Colorado, Montana, and Other Western States and Territories, 1812–1866 (Urbana: University of Illinois Press, 1988). Mattes estimated five thousand cholera deaths on the trail in 1850 alone (p.3). The horrific impact of diseases at this time on the native peoples is discussed in Hyde, *Spotted Tail's Folk*, 50–52.

17. "An Emigrant" remembered Kearny when he wrote from Fort Laramie on August 1, 1849; his letter appeared in the *Missouri Republican* (St. Louis), Aug. 29, 1849, and reprinted in part in Albert Watkins, ed., "Notes on the Early History of the Nebraska Country," *Publications of the Nebraska State Historical Society* 20 (1922): 207–8. The anonymous correspondent commenting about Indian conduct wrote from Fort Laramie on September 18, 1849; the letter was published in the *Missouri Republican*, October 25. Watkins, "Notes," 214–16.

18. Watkins, "Notes," 159.

19. The term "key of communication" came from Prince Paul Wilhelm of Wurttemberg, the German duke and perceptive globetrotter, who arrived at Fort Laramie after the treaty's conclusion. Louis C. Butscher, ed., "An Account of Adventures in the Great American Desert by His Royal Highness, Duke Paul Wilhelm von Wurttemberg," *New Mexico Historical Review* 17 (July–Oct., 1942): 210.

20. *Frontier Guardian*, Sept. 5, 1851.

21. Richard White, "The Winning of the West: The Expansion of the Western Sioux in the Eighteenth and Nineteenth Centuries," *Journal of American History* 65 (Sept. 1978): 340–41. Father Pierre Jean De Smet, a witness to the 1851 treaty council, provided its description of "union, harmony, and amity." Pierre J. De Smet, *Western Missions and Missionaries: A Series of Letters* (New York: James B. Kirker, 1863), 101. For more on this interesting character, see Robert C. Carriker, *Father Peter John DeSmet: Jesuit in the West* (Norman: University of Oklahoma Press, 1995).

22. Samuel Cooper's diary, entry for Sept. 8, 1851, "Recollections of Incidents and Characters during Fifty Years of Military Service," Samuel Cooper Papers, Southern Historical Collection, University of North Carolina, Chapel Hill. It joins a rich array of sources on the 1851 treaty council. R. Eli Paul, ed., "George Wilkins Kendall and a Party of Pleasure Seekers on the Prairie, 1851," *Nebraska History* 64 (Summer 1983): 35–80.

23. Harry Anderson, "The Controversial Sioux Amendment to the Fort Laramie Treaty of 1851," *Nebraska History* 37 (Sept. 1956): 202.

24. A civilian observer commented similarly on the Sioux difficulty of selecting "a principal chief for the whole nation." *Missouri Republican*, Nov. 9, 1851, dateline Sept. 11.

25. The dialogue, as well as more details on Conquering Bear, appeared in the *Missouri Republican*, Nov. 23, 1851, reporting from the treaty ground on Sept. 15. In this account the new leader's name is given as Frightening Bear, one of many variations that appears in the historical record, including Brave Bear, Scattering Bear, Bear who Scatters His Enemies, and sometimes just—almost in exasperation—the Bear. Conquering Bear appears to be the name that has won out in current usage.

26. The dispersion of the presents and this formal use of a cannon to mark such an occasion are described in De Smet, *Western Missions and Missionaries*, 109–10. For the name "The Big Issue," see the 1907 interview of William Garnett in Tablet 1, Eli S. Ricker Collection, Nebraska State Historical Society Archives, Lincoln.

27. De Smet, *Western Missions and Missionaries*, 97.

28. Elsewhere (Fort Atkinson, 1853) and to no avail, Capt. Robert H. Chilton, First Dragoons, raised this same concern, the issuance of Indian annuities along a major trail. Oliva, "Fort Atkinson," 227.

29. De Smet, *Western Missions and Missionaries*, 111; Kingsley M. Bray, "Lone Horn's Peace: A New View of Sioux–Crow Relations, 1851–1858," *Nebraska History* 66 (Spring 1985): 28–47.

30. Lt. Hugh B. Fleming to Lt. Richard B. Garnett, Fort Laramie, June 16, 1853; Garnett, Fort Laramie, to Capt. Francis. M. Page, assistant adjutant general, Department of the West, Jefferson Barracks, Mo., June 30, 1853, LR, AGO, RG 94, NA.

31. Ibid. The government damaged its credibility by almost routinely delivering the Indians their goods late in the 1852 and 1853 seasons. Anderson, "Controversial Sioux Amendment," 209. An insightful study that gives endless examples of poor Indian-white communication, especially regarding political customs, is Catherine Price, *The Oglala People, 1841–1879: A Political History* (Lincoln: University of Nebraska Press, 1996).

32. Unless otherwise noted, quotes by Winship come from his previously cited report.

33. Lloyd E. McCann, "The Grattan Massacre," *Nebraska History* (Mar. 1954): 1–25, has been the standard secondary source. The narrative presented here depends more on contemporary eyewitnesses.

34. A variation of the name for this Miniconjou man is Straight Foretop. Price, *Oglala Politics*, 37.

35. George W. Cullum, *Biographical Register of the Officers and Graduates of the U.S. Military Academy at West Point, N.Y., from Its Establishment in 1802 to 1890* (Boston: Houghton, Mifflin, 1891), class of 1853. Grattan's grades at West Point are mentioned in John D. McDermott, *A Guide to the Indian Wars of the West* (Lincoln: University of Nebraska Press, 1998), 151–52.

36. Schnyder mentioned his role in the "Laramie Massacre of 1854" in a reminiscence reprinted in the *Omaha Daily Herald*, Oct. 16, 1879, "from a letter to the N.Y. Times."

37. Statement of Man Afraid of His Horses, Letters Received, Dept. of the West, Records of the U.S. Army Continental Commands, 1821–1920, RG 393, NA. This is cited at length in McCann, "Grattan Massacre," 9–10, and a copy can be found in the papers of Remi A. Nadeau at the American Heritage Center, University of Wyoming, Laramie.

38. Obridge Allen provided two eyewitness accounts recorded soon after the fight; see appendix.

39. Allen statements.

40. Man Afraid of His Horses statement.

41. Allen statements.

42. Ibid. (concerning loading the cannon). James Bordeaux provides three eyewitness accounts recorded soon after August 19, 1854, all of which mention his recommendation to Grattan; see appendix. Biographical information on Bordeaux, a Fort Laramie fixture for years, can be found in John D. McDermott, "James Bordeaux," in *The Mountain Men and the Fur Trade of the Far West*, eds. LeRoy R. Hafen and Ann W. Hafen, 5 (Glendale, Calif.: The Arthur H. Clark Co., 1965–72): 65–80. Statement of Big Partisan, taken down by Mr. [Seth] Ward at the trading house of Bordeau, Dec. 7, 1854, and copied by Oscar F. Winship, Jan. 8, 1855. LR, Dept. of the West, RG 393, NA. To the author's knowledge, Big Partisan's account has not been previously cited.

43. Man Afraid of His Horses statement.

44. Allen statements.

45. Ibid.

46. Man Afraid of His Horses statement.

47. Big Partisan statement.

48. Statement of Little Thunder, taken down by Mr. [Seth] Ward at the trading house of Bordeau, Dec. 7, 1854, and copied by Oscar F. Winship, Jan. 8, 1855. LR, Dept. of the West, RG 393, NA. Little Thunder's account has not been previously cited.

49. Big Partisan statement.

50. Man Afraid of His Horses statement.

51. Man Afraid of His Horses statement. In this context, "soldiers" means *akicita*, the Lakota group of men who served as "policemen," and enforced tribal rules.

52. Man Afraid of His Horses statement; Allen statements; Bordeaux statements, *House of Representatives Report No. 63*, Serial 788.

53. Man Afraid of His Horses statement.

54. Little Thunder statement.

55. Big Partisan statement. Bordeaux confirmed the wounding of Conquering Bear's brother. *Missouri Republican*, Sept. 13, 1854.

56. Man Afraid of His Horses statement.

57. Bordeaux statement of Nov. 1854, *House of Representatives Report No. 63*, Serial 788.

58. Big Partisan statement.

59. Allen statements; McCann, "Grattan Massacre," 19–21.

60. Bordeaux statement, Nov. 19, 1854; Man Afraid of His Horses statement.

61. Big Partisan statement; Little Thunder statement; McCann, "Grattan Massacre," 21–23.

62. Mattes, *Platte River Narratives*, 205. The description of old Fort John, the adobe fort, came from an army officer's wife. Annie Dougherty Ruff, "Camp Near Laramie, June 24, 1849," to Mary Dougherty, her mother, Liberty, Mo. Mattes secured a transcript of this and other family letters, which may be found in his papers held at the National Frontier Trails Center, Independence, Mo.

63. McCann, "Grattan Massacre," 23–24; *Missouri Republican*, Sept. 13, 1854.

64. Capt. Edward J. Steptoe, Salt Lake City, Utah, to Jefferson Davis, secretary of War, Washington, D.C., Sept. 29, 1854, *House of Representatives*

Report No. 63; John W. Whitfield, Upper Platte Agency, to Alfred Cumming, superintendent of Indian affairs, St. Louis, Sept. 27, 1854, in *Report of the Commissioner of Indian Affairs*, Nov. 25, 1854, *House Executive Documents*, 33rd U.S. Cong., 2nd sess., 1854–55, No. 1, Serial 777; Hafen and Young, *Fort Laramie*, 232.

65. McCann, "Grattan Massacre," 24.

Chapter 2. Reluctant Executioner

1. Report of the Secretary of War, Dec. 4, 1854, in *House Executive Documents*, 33rd U.S. Cong., 2nd sess., 1854–55, No. 1, Serial 778. Unless otherwise cited the following quotes come from this report.

2. R. Eli Paul, "Frontier Forts," in *Encyclopedia of the Great Plains*, ed. by David J. Wishart (Lincoln: University of Nebraska Press, forthcoming). The erosion and collapse of the Permanent Indian Frontier is discussed at length in Robert M. Utley, *The Indian Frontier of the American West, 1846–1890* (Albuquerque: University of New Mexico Press, 1884), chap. 2.

3. Davis's report provided the garrison strength of Fort Laramie. The old adobe fort as sanctuary is mentioned in Ethel Massie Withers, ed., "Experiences of Lewis Bissell Dougherty on the Oregon Trail, Part II," *Missouri Historical Review* 24 (July 1930): 552.

4. Col. Newman S. Clarke, Headquarters, Department of the West, Jefferson Barracks, Mo., to Col. Samuel Cooper, adjutant general, Washington, D.C., Sept. 7, 1854, in Reports from the Department of the West, *House Executive Document No. 1*, Serial 778; Hafen and Young, *Fort Laramie*, 236.

5. Winship report. His informant for the Sioux tribe was named "Jouett," probably Joseph Jewett. James A. Hanson, *Little Chief's Gatherings: The Smithsonian Institution's G. K. Warren 1855–1856 Plains Indian Collection and The New York State Library's 1855–1857 Warren Expeditions Journals* (Chadron, Nebr.: The Fur Press, 1996), 117. For a synopsis of Winship's wartime experience, see Theophilus F. Rodenbough, *From Everglade to Canyon with the Second United States Cavalry: An Authentic Account of Service in Florida, Mexico, Virginia, and the Indian Country, 1836–1875* (Norman: University of Oklahoma Press, 2000), 454.

6. Ibid. Others in government shared this idea of thrashing, then treating with the Indians. Utley, *Indian Frontier*, 60–63.

7. Winship's report was endorsed by Lt. Col. Lorenzo Thomas, assistant adjutant general, Headquarters of the Army, New York, N.Y., on Jan. 15, 1855, then sent to Washington, D.C.

8. Whitfield to Cumming, Sept. 27, Oct. 2, 1854, *House Executive Document No. 1*, Serial 777; Report of Lieutenant Fleming, Aug. 30, 1854, *House of Representatives Report No. 63*, Serial 788.

9. Carolyn Minnette McClellan, "The Sioux Expedition, 1854–1856," Master's thesis, Washington University, St. Louis, Mo., 1945, 58. McClellan surveyed many extant Missouri newspapers and determined this Sept. 10 date. The *Missouri Republican* letter of James Bordeaux, was dated Aug. 21 and appeared on Sept. 13, 1854. The Mitchell letter appeared two days later in this influential daily. Watkins, "Notes," 259–61.

10. Letter from the Secretary of War, transmitting information relating to an engagement between the United States troops and the Sioux Indians near Fort Laramie, Feb. 9, 1855, *House of Representatives Report No. 63*, Serial 788 (for Davis quote); Report of Brevet Lieutenant Colonel Hoffman, Nov. 19, 1854, *ibid.*, which also appears in "Correspondence respecting the massacre of Lieutenant Grattan and his command by Indians," Report of the Secretary of War, July 10, 1856, *Senate Executive Documents*, 34th U.S. Cong., 1st sess., 1855–56, No. 91, Serial 823; Hafen and Young, *Fort Laramie*, 233. The question of who fired first persisted for months. An anonymous, but knowledgeable correspondent from the "Platte River, March 12th, 1855," wrote a lengthy account of the Grattan fight, concluding that Conquering Bear had not been treacherous, inexperienced officers were to blame, and the soldiers had fired first. *Missouri Republican*, Apr. 13, 1855, in Watkins, "Notes," 266–68.

11. *Missouri Republican*, Dec. 12, 1854, in Watkins, "Notes," 263.

12. Letter of Bvt. 2nd Lt. John T. Mercer, Sixth Infantry, from Jefferson Barracks, Mo., Nov. 23, 1854, to "Cousin" in Cedar Town, Georgia, U.S. Army Officers' and Soldiers' Miscellany Papers, William R. Perkins Library, Duke University, Durham, N.C.

13. *Ibid.*

14. Winship report.

15. James L. Morrison, Jr., ed., *The Memoirs of Henry Heth* (Westport, Conn.: Greenwood Press, 1974), 123.

16. Eugene Bandel, *Frontier Life in the Army, 1854–1861*, ed. Ralph P. Bieber (Glendale, Calif.: The Arthur H. Clark Company,

1932), 28. George Rollie Adams, *General William S. Harney: Prince of Dragoons* (Lincoln: University of Nebraska Press, 2001), 119n.31.

17. Col. William S. Harney, Headquarters, Sioux Expedition, St. Louis, Mo., to Thomas, New York, Apr. 5, 1855, Letters Sent, Sioux Expedition, 1855–56 (hereafter "LSSE"), Dept. of the West, RG 393, NA. Harney's "Orders No. 1," Apr. 3, 1855, can be found in its entirety in Rodenbough, *From Everglade to Canyon*, 526–27. Biographical information comes primarily from the recent—and best—biography of Harney: Adams, *Prince of Dragoons*. Chapter seven, "'Great White Chief' on the Plains," covers the Sioux Expedition, as do three pieces by Richmond L. Clow: "Mad Bear: William S. Harney and the Sioux Expedition of 1855–1856," *Nebraska History* 61 (Summer 1980): 132–51; "General William S. Harney on the Northern Plains," *South Dakota History* 16 (Fall 1986): 229–48; and "William S. Harney," in *Soldiers West: Biographies from the Military Frontier*, ed. Paul Andrew Hutton (Lincoln: University of Nebraska Press, 1987), 42–58. For a contemporary definition of brevet ranks, see H. L. Scott, *Military Dictionary: Comprising Technical Definitions; Information on Raising and Keeping Troops; Actual Service, Including Makeshifts and Improved Materiel; and Law, Government, Regulation, and Administration Relating to Land Forces* (New York: D. Van Nostrand, 1864), 110–11.

18. The reminiscent description of Harney in 1855 came from George L. Miller, "The Military Camp on the Big Sioux River in 1855," *Transactions and Reports of the Nebraska State Historical Society* 3 (1892): 119–20. Miller's effusive description went on to say, "He was yet so tender of heart . . . that even a wronged army mule could arouse in him the most practical sympathy." The nicknames "white beard" and "hornet" (or "wasp") accompanied Lakota translations of tribal winter counts (discussed in chap. 8). The origin of "prince of dragoons" can be found in Adams, *Prince of Dragoons*, 115. Brigham Young, the leader of the Latter-day Saints in Utah, sarcastically referred to Harney in 1857 as "the saintly squaw killer." Wilford Hill LeCheminant, "A Crisis Averted: General Harney and the Change in Command of the Utah Expedition," *Utah Historical Quarterly* 51 (Winter 1983): 34. See also J. P. Dunn, Jr., *Massacres of the Mountain: A History of the Indian Wars of the Far West* (New York: Harper & Brothers, 1886), 251.

19. The official date of Harney's appointment to command the Sioux Expedition was March 22, 1855. Bieber, citing Samuel Cooper to Harney, Mar. 22, 1855, in Bandel, *Frontier Life*, 29. The too-good-to-be-true Pierce quote comes from Harney's eventual hagiographer, who included a lengthy biographical sketch of and dedicated his book to this "distinguished soldier . . . devoted patriot . . . [and] veteran chieftain." Logan Uriah Reavis, *St. Louis: The Future Great City of the World* (St. Louis: C. R. Barns, 1876), 349–50.

20. Durwood Ball, *Army Regulars on the Western Frontier, 1848–1861* (Norman: University of Oklahoma Press, 2001, xx–xxiii; and Robert M. Utley, *Frontiersmen in Blue: The United Army and the Indian, 1848–1865* (New York: Macmillan Publishing, 1967), 12.

21. Orders No. 1, Sioux Expedition, Apr. 3, 1855, repr. Rodenbough, *From Everglade to Canyon*, 526–27. These are identical to General Orders No. 2 from the Headquarters of the Army.

22. Winship, St. Louis, to Lt. Col. Philip St. George Cooke, Second Dragoons, commanding, Fort Leavenworth, Apr. 23, 1855, LSSE.

23. Examples of army frugality abound in Robert W. Frazer, *Forts and Supplies: The Role of the Army in the Economy of the Southwest, 1846–1861* (Albuquerque: University of New Mexico Press, 1983).

24. Winship, St. Louis, to Maj. Albemarle Cady, commanding battalion, Sixth Infantry, St. Louis, Apr. 18, 1855, LSSE.

25. Winship, St. Louis, to Col. Edwin V. Sumner, Cavalry Depot, Apr. 25, 1855; Winship to Cooke, Fort Leavenworth, Apr. 26, 1855; Harney, St. Louis, to Thomas, New York, May 13, 1855, LSSE. Harney had an occasion to admonish Cooke later on another matter. Winship, St. Louis, to Cooke, Oregon Route, July 2, 1855, LSSE. For the origin of Sumner's nickname, see Utley, *Frontiersmen in Blue*, 121; and William Y. Chalfant, *Cheyennes and Horse Soldiers: The 1857 Expedition and the Battle of Solomon's Fork* (Norman: University of Oklahoma Press, 1989), 321.

26. Quotations come from a Winship confidante, 1st Lieut. George T. Balch, Ordnance Dept., St. Louis, to Harriet Balch, his wife, May 13, May 20, 1855, Balch Papers, Bancroft Library, University of California, Berkeley. Harney added, "The remaining staff officers to be

attached to the expedition will be announced so soon as their assignments to the same shall become known." Rodenbough, *From Everglade to Canyon*, 526–27. Officers who filled these staff positions included: Lt. Col. Timothy P. Andrews (paymaster), 1st Lt. George T. Balch (ordnance officer), assistant surgeons David L. Magruder and Aquila T. Ridgely, Capt. Marcus De Lafayette Simpson (commissary of subsistence), and 2nd Lt. Gouverneur K. Warren (topographical engineer). Harney to Thomas, Apr. 5, 1855, LSSE; this is reprinted, as is a significant portion of "Official Correspondence Relating to Fort Pierre," in *South Dakota Historical Collections* 1 (1902): 385–86.

27. Emerson Gifford Taylor, *Gouverneur Kemble Warren: The Life and Letters of an American Soldier, 1830–1882* (Boston: Houghton Mifflin Company, 1932), 19–20, which reprinted a letter from Capt. Andrew A. Humphreys, Topographical Engineers, Washington, to Jefferson Davis, Feb. 5, 1855. For more on the Pacific Railroad Surveys and Warren's role, see Frank N. Schubert, *Vanguard of Expansion: Army Engineers in the Trans-Mississippi West, 1819–1879* (Washington: U.S. Government Printing Office, 1980), chaps. 6, 7.

28. Winship, St. Louis, to Cooke, Fort Leavenworth, Apr. 27, 1855; Harney, St. Louis, to Cooper, Washington, June 2, 1855; Morrison, *Memoirs of Henry Heth*, 123–25.

29. Harney, St. Louis, to Col. Newman L. Clarke, commanding, Dept. of the West, St. Louis, Apr. 10, 1855; Winship, St. Louis, to Cady, Jefferson Barracks, Apr. 10, 1855; Harney to Cooper, Washington, Apr. 12, 1855; Harney to Thomas, New York, Apr. 13, 1855; Harney to Thomas, Apr. 20, 1855, LSSE.

30. Harney, St. Louis, to Thomas, New York, Apr. 30, 1855, LSSE.

31. Winship, St. Louis, to Cooke, Fort Leavenworth, Apr. 23, 1855; Harney, St. Louis, to Brig. Gen. Thomas S. Jesup, quartermaster general, Washington, May 16, 1855; Winship to Cooke, May 17, 1855; Harney to Jesup, June 4, 1855; Winship to Cooke, commanding, Second Dragoons, Oregon Route, June 13, 1855; Randy Steffen, *The Horse Soldier, 1776–1943: The United States Cavalryman; His Uniforms, Arms, Accoutrements, and Equipments; Vol. 2, The Frontier, the Mexican War, the Civil War, the Indian Wars, 1851–1880* (Norman: University of Oklahoma Press, 1978), 21.

32. Commanding officers were to send "returns exhibiting the strength, condition, and disposition of their respective commands; also, special estimates for clothing, camp and garrison equipage, ordnance and ordnance stores . . . for a year's service in the field." Orders No. 1, Apr. 3, 1855, in Rodenbough, *From Everglade to Canyon*, 526–27. Harold H. Schuler, *Fort Pierre Choteau* (Vermillion: University of South Dakota Press, 1990), 133.

33. Harney, St. Louis, to Thomas, New York, Apr. 5, 1855, LSSE.

34. Harney, St. Louis, to Thomas, New York, Apr. 30, 1855, LSSE. Harney asked again in May, "I wish to visit Fort Pierre and some other points on the Missouri so soon as the river is navigable—if no objection is made by the Department?" Harney, St. Louis, to Cooper, Washington, May 19, 1855, LSSE. Again, he was turned down.

35. Harney to Thomas, Apr. 5, 1855, LSSE. For more on the use of steamboats, see also "Official Correspondence, Fort Pierre," SDHC. For more on Harney's earlier experiences on the Upper Missouri and Florida experiences, see Adams, *Prince of Dragoons*, 23–31, 55–79.

36. For these and other examples of Harney's attempt to lower expectations: Harney, St. Louis, to Thomas, New York, Apr. 5, 1855; Harney to Thomas, June 2, 1855; Harney to Thomas, June 14, 1855; Harney, Fort Leavenworth, to Cooper, Washington, July 26, 1855; Harney, Camp near Fort Leavenworth, to Burton A. James, Agent for Sacs and Foxes, Sac and Fox Agency, July 28, 1855; Harney, Camp near Fort Leavenworth, to Thomas, July 30, 1855; Harney, Camp near Oak Grove, Kansas Territory, to Agent of the Delaware Indians, Aug. 5, 1855, LSSE.

Chapter 3. Overland

1. Capt. Stewart Van Vliet, assistant quartermaster, Fort Leavenworth, to Cady, commanding battalion, Fort Leavenworth, May 7, 1855; Van Vliet to A. P. Howe, Fort Leavenworth, May 7, 1855; Van Vliet to Cooke, commanding, Fort Leavenworth, May 7, 1855; Van Vliet, Jefferson City, Mo., to Cooke, May 9, 1855, LSSE.

2. Harney, St. Louis, to Thomas, New York, May 12, 1855, LSSE.

3. Harney, St. Louis, to Cooper, Washington, May 19, 1855, LSSE.

4. Winship, St. Louis, to Cooke, Fort Leavenworth, May 24, 1855, LSSE.

5. Harney, St. Louis, to Thomas, New York, May 31, 1855; Winship, St. Louis, to Thomas, New York, June 10, 1855, LSSE.

6. Winship, St. Louis, to Capt. Samuel Woods, commanding, Fort Riley, June 12, 1855; Winship, St. Louis, to Woods, Fort Riley, June 14, 1855, LSSE.

7. Winship, St. Louis, to Hoffman, commanding, Fort Laramie, June 9, 1855, LSSE.

8. Winship, St. Louis, to Cooke, commanding, Second Dragoons, Oregon Route, June 13, 1855; Winship to Cooke, June 15, 1855, LSSE.

9. Louis A. Garavaglia and Charles G. Worman devote a section, "Muzzle-loaders or Breechloaders," in their comprehensive *Firearms of the American West, 1803–1865* (Albuquerque: University of New Mexico Press, 1984), 181–90. The Sharps carbine is prominently featured in this story.

10. Winship, St. Louis, to Cooke, Fort Leavenworth, June 2, 1855, LSSE.

11. Harney, St. Louis, to Thomas, New York, May 19, 1855, LSSE. Charles Galpin had worked in Sioux country since 1839, married a Lakota woman, and transferred Fort Pierre to the military in 1855. John E. Sunder, *The Fur Trade on the Upper Missouri, 1840–1865* (Norman: University of Oklahoma Press, 1965), 133, 170.

12. Harney, St. Louis, to Cooper, Washington, Apr. 26, 1855, LSSE. Harney wanted his letter shown to Secretary of War Jefferson Davis.

13. Winship, St. Louis, to Hoffman, commanding, Fort Laramie, June 9, 1855; Winship to Thomas, New York, June 10, 1855; Winship to Hoffman, June 13, 1855, LSSE. Early reports from the field include: Hoffman, Fort Laramie, to Page, asst. adj. gen., Dept. of the West, Jefferson Barracks, Mo., Nov. 19, 1854; Hoffman to Cooper, Washington, Nov. 29, 1854; Hoffman to Page, Dec. 12, 1854; Hoffman to Cooper, Dec. 15, 1854, LR, Dept. of the West, RG 393, NA. Hoffman's reports also included valuable enclosures, including the December statements of Big Partisan and Little Thunder, which contained more information than just the Grattan fight and figure in chap. 5.

14. Winship, St. Louis, to a Mr. Nave and Mr. McCord, Savannah, Mo., June 16, 1855, LSSE; Louise Barry, *The Beginning of the West: Annals of the Kansas Gateway to the American West, 1540–1854* (Topeka: Kansas State Historical Society, 1972), 1085, mentions a Savannah businessman by the name of McCord.

15. Winship to Hoffman, June 9, 1855, LSSE.

16. Winship to Cooke, Fort Leavenworth, June 2, 1855, LSSE.

17. *Ibid.*

18. Harney, St. Louis, to Thomas, New York, June 2, 1855, LSSE. The "decisive blow" quote came from a letter Lt. George Balch, St. Louis, wrote to his wife Harriet, May 20, 1855, Balch Papers. Francis Paul Prucha, *The Sword and the Republic: The United States Army on the Frontier, 1783–1846* (New York: Macmillan Publishing Company, 1969), 20–24.

19. Harney to Thomas, June 2, 1855, LSSE.

20. Winship, St. Louis, to Cooke, Oregon Route, June 21, 1855, LSSE.

21. Diary entry for July 21, 1855, in Ray H. Mattison, ed., "The Harney Expedition Against the Sioux: The Journal of Capt. John B. S. Todd," *Nebraska History* 43 (June 1962): 105–6.

22. *Ibid.*, 93–94. On August 5, Harney wrote a letter to the agent for the Delaware Indians from "Camp near Oak Grove, K.T." which means he camped there as well after a short march from Fort Leavenworth.

23. John Parker Hawkins, *Memoranda Concerning Some Branches of the Hawkins Family and Connections* (Indianapolis: Privately printed, 1913), 86.

24. J. Henry Carleton, *The Prairie Logbooks: Dragoon Campaigns to the Prairie Villages in 1844, and to the Rocky Mountains in 1845*, ed. Louis Pelzer (Chicago: Caxton Club, 1943), 10–16.

25. Mattison, "Todd Journal," 94.

26. Ibid., 94–96; William E. Lass, *From the Missouri to the Great Salt Lake: An Account of Overland Freighting* (Lincoln: Nebraska State Historical Society, 1972), 28. For more on the standard operating procedures of this and other freighting firms, see Lass's first chapter.

27. Mattison, "Todd Journal," 97–99.

28. Ibid.

29. Ibid., 99. See also Robert L. Girardi and Nathaniel Cheairs Hughes, Jr., eds., *The Memoirs of Brigadier General William Passmore Carlin, U.S.A.* (Lincoln: University of Nebraska Press, 1999), 11–13.

30. Harney, Fort Pierre, to Thomas, New York, Dec. 11, 1855, which includes the attached "Report of a Board of Officers made in compliance with Orders No. 10, Head Quarters, Sioux Expedition, on the subject of the armament of the troops of the Expedition," Fort Pierre, Oct. 23, 1855, LR, AGO, RG 94, NA.

31. For explanations of the importance of the minie ball and the rifles that fired them, see Garavaglia and Worman, "Frontier Forts Counted on Minie," *The American Rifleman* 125 (Apr. 1977): 32–34; Garavaglia and Worman, *Firearms of the American West*, chap. 11, "Infantry Arms."

32. Winship, St. Louis, to Cooke, Oregon Route, June 15, 1855, LSSE.

33. Paul D. Johnson, *Civil War Cartridge Boxes of the Union Infantryman* (Lincoln, R.I.: Andrew Mowbray Publishers, 1998), chap. 3, "Development of the Rifle-Musket Cartridge Box;" Garavaglia and Worman, *Firearms of the American West*, 115–16.

34. Winship, Camp near Fort Leavenworth, to Hoffman, Fort Laramie, July 30, 1855, LSSE; Mattison, "Todd Journal," 107.

35. Washington Irving's quote came from Carleton, *Prairie Logbooks*, 57; Mattison, "Todd Journal," 100.

36. Mattison, "Todd Journal," 100. For pages worth of unflattering overlander comments about Fort Kearny, see Mattes, *Great Platte River Road*, chaps. 6, 7.

37. Winship, St. Louis, to Cady, commanding, Fort Kearny, June 12, 1855, LSSE; Mattison, "Todd Journal," 105–6.

38. Hawkins, *Memoranda*, 87.

39. Mattison, "Todd Journal," 94–95. Another mention of Indians at Ash Hollow appeared in *ibid.*, 103.

40. Todd mistakenly gave the surveyor general's name as Burris. Ibid., 96–97, 100–2; Mattes, *Platte River Road Narratives*, 449. One of these officers was Henry Heth. According to Todd, "Heath [note the misspelling, hence its pronunciation—AU] confirms the reports brought by the mail carrier about the temper of the Indians—says that there is no doubt but that we shall have plenty to do this summer and fall."

41. Harney, St. Louis, to Thomas, New York, June 2, 1855, LSSE.

42. Balch made a detailed "report" about his inspection trip to his spouse. G. Balch, St. Louis, to H. Balch, May 26, 1855, and continued

through June 11, Balch Papers. The state of the artillery battery was mentioned in the following dispatches: Harney, St. Louis, to Thomas, New York, Apr. 7, 1855; Harney to Thomas, May 24, 1855; Winship, St. Louis, to Cady, Fort Leavenworth, May 24, 1855; Harney to Thomas, June 14, 1855, LSSE.

43. Testimony of Lieut. John Mendenhall, Fourth Artillery, "Proceedings of a General Court Martial Convened at Fort Laramie, N.T., Sept. 18th, 1855," Court Martial File #HH551, Court Martial Case Files, 1809–1894, Records of the Judge Advocate General, RG 153, NA.

44. Harney to Thomas, June 14, 1855; Winship, St. Louis, to Cooke, commanding, Second Dragoons, Oregon Route, June 13, 1855, LSSE.

45. Harney to Thomas, June 14, 1855, LSSE.

46. Mattison, "Todd Journal," 104–5.

47. Ibid., 105–7; Harney, Headquarters, Sioux Expedition, on the Missouri River, to Cooper, Washington, July 14, 1855, LSSE. The officers from Fort Laramie, all destined for the newly formed regiments, were second lieutenants Alden Sargent, John T. Shaaf, and Hugh B. Fleming. This last person was the same Fleming who sent Grattan off to his death; he would play no further role in the First Sioux War.

48. *Missouri Republican*, July 13, 1855, in Watkins, "Notes," 273.

49. Winship, Camp near Fort Leavenworth, to Cady, commanding, Fort Kearny, July 24, 1855, LSSE; Mattison, "Todd Journal," 107–8.

50. Harney, Camp near Fort Leavenworth, to Thomas, New York, Aug. 3, 1855, LSSE.

51. Mattison, "Todd Journal," 108; Harney, Camp near Fort Kearny, to Thomas, New York, Aug. 23, 1855, LSSE; G. Balch, Fort Leavenworth, to H. Balch, Aug. 3, 1855, Balch Papers. The letter by the anonymous Sioux Expedition correspondent appeared in the *Missouri Republican*, Sept. 11, 1855, in Watkins, "Notes," 276–77. One reason for guessing this person was a civilian is that he later served as a volunteer aide to the army surgeon. Lieutenant Nathan A. M. Dudley, Tenth Infantry, described these mounts as "fine, good sized ponies." R. Eli Paul, ed., "Battle of Ash Hollow: The Recollections of General N. A. M. Dudley," *Nebraska History* 62 (Fall 1981): 378, 392.

52. Harney, Camp near Fort Kearny, to Thomas, New York, Aug. 23, 1855, LSSE. Harney had left an order for Warren at Fort Leavenworth, then at Fort Pierre, to follow as soon as possible. Warren's cross-country

trek made this order moot. Winship, Camp near Fort Leavenworth, to Warren, Fort Leavenworth, Aug. 3, 1855, LSSE. *New York Times*, Sept. 4, 1855, reprinted from *Missouri Republican*, Aug. 31, 1855.

53. The term "mountain men" appeared in the *New York Times*, *ibid.* Sources for this trip include: Warren's daily journal in Hanson, *Little Chief's Gatherings*, 101; and Frank N. Schubert, introduction to *Explorer on the Northern Plains: Lieutenant Gouverneur K. Warren's Preliminary Report of Explorations in Nebraska and Dakota, in the Years 1855–'56–'57* (Washington: U.S. Government Printing Office, 1981), xii–xiii, which includes a map by Warren of the route between Fort Pierre and Fort Kearny.

54. Warren's evaluations and conclusions on new routes of military roads, based on three years of explorations, are summarized in Schubert, *Explorer on the Northern Plains*, 6. See also W. Turrentine Jackson, *Wagon Roads West: A Study of Federal Road Surveys and Construction in the Trans-Mississippi West, 1846–1869* (New Haven, Conn.: Yale University Press, 1964), 139.

55. Hanson, *Little Chief's Gatherings*, 102; Harney, Camp near Fort Kearny, to Thomas, New York, Aug. 23, 1855, LSSE. Earlier Warren had been given explicit instructions for gathering intelligence. "In the mean time you will collect from traders and other people of the country all the reliable information that can be obtained as to the locality, disposition, and probable movements of the various Indians inhabiting or visiting that region." Winship, St. Louis, to Warren, St. Louis, June 4, 1855, LSSE.

56. Circular from Harney, Camp near Fort Kearny, Aug. 22, 1855, LSSE; Mattison, "Todd Journal," 108; Hanson, *Little Chief's Gatherings*, 102.

57. Monthly return for the Sioux Expedition, Aug. 1855, Returns of "Expeditions," 1806–1916, AGO, RG 94, NA; Harney, Camp near Fort Kearny, to Thomas, New York, Aug. 23, 1855, LSSE. Capt. Thomas Hendrickson's exact words—in an Aug. 28, 1855, letter that describe his Fort Kearny command—were "the lame and the sick." LS, Fort Kearny, RG 393, NA. A list of officers and their units on the Sioux Expedition can be found in Fredrick T. Wilson, "Old Fort Pierre and Its Neighbors," *South Dakota Historical Collections* 1 (1902): 282–84.

58. Mattison, "Todd Journal," 108–9.

59. Harney, Fort Leavenworth, to Cooper, Washington, July 26, 1855, LSSE.

60. Harney, Camp near Fort Leavenworth, to Agent Burton A. James, Sac and Fox Agency, July 28, 1855, LSSE.

61. Harney, Camp near Fort Leavenworth, to Thomas, New York, July 30, 1855; Harney, Camp near Oak Grove, K.T., to Agent of the Delaware Indians, Aug. 5, 1855, LSSE.

62. These times came from an August 9 circular by Harney during his trip between Fort Leavenworth and Fort Kearny. There is no reason to assume he radically changed the schedule after Aug. 24. Circular, Headquarters, Sioux Expedition, Camp on the Vermillion, Aug. 9, 1855, LSSE.

63. Hanson, *Little Chief's Gatherings*, 102–4. For more on overland trail odometers, see Norman E. Wright, "Odometers," *Overland Journal* 13 (No. 3, 1995): 14–24.

64. Bandel, *Frontier Life*, 20, 21, 80; Carleton, *Prairie Logbooks*, 209–10.

65. Mattison, "Todd Journal," 109; Hanson, *Little Chief's Gatherings*, 103.

66. G. Balch, Fort Laramie, to H. Balch, Sept. 18, 1855, Balch Papers.

67. Mattison, "Todd Journal," 110; Hanson, *Little Chief's Gatherings*, 103; Winship, Camp No. 6 (on the Platte), to Cooke, "Present," Aug. 27, 1855; Circular from Winship, Camp No. 9 (O'Fallon's Bluffs), to Cooke, Cady, and Balch, Aug. 31, 1855, LSSE.

68. Mattison, "Todd Journal," 109–10; G. Balch, Camp on the South Fork, Platte River, to H. Balch, Aug. 30, 1855, Balch Papers. The 1853 publication to which Balch referred was Howard Stansbury, "Exploration and Survey of the Valley of the Great Salt Lake of Utah, Including a Reconnaissance of a New Route through the Rocky Mountains," *Senate Executive Documents*, U.S. 32nd Cong., spec. sess., Mar. 1851, No. 3, Serial 608.

69. *Missouri Republican*, Sept. 27, 1855, in Watkins, "Notes," 278.

70. Hanson, *Little Chief's Gatherings*, 103.

71. Mattison, "Todd Journal," 110–11; Hanson, *Little Chief's Gatherings*, 103–4; Mattes, *Great Platte River Road*, 316; Bandel, *Frontier Life*, 80;. John P. Langellier, *Army Blue: The Uniform of Uncle Sam's*

Regulars, 1848–1873 (Atglen, Penn.: Schiffer Military History, 1998), 37, 40–41.

72. Bandel, *Frontier Life*, 82; Hanson, *Little Chief's Gatherings*, 103–4.

Chapter 4. Upriver

1. Maj. David H. Vinton, quartermaster, St. Louis, to Brig. Gen. Thomas S. Jesup, quartermaster general, Washington, Mar. 30, 1855, in "Official Correspondence, Fort Pierre," 382–84. Army quartermasters needed good mileage figures to prepare their freighting contracts.

2. Vinton, St. Louis, to Jesup, Washington, Mar. 30, 1855, "Official Correspondence, Fort Pierre," 382–84; Winship, St. Louis, to Capt. Edmund A. Ogden, asst. quartermaster, St. Louis, May 7, 1855; Winship to Hitchcock, Carlisle Barracks, May 23, 1855; Harney, St. Louis, to Thomas, Headquarters of the Army, New York, May 24, 1855; Winship to Commanding Officer, Second Infantry, Carlisle, May 24, 1855; Winship to Commanding Officer, Second Infantry, Alton, Ill., June 4, 1855; Winship to Warren, St. Louis, June 4, 1855; Winship to Commanding Officer, Battalion Second Infantry, Alton, June 6, 1855; Winship to Commanding Officer, Newport Barracks, Ky., June 6, 1855; Winship to Commanding Officer, Battalion Second Infantry, Fort Leavenworth, June 7, 1855; Winship to Bvt. 2nd Lieut. John McCleary, Third Infantry, commanding detachment of recruits, Alton, June 8, 1855; Winship to Commanding Officer, Fort Leavenworth, June 8, 1855; Harney, St. Louis, to Page, St. Louis, June 9, 1855; Winship to Van Vliet, Steamer Kate Kinney [Kate Sweeney?], Alton, June 9, 1855; Winship to Thomas, New York, June 10, 1855; Winship to Thomas, June 12, 1855; Winship to Ogden, St. Louis, June 12, 1855; Harney to Page, June 13, 1855, LSSE; Richard Joseph Coyer, ed., "'This Wild Region of the Far West': Lieutenant Sweeny's Letters from Fort Pierre, 1855–56," *Nebraska History* 63 (Summer 1982):236–37; Hanson, *Little Chief's Gatherings*, 94. The four infantry companies were divided one per boat with the band assigned to the largest vessel, presumably *Australia*. The ordnance stores alone amounted to thirty to forty tons, divided into four lots, each complete to itself, and transported on a separate boat. G. Balch, St. Louis, to H. Balch, May 26, 1855, Balch Papers.

3. Winship, St. Louis, to Maj. William R. Montgomery, commanding battalion, Second Infantry, Fort Leavenworth, June 7, 1855;

Winship to Commanding Officer, St. Louis Arsenal, June 7, 1855; Winship, St. Louis to Commanding Officer, Fort Leavenworth, June 8, 1855; Harney, St. Louis, to Page, St. Louis, June 9, 1855; Winship to Thomas, New York, June 10, 1855; Winship to Thomas, June 12, 1855; Harney to Page, June 13, 1855, LSSE; Hanson, *Little Chief's Gatherings*, 94.

4. Hanson, *Little Chief's Gatherings*, 94–95.

5. Mary K. Dains, "Midwestern River Steamboats: A Pictorial History," *Missouri Historical Review* 66 (July 1972): 589; *Missouri Republican*, Aug. 8, 1851. The probable author of the quotation is B. Gratz Brown of St. Louis, later the governor of Missouri, on his way to the Fort Laramie treaty council. Coincidentally *Cataract* was the steamboat Harney and his staff boarded at St. Louis for Fort Leavenworth in July 1855. *Ibid.*, July 13, 1855, in Watkins, "Notes," 273.

6. Van Vliet, St. Louis, to Captain George G. Waggaman, commissary of subsistence, St. Louis, June 10, 1855; Van Vliet to Capt. George D. Ramsay, Ordnance Corps., commanding, St. Louis Arsenal, June 10, 1855; Harney, St. Louis, to Thomas, New York, June 14, 1855, LSSE; Coyer, "Sweeny Letters," 236; Hanson, *Little Chief's Gatherings*, 95; Mary K. Dains, "Steamboats of the 1850s–1860s: A Pictorial History," *Missouri Historical Review* 67 (Jan. 1973): 278.

7. Augustus Meyers, *Ten Years in the Ranks, U.S. Army* (New York: The Stirling Press, 1914), 53–57. Meyers' enlistment, training, and participation in the Sioux Expedition cover the first five chapters of his autobiography.

8. Harney, St. Louis, to Thomas, New York, June 14, 1855; Winship, St. Louis, to Capt. William M. Gardner, commanding, Company D, Second Infantry, Fort Leavenworth, June 26, 1855, LSSE; Hanson, *Little Chief's Gatherings*, 95.

9. Hanson, *Little Chief's Gatherings*, 96.

10. Ibid., 96–97.

11. Ibid.

12. For his reminiscences of this episode in his career, see George L. Miller, "The Fort Pierre Expedition," *Transactions and Reports of the Nebraska State Historical Society* 3 (1892): 110–19; "The Military Camp on the Big Sioux River in 1855," *Ibid.*:119–24; and "Personal and Other Notes of the Early Days," *Transactions and Reports of the Nebraska State Historical Society* 4 (1892):194–98.

13. Hanson, *Little Chief's Gatherings*, 97.

14. *Ibid.*, 97–98.

15. Record of events, "Official Correspondence, Fort Pierre," 430–31; the arrival date is repeated in Montgomery, Fort Pierre, to Cooper, Washington, July 31, 1855, in ibid., 389–90. Coyer, "Sweeny's Letters," 236–38; Hanson, *Little Chief's Gatherings*, 98–99.

16. Winship, St. Louis, to Commanding Officer of the Second Infantry, Alton, Ill., June 4, 1855; Winship to Simpson, commissary of subsistence, St. Louis, June 4, 1855, LSSE.

17. Coyer, "Sweeny's Letters," 236–37.

18. Record of events, "Official Correspondence, Fort Pierre," 431.

19. Coyer, "Sweeny's Letters," 236–37.

20. Hanson, *Little Chief's Gatherings*, 99–100, Taylor, *Gouverneur Kemble Warren*, 20–21; Cooper, Washington, to Harney, St. Louis, Apr. 25, 1855, in "Official Correspondence, Fort Pierre," 386. Inevitably, in addition to all these tasks, General Harney told Warren to gather intelligence on the Indians. Winship, St. Louis, to Warren, St. Louis, June 4, 1855, LSSE.

21. Jesup to Vinton, Mar. 23, 1855, in "Official Correspondence, Fort Pierre," 381; Schuler, *Fort Pierre Chouteau*, 29, 32–34.

22. "Official Correspondence, Fort Pierre," 382–84; Cooper, Washington, to Harney, St. Louis, Apr. 25, 1855, in *ibid.*, 386.

23. *Ibid.*

24. "Official Correspondence, Fort Pierre," 348–50, 382–84, 394.

25. The best articles on the Turnley experiment are two studies by Timothy R. Nowak: "The Army's Use of Portable Cottages at Fort Pierre Chouteau during the Sioux Expedition, 1855–56," Paper presented at the annual meeting of the South Dakota State Historical Society, Rapid City, S. Dakota, March 28, 1998; and "From Fort Pierre to Fort Randall: The Army's First Use of Portable Cottages," *South Dakota History* 32 (Summer 2002): 95–116. See also Harney, St. Louis, to Cooper, Washington, Apr. 21, 1855, LSSE; and Parmenus Taylor Turnley, *Reminiscences of Parmenus Taylor Turnley: From the Cradle to Three-Score and Ten* (Chicago: Donahue & Henneberry, 1892), 127–29. The term "knocked-down houses" came from P. J. O'Reilly, an old steamboat man who "brought 300 knocked-down houses here [Omaha] from Cincinnati,"

the same city that provided the military cottages for Fort Pierre. *Omaha Daily Bee*, June 27, 1913. Curiously a "Cincinnati house" was used in Kansas as early as 1844. Barry, *Beginning of the West*, 505–506.

26. Winship, St. Louis, to Capt. Parmenus T. Turnley, asst. quartermaster, Cincinnati, May 14, 1855, LSSE.

27. Harney, St. Louis, to Cooper, Washington, May 25, 1855, LSSE; Hanson, *Little Chief's Gatherings*, 100; Coyer, "Sweeny's Letters," 238–39. The garrison seemed well provisioned if the post sutler's variety of goods for the winter of 1855–1856 is any indication. See Elizabeth Soderberg, "Fort Pierre Sutler, 1855," *Military Collector & Historian* 49 (Summer 1997): 50–57.

28. Winship, Camp near Fort Kearny, to Commanding Officer, Fort Pierre, Aug. 21, 1855; Winship to Montgomery, commanding, Fort Pierre, Aug. 21, 1855, LSSE. Earlier, Harney had ordered the commander to "spare no pains in putting your command in the best possible condition for the field, as it will be liable to be ordered to do so at a moment's warning." Winship, St. Louis, to Commanding Officer of the Second Infantry, Alton, Ill., June 4, 1855, LSSE.

29. Ibid.

30. Harney, Camp near Fort Leavenworth, to Thomas, New York, Aug. 3, 1855; Harney, Camp near Fort Kearny, to Thomas, Aug. 23, 1855, LSSE; *Omaha Nebraskian*, Aug. 29, 1855, repr. *New York Times*, Sept. 14, 1855; Coyer, "Sweeny's Letters," 236–37, 239–40.

31. Harney, Camp near Fort Leavenworth, to Thomas, New York, Aug. 3, 1855; Harney, Camp near Fort Kearny, to Thomas, Aug. 23, 1855, LSSE. The anonymous correspondent was termed "an outsider." *Omaha Nebraskian*, Sept. 16, 1855, repr. *New York Times*, Oct. 18, 1855.

Chapter 5. Since Killing the Soldiers

1. Many authors can be excused because, for most, the First Sioux War was not the focus of their studies; however, it is interesting how quickly they scoot through the months between August 1854 and September 1855. The exceptions are McClellan's thesis on the Sioux Expedition, which devoted a lengthy chapter to this period, and ethnohistorian Kingsley Bray of Manchester, England, whose forthcoming biography of Crazy Horse examines this period in detail and with great insight.

2. Winship report. Winship's source of information may have been Paul Carrey, a "French gentleman" from St. Louis, who had accompanied him to Fort Laramie. Winship's locations for the Sioux tribes read similar to those that Lieutenant Warren copied in St. Louis, June 1855, from "a memorandum by Mr. Carrey." Warren hired the knowledgeable and ubiquitous Carrey as his assistant and together they traveled to Fort Pierre. "Extract from my journal of a trip from Fort Leavenworth, Missouri, via Forts Atkinson and Laramie, to Fort Kearney, O[regon]. R[oute]., furnished at request of First Lieutenant W[infield]. S[cott]. Hancock, Adjutant 6th Regiment of Infantry," *House of Representatives Report No. 63*, Serial 788; Hanson, *Little Chief's Gatherings*, 94.

3. Hafen and Young, *Fort Laramie*, 233–34; Hoffman, Fort Laramie, to Cooper, Washington, Nov. 29, 1854, LR, Dept. of the West, RG 393, NA.

4. Hoffman to Cooper, Nov. 29, 1854; Thomas S. Twiss, Fort Laramie, to George W. Manypenny, commissioner of Indian affairs, Washington, Sept. 3, 1855, in Report of the Commissioner of Indian Affairs, Nov. 26, 1855, *Senate Executive Documents*, 34th U.S. Cong., 1st sess., 1855–56, No. 1, Serial 810.

5. Hoffman, Fort Laramie, to Page, Jefferson Barracks, Dec. 12, 1854, LR, Dept. of the West, RG 393, NA; copy made by Winship and which also contained a Dec. 8, 1854, message to Hoffman from Big Partisan and Little Thunder and their statements about the Grattan fight. Anonymous correspondent, "Platte River, March 12th, 1855," *Missouri Republican*, Apr. 13, 1855. The question of Indian surrenders cropped up in later stories. *Missouri Republican*, July 3, 7, Aug. 11, 14, 1855.

6. Little Thunder statement, LR, Dept. of the West, RG 393, NA.

7. *Missouri Republican*, Apr. 13, 1855. Author Mari Sandoz claimed that the site of Conquering Bear's scaffold burial was in her father's Sand Hills orchard! Mari Sandoz, "Some Oddities of the American Indian," in *Hostiles and Friendlies: Selected Short Writings of Mari Sandoz* (Lincoln: University of Nebraska Press, 1959), 85.

8. Entry for "Little Thunder," Frederick Webb Hodge, ed., *Handbook of American Indians North of Mexico* (Washington: U.S. Government Printing Office, 1912), 771; Susan Bordeaux Bettelyoun and Josephine Waggoner, *With My Own Eyes: A Lakota Woman Tells Her People's*

History, ed. by Emily Levine (Lincoln: University of Nebraska Press, 1998), 154; Hanson, *Little Chief's Gatherings*, 116.

9. Little Thunder statement, LR, Dept. of the West, RG 393, NA.

10. Ibid.

11. Ibid.; Hoffman to Page, Nov. 19, 1854, LR, Dept. of the West, RG 393, NA, with an attachment reporting an inspection of the mail party murder site, Capt. William Scott Ketchum, Sixth Infantry, Fort Laramie, to Hoffman, Nov. 19, 1854; Hoffman to Cooper, Nov. 29, 1854; Bieber introduction to Bandel, *Frontier Life*, 27–28; McClellan, "Sioux Expedition," 69–71; *Missouri Republican*, Dec. 12, 1854, in Watkins, "Notes," 263.

12. Hoffman to Page, Dec. 12, 1854, esp. Little Thunder statement. Little Thunder apparently contradicted Alfred Vaughan, who wrote, "All of the Indians who were present at the unfortunate massacre of Lieut. Grattan and his party are now in this vicinity. . . ." Alfred J. Vaughan, Indian agent, Fort Pierre, to Hoffman, Nov. 21, 1854. LR, Dept. of the West, RG 393, NA.

13. Hyde, *Red Cloud's Folk*, 76.

14. Charles E. Galpin, Fort Pierre, to J. P. B. Gratiot, North Platte River, Nov. 20, 1854, an attachment of Hoffman's letter of Nov. 29, 1854, LR, Dept. of the West, RG 393, NA; Hyde, *Red Cloud's Folk*, 77.

15. *Nebraska Palladium* (Bellevue, Nebr. Terr.), Nov. 8, 1854; "Trouble Among the Indians of Nebraska," dateline of Bellevue, Nebr., Nov. 10, 1854, *New York Tribune*, n.d., clipping found in the Robert W. Furnas scrapbooks, Nebraska State Historical Society Library, Lincoln.

16. Mattes, *Platte River Road Narratives*, 432–55; Unruh, *Plains Across*, 120.

17. William G. Bek, trans., "From Bethel, Missouri, to Aurora, Oregon: Letters of William Keil, 1855–1870, Part I," *Missouri Historical Review* 48 (Oct. 1953): 23–41; "Part II," *Missouri Historical Review* 48 (Jan. 1954): 141–53.

18. McClellan, "Sioux Expedition," 66, 87. Little Thunder denied at least one raid attributed to the Brulés, the one involving a theft of military horses at Fort Kearny. Little Thunder statement, LR, Dept. of the West, RG 393, NA. Juanita Brooks, ed., *On the Mormon Frontier: The Diary of Hosea Stout, 1844–1861* 2 (Salt Lake City: University of Utah Press, 1964): 549, 550.

19. McClellan, "Sioux Expedition," chaps. 4, 5. Her detailed, but uncritical, survey of the months after the Grattan fight depended on newspaper accounts for its content, if not its tone.

20. Ibid., 63.

21. Ibid., 88–90; Hoffman, Fort Laramie, to Winship, St. Louis, Febr. 9, 1855, LR, AGO, RG 94, NA; copies and transcriptions of this and other key military and Indian affairs documents were provided by Kingsley Bray.

22. Hoffman to Winship, Febr. 9, 1855.

23. Hoffman to Winship, Febr. 14, 1855, LR, AGO, RG 94, NA. In 1855, Geminien Beauvais kept a trading post five miles east of Fort Laramie. Charles E. Hanson, Jr., "Geminien P. Beauvais," in Hafen and Hafen, *Mountain Men and the Fur Trade*, 7:39–41.

24. McClellan, "Sioux Expedition," 99–100; *Missouri Republican*, Sept. 15, 1855; Bek, "Letters of William Keil," 30; James E. Enos, "Recollections," unpublished typescript, Newberry Library, Chicago, copy in the Mattes Collection, National Frontier Trails Center, Independence, Mo. Enos identified the milkmaid as part of the "Hargreaves" train. Bieber introduction to Bandel, *Frontier Life*, 27–28. In 1855, too, Edward Morin returned the body of Robert Gibson to St. Joseph in late summer. *Council Bluffs* (Iowa) *Chronotype*, Sept. 12, 1855.

25. Bettelyoun and Waggoner, *With My Own Eyes*, 6–7, 128; George E. Hyde, *The Pawnee Indians* (Norman: University of Oklahoma Press, 1974), 242; Watkins, "Notes," 274–75; *New York Times*, Sept. 13, 1855, repr. *Missouri Republican*, Sept. 8.

26. *Missouri Republican*, Aug. 13, 1855, in Watkins, "Notes," 274–76.

27. George Hepner, agent for the Pawnee tribe, Nebraska City, N.T., to Alfred Cumming, superintendent of Indian affairs, St. Louis, Sept. 24, 1855. LR, Council Bluffs Agency, Records of the Office of Indian Affairs, RG 75, NA. For more about the Pawnee tribe in the summer of 1855, see Hyde, *Pawnee Indians*, 242–43; and John M. Thayer, "My Very First Visit to the Pawnee Village in 1855," *Proceedings and Collections of the Nebraska State Historical Society* 15 (1907): 119–27. Mattison, "Todd Journal," 104–105.

28. Alban W. Hoopes, "Thomas S. Twiss, Indian Agent on the Upper Platte, 1855–1861," *Mississippi Valley Historical Review* 20

(Dec. 1933–34): 353. See also Burton S. Hill, "Thomas S. Twiss, Indian Agent," *Great Plains Journal* 6 (Spring 1967): 85–96.

29. Twiss, Buffalo, N.Y., to secretary of War, Mar. 17, 1855; Twiss to Cumming, St. Louis, Aug. 13, 1855, LR, Office of Indian Affairs, RG 75, NA. Twiss's correspondence is available on *National Archives Microfilm Publication M234*, roll 889. Superintendent Cumming turned over the annuity goods for the Upper Platte Agency to Agent Twiss on May 28, 1855, before embarking himself on the steamboat *St. Mary*, June 6, 1855, with the annuity goods for the Upper Missouri Agency tribes. "A report in regard to the expedition among the Indians on the Upper Missouri," Cumming, superintendent of Indian Affairs, St. Louis, to Manypenny, commissioner of Indian affairs, Febr. 14, 1856, in *House Executive Documents*, 34th U.S. Cong., 1st sess., 1855–56, No. 65, Serial 853.

30. Twiss, Fort Laramie, to Cumming, Aug. 13, 1855, LR, OIA, RG 75, NA.

31. Twiss to Robert McClelland, sec. of Interior, Aug. 20, 1855; Twiss to Manypenny, Oct. 1, 1855, both in *Senate Executive Document No. 1*, Serial 810; the latter letter was printed in large part in Hoopes, "Twiss, Indian Agent," 356.

32. Twiss to McClelland, Aug. 20, 1855; Hyde, *Red Cloud's Folk*, 96.

33. Twiss to Manypenny, Sept. 3, 1855, *Senate Executive Document No. 1*, Serial 810. Lieutenant Warren noted on Sept. 22, 1855, "A large delegation of Brules and Ogallallah came at 12 o'clock, with the Indian Agent Mr. Twiss. . . .The Ogal. Chief 'the man whose horses are a terror to his foes,' or 'the man who is afraid of his horses,' 'Tah-shone-kee-Ko-Kee Pah Pee,' said that his band had been waiting 3 months and killed no buffalo. . . ." Hanson, *Little Chief's Gatherings*, 110.

34. The Lakota name for the North Platte River was recorded by Rufus B. Sage, *Rocky Mountain Life, or, Startling Scenes and Perilous Adventures in the Far West, during an Expedition of Three Years [1841 to 1844]* (Lincoln: University of Nebraska Press, 1982), 54.

35. Chief Red Cloud, reminiscing in 1897, claimed to have been born along "Blue Creek" in 1821. R. Eli Paul, ed., *Autobiography of Red Cloud: War Leader of the Oglalas* (Helena: Montana Historical Society, 1997), 31. Lieutenant Warren wrote in his diary, "The Sioux call it

Meena-To Wauk-pa-lah, or Blue Water Creek," although on his map he spells it "Mini To Wakpala." Hanson, *Little Chief's Gatherings*, 104–105.

Chapter 6. *Blue Water Creek and the Day of Retribution*

1. Mattison, "Todd Journal," 110–11; Mattes, *Great Platte River Road*, 304. Mattes devotes a chapter of his book to Ash Hollow. See also Robert L. Munkres, "Ash Hollow: Gateway to the High Plains," *Annals of Wyoming* 42 (Apr. 1970): 5–43; and R. F. Diffendal, Jr., R. K. Pabian, and J. R. Thompson, *Geologic History of Ash Hollow Park, Nebraska* (Lincoln: Conservation and Survey Division, University of Nebraska, 1982).

2. The ten Indians per tipi ratio appears throughout the literature, particularly for the Sioux. Some examples: *Missouri Republican*, Oct. 24, 1851, from the Horse Creek treaty ground in Sept., "I have taken pains to form an estimate of the number present, and by the number of lodges, estimating, as is common with those familiar with the Indians. . . ." De Smet, *Western Missions and Missionaries*, 100, also at Horse Creek, "we found about a thousand lodges, that is to say, ten thousand Indians. . . ." Henry R. Schoolcraft, *Information Respecting the History, Condition and Prospects of the Indian Tribes of the United States* 3 (Philadelphia: Lippincott, Grambo & Company, 1853): 629, "Sioux, on Missouri, about 3,000 lodges, about 30,000 souls."

3. Harney, Camp on Blue Water Creek, to Thomas, New York, Sept. 5, 1855; Harney, Fort Pierre, to J. Davis, Washington, Nov. 10, 1855, LSSE; Van Vliet, captain and asst. quartermaster, "Camp on Blue Water," to Jesup, quartermaster general, Sept. 3, 1855, Consolidated Correspondence File, 1794–1915, Special File: "Sioux Expedition, 1855," Records of the Office of Quartermaster General, RG 92, NA; Hanson, *Little Chief's Gatherings*, 103–4; Mattison, "Todd Journal," 110–11; Anonymous correspondent, writing from "Mineto, or Blue Creek, Near Ash Hollow, 150 miles from Fort Laramie," Sept. 5, 1855, *Missouri Republican*, Sept. 27, 1855, in Watkins, "Notes," 278–81; John M. Sullivan, "Camp on the Blue Water," Sept. 5, 1855, *Leavenworth* (Kans.) *Herald*, Sept. 22, 1855; Bandel, *Frontier Life*, 84; Samuel H. Starr, "Camp 10 miles up the Laramie River, N.T." to his wife Eliza, Sept. 7, 1855, Samuel H. Starr Correspondence, William K. Bixby Collection, Missouri Historical Society, St. Louis, Mo.; Lt. Col. Philip St. George Cooke,

"Report of September 5, 1855," *Senate Executive Documents*, 34th U.S. Cong., 3rd sess., No. 58, Serial 881.

4. Cooke's instructions to his company commanders on Sept. 2, came from Heth during testimony taken at the A. P. Howe court martial, previously cited as "Proceedings of a General Court Martial Convened at Fort Laramie, N.T., Sept. 18th, 1855," hereafter "Howe Court Martial." This important source contains the previously unused testimony of several Sept. 3 participants.

5. Mattison, "Todd Journal," 110–11.

6. Paul, "Recollections of Dudley," 380–81, 390; William Chandless, *A Visit to Salt Lake: Being a Journey across the Plains and a Residence in the Mormon Settlements at Utah* (London: Smith, Elder, and Co., 1857), 74–75. Chandless's published account of Harney's speech had the expletives deleted, all but two of which can be restored confidently.

7. *Ibid.*

8. Paul, "Recollections of Dudley," 381, 384; Harvey, "Battle Ground of Ash Hollow," 156; Richard C. Drum, "Reminiscences of the Indian Fight at Ash Hollow, 1855," *Collections of the Nebraska State Historical Society* 16 (1911): 144–45; Cooke, "Report of Sept. 5, 1855." See also the John Talbot interview that formed this old Second dragoon's obituary in a Cheyenne, Wyo., newspaper (perhaps the *Tribune*?), July 1910; clipping found in the Wyoming State Archives by John Ludwickson, Nebraska State Historical Society, who provided the author with a copy.

9. Mattison, "Todd Journal," 108, 111; Harney, "Report of Sept. 5, 1855" Hanson, *Little Chief's Gatherings*, 104; Bandel, *Frontier Life*, 84; D. C. Beam, "Reminiscences of Early Days in Nebraska," *Transactions and Reports of the Nebraska State Historical Society* 3 (1892): 302. Captain Todd mentioned the Woods family tragedy in his diary. By the time the news reached Fort Laramie, the number of reported victims had increased to four children and two servants. S. Starr to E. Starr, Sept. 7, 1855, Bixby Collection.

10. Anonymous correspondent, *Missouri Republican*, Sept. 27, 1855; S. Starr to E. Starr, Sept. 7, 1855, Bixby Collection; Hanson, *Little Chief's Gatherings*, 103–6; Lieut. Gouverneur K. Warren, "Report of September 4, 1855, and Sketch of Battle Ground at Blue Water Creek," in *Senate Executive Documents*, 34th U.S. Cong., 1st and 2nd sess., No. 76, Serial 811; Harvey, "Battle Ground of Ash Hollow," 158–62; Mattison,

"Todd Journal," 111–12; Reminiscence of Samuel Walsh, an enlisted man, *Omaha Daily Herald*, July 15, 1876; Harney, "Report of Sept. 5, 1855."

11. Hanson, *Little Chief's Gatherings*, 104.

12. Cooke, "Report of Sept. 5, 1855;" Hanson, *Little Chief's Gatherings*, 103–4, 116–17 (for biographical note on Honore Tesson); Morrison, *Memoirs of Henry Heth*, 128; Paul, "Recollections of Dudley," 390–91, 393; Drum, "Reminiscences of the Indian Fight," 145, 150; Talbot obituary, Cheyenne, Wyo., newspaper clipping, July 1910.

13. Anon. correspondent, *Missouri Republican*, Sept. 27, 1855; Harney, "Report of Sept. 5, 1855;" Hanson, *Little Chief's Gatherings*, 104, 116 (for a biographical note on Colin Campbell, who had accompanied Lieutenant Warren from Fort Pierre); Mattison, "Todd Journal," 112.

14. Harney to Davis, Nov. 10, 1855, LSSE; Paul, "Recollections of Dudley," 381; Walsh reminiscence, *Omaha Daily Herald*, July 15, 1876; Hanson, *Little Chief's Gatherings*, 104; Warren, "Report of Sept. 4, 1855;" Mattison, "Todd Journal," 112; Chandless, *Trip to Salt Lake*, 75; Beam, "Reminiscences of Early Days," 301–2.

15. Harney, "Report of Sept. 5, 1855;" Mattison, "Todd Journal," 112; Anon. correspondent, *Missouri Republican*, Sept. 27, 1855.

16. For the Harney–Little Thunder dialogue here and to follow, see Hanson, *Little Chief's Gatherings*, 104; Harney, "Report of Sept. 5, 1855;" and Harney to Davis, Nov. 10, 1855, LSSE.

17. Ibid.

18. Hanson, *Little Chief's Gatherings*, 104.

19. Ibid.; Mattison, "Todd Journal," 112–13.

20. Harney, "Report of Sept. 5, 1855;" Mattison, "Todd Journal," 113; Hanson, *Little Chief's Gatherings*, 104; Maj. Albemarle Cady, Camp on Blue Water Creek, to Winship, Sept. 4, 1855, LR, AGO, RG 94, NA; S. Starr to E. Starr, Sept. 7, 1855, Bixby Collection.

21. Cady to Winship, Sept. 4, 1855, RG 94, NA; Harney, "Report of Sept. 5, 1855;" Bandel, *Frontier Life*, 84.

22. Cooke, "Report of Sept. 5, 1855;" Anon. correspondent, *Missouri Republican*, Sept. 27, 1855; Harvey, "Battle Ground of Ash Hollow," 156–57; Drum, "Reminiscence of the Indian Fight," 145–46; Cooke, "Report of Sept. 5, 1855."

23. Cooke, "Report of Sept. 5, 1855;" Drum, "Reminiscence of the Indian Fight," 157; Mattison, "Todd Journal," 113–14; Hanson, *Little Chief's Gatherings*, 104; Harney, "Report of Sept. 5, 1855." Regarding adjustable sights, the anonymous correspondent of the *Missouri Republican*, Sept. 27, 1855, noted that "the Infantry were ordered to place their rifles at long range of from six hundred to one thousand yards. . . ." John Talbot, a dragoon comrade, was the source for the chief bugler's nickname of John M. "Yankee" Sullivan, a native of Concord, New Hampshire. Talbot obituary; Sullivan enlistment papers, compiled by Dennis Shimmin and on file at Ash Hollow State Historical Park, Lewellen, Nebraska.

24. Mattison, "Todd Journal," 113.

25. Cooke, "Report of Sept. 5, 1855;" Drum, "Recollections of the Indian Fight," 146.

26. S. Starr to E. Starr, Sept. 7, 1855, Bixby Collection; "Report of a Board of Officers on the armament of the troops of the Expedition," Fort Pierre, Oct. 23, 1855, LR, AGO, RG 94, NA.

27. Cooke, "Report of Sept. 5, 1855;" Van Vliet to Jesup, Sept. 3, 1855, QM Cons. Corr., RG 92, NA; Mattison, "Todd Journal," 113; Hanson, *Little Chief's Gatherings*, 104. Classic Lakota tactics—and those of their Plains Indian enemies—are discussed throughout Paul, *Autobiography of Red Cloud*.

28. Cooke, "Report of Sept. 5, 1855;" Harvey, "Battle Ground of Ash Hollow," 157; Drum, "Reminiscence of the Indian Fight," 146; Cooke and Heth testimony, Howe Court Martial.

29. Cokawin's account can be found in Bettelyoun and Waggoner, *With My Own Eyes*, 57-58, 62–65, originals of which can be found in the Susan Bordeaux Bettelyoun Collection, Nebraska State Historical Society Archives, Lincoln.

30. Anon. correspondent, *Missouri Republican*, Sept. 27, 1855.

31. Cady to Winship, Sept. 4, 1855, RG 94, NA; Hanson, *Little Chief's Gatherings*, 104.

32. Mattison, "Todd Journal," 114.

33. Hanson, *Little Chief's Gatherings*, 106, 116 (for a biographical note on Mr. Desomet).

34. Drum, "Reminiscences of the Indian Battle," 146; Mattison, "Todd Journal," 114.

35. Paul, "Recollections of Dudley," 392; Harney, "Report of Sept. 5, 1855;" Drum, "Reminiscence of the Indian Battle," 146.

36. Morrison, *Memoirs of Henry Heth*, 128; Cooke, "Report of Sept. 5, 1855;" Harvey, "Battle Ground of Ash Hollow," 157; Paul, "Recollections of Dudley," 381, 392, 395; Hanson, *Little Chief's Gatherings*, 106; Cooke and Heth testimony, Howe Court Martial; Drum, "Reminiscence of the Indian Fight," 146; Warren, "Report of Sept. 4, 1855."

37. Mendenhall testimony, Howe Court Martial.

38. Cooke, "Report of Sept. 5, 1855;" Statement of accusation and testimony of Cooke, Mendenhall, Sullivan, Walsh, and Wright, Howe Court Martial; Morrison, *Memoirs of Henry Heth*, 128. Sullivan mentioned in his published letter the effect "when the Glorious Charge rang out from 'my old bugle'. . . ." *Leavenworth Herald*, Sept. 22, 1855.

39. Chandless, *Visit to Salt Lake*, 75; Morrison, *Memoirs of Henry Heth*, 128; Paul, "Recollections of Dudley," 395.

40. Cooke, "Report of Sept. 5, 1855;" Mendenhall testimony, Howe Court Martial.

41. Bettelyoun and Waggoner, *With My Own Eyes*, 63.

42. Van Vliet to Jesup, Sept. 3, 1855, RG 92, NA; Harney, "Report of Sept. 5, 1855;" Hanson, *Little Chief's Gatherings*, 104; Mattison, "Todd Journal," 114; S. Starr to E. Starr, Sept. 7, 1855, Bixby Collection; Coyer, "Sweeny's Letters," 240; Harvey, "Battle Ground of Ash Hollow," 157; Paul, "Recollections of Dudley," 388; Cooke, "Report of Sept. 5, 1855;" Steele testimony, Howe Court Martial; Drum, "Reminiscence of the Indian Fight," 146.

43. Drum, "Reminiscences of the Indian Fight," 147–48; Paul, "Recollections of Dudley," 381–82, 386, 388; Harvey, "Battle Ground of Ash Hollow," 157; Steele testimony, Howe Court Martial; Sullivan letter, *Leavenworth Herald*, Sept. 22, 1855; Hanson, *Little Chief's Gatherings*, 106.

44. Cooke, "Report of Sept. 5, 1855;" Paul, "Recollections of Dudley," 381–82, 387–88. Lieutenant Warren wrote, "A poor Ogallalah woman was shot badly in the shoulder by a dragoon after the fight was over; he saw her concealed in the grass and mistook her for a man." Hanson, *Little Chief's Gatherings*, 106.

45. Bettelyoun and Waggoner, *With My Own Eyes*, 63. Bettelyoun and Waggoner recorded, edited, and re-edited Cokawin's story, which

explains the additional word or two that crops up from using the published and manuscript accounts.

46. Ibid.

47. Mattison, "Todd Journal," 113. "Minnies," of course, refer to minie balls fired by the long-range rifles.

48. *Missouri Republican*, Oct. 25, 1855, in Watkins, "Notes," 281–82. Biographies of Iron Shell and Spotted Tail can be found in the Josephine Waggoner Papers, Museum of the Fur Trade, Chadron, Nebr. Iron Shell was born about 1818, the son of Bull Tail, Spotted Tail about 1822. Considerable biographical information on the pair can also be gleaned from Bettelyoun and Waggoner, *With My Own Eyes*; Hyde, *Spotted Tail's Folk*; and Royal B. Hassrick, *The Sioux: Life and Customs of a Warrior Society* (Norman: University of Oklahoma Press, 1964).

The person conspicuous by his absence, everywhere in the historical record of Blue Water Creek but Mari Sandoz's novel, is Crazy Horse. Sandoz devotes a chapter to getting the young Oglala to Little Thunder's village and witnessing the fight's aftermath, the result being a defining moment in his life. Mari Sandoz, *Crazy Horse, the Strange Man of the Oglalas* (Lincoln: University of Nebraska Press, 1992), chap. 4, "Soldiers on the Blue Water." Kingsley Bray, Crazy Horse's biographer, places him elsewhere and will probably put this imagined episode to rest.

49. Hanson, *Little Chief's Gatherings*, 106; Beam, "Reminiscences of Early Days," 302.

50. Cooke, "Report of Sept. 5, 1855."

51. Statement of accusation and testimony of Drum, Howe Court Martial; Beam, "Reminiscences of Early Days," 302; Harvey, "Battle Ground of Ash Hollow," 157; Drum, "Reminiscences of the Indian Fight," 146–48; Warren, "Report of Sept. 4, 1855;" Hanson, *Little Chief's Gatherings*, 106; Paul, "Recollections of Dudley," 381, 392–95, where the name "Hudson's Hole" (also "Hudson's Cave") appeared.

52. Harney, "Report of Sept. 5, 1855;" Drum, "Reminiscences of the Indian Fight," 146–48; Cooke, "Report of Sept. 5, 1855;" Assistant Surgeon Aquila T. Ridgely, Fort Laramie, to Surgeon General Thomas Lawson, Washington, Sept. 17, 1855, LR, Records of the Office of the Surgeon General, RG 112, NA; Hanson, *Little Chief's Gatherings*, 106.

53. Warren, "Report of Sept. 4, 1855;" Hanson, *Little Chief's Gatherings*, 104, 106.

54. Ibid.; Drum, "Reminiscence of the Indian Fight," 149–50; Bandel, *Frontier Life,*" 88.

55. Cooke, "Report of Sept. 5, 1855;" Mattison, "Todd Journal," 114; Ridgely to Lawson, Sept. 17, 1855, LR, Office of the Surgeon General, RG 112, NA.

56. Warren, "Report of Sept. 4, 1855."

57. Bandel, *Frontier Life,*" 87; Mattison, "Todd Journal," 114; Anon. correspondent, *Missouri Republican*, Sept. 27, 1855; Chandless, *Visit to Salt Lake*, 75; Beam, "Reminiscences of Early Days," 302; Paul, "Recollections of Dudley," 388.

58. Cooke, "Report of Sept. 5, 1855;" Cady to Winship, Sept. 4, 1855, RG 94, NA; Van Vliet to Jesup, Sept. 3, 1855, RG 92, NA; Coyer, "Sweeny's Letters," 240; Mattison, "Todd's Journal," 114.

59. Chief Bugler Sullivan gave the surnames of the deceased soldiers. *Leavenworth Herald*, Sept. 22, 1855. Years later D. C. Beam remembered one soldier, "a man by the name of McDonald, with whom I had served two years in the first dragoons." Beam, "Reminiscences of the Early Days," 303. Their first names come from a list of killed, wounded, and missing (the last being Pvt. Marshall Ryder, Second Dragoons), the transcript of which was found in the records of the Adjutant General's Office, RG 94, NA, and provided to the author by John D. McDermott.

60. S. Starr to E. Starr, Sept. 7, 1855, who, besides this judgment, passed along the statistics of Captain Steele, a fellow dragoon officer: "The indians lost 50 or 60 killed. One compy. of dgns. lost 3 killed and 5 wounded—the other compy. 1 wounded. The artillery company lost 2 killed. The infantry, none. The dgns. you see did the fighting." William Chandless, though, "[h]eard plenty about the fight, infantry and dragoons each making out they had borne the brunt of it." Chandless, *Visit to Salt Lake*, 74.

61. Capt. William M. Gardner, Second Infantry, Fort Pierre, to his mother, Oct. 18, 1855, William M. Gardner Papers, Southern Historical Collection, University of North Carolina, Chapel Hill.

62. Harney, "Report of Sept. 5, 1855;" Cady to Winship, Sept. 4, 1855, RG 94, NA; Anon. correspondent, *Missouri Republican*, Sept. 27, 1855; S. Starr to E. Starr, Sept. 7, 1855, Bixby Collection; Cooke, "Report of Sept. 5, 1855;" Mattison, "Todd Journal," 114; Bandel, *Frontier Life*, 87–88; Chandless, *Visit to Salt Lake*, 75.

63. Beam, "Reminiscences of Early Days," 302–3.

64. Walsh letter, *Omaha Daily Herald*, July 15, 1876.

65. Lieutenant Dudley, the sole chronicler to mention Warren's collecting effort, recalled "his bringing a wagon load of Indian relics into Fort Laramie after the fight," Paul, "Recollections of Dudley," 393.

66. Harney, "Report of Sept. 5, 1855;" Captain Todd wrote that the Indian painting was executed on a U.S. Post Office document. Mattison, "Todd Journal," 114.

67. Sullivan letter, *Leavenworth Herald*, Sept. 22, 1855. See also *Missouri Republican*, Sept. 27, 1855; Chandless, *Visit to Salt Lake*, 82, 86: "Went in the evening to the sergeant's [Trumbull's?] tent; saw there a number of trophies, leggings, quivers, and saddle-cloths, covered with very handsome bead-work."

68. Harney, "Report of Sept. 5, 1855."

69. See also Cooke, "Report of Sept. 5, 1855," who mentioned Buford and Wright.

70. Ibid.

71. Paul, "Recollections of Dudley," 386; Beam, "Reminiscences of Early Days," 303; G. Balch, Fort Laramie, to H. Balch, Sept. 18, 1855, Balch Papers. See also Randy Brown, "Buried in Ash Hollow," *Overland Journal* 8 (No. 3, 1990): 18-25.

72. Hanson, *Little Chief's Gatherings*, 106; Drum, "Reminiscence of the Indian Fight," 144–45; Harvey, "Battle Ground of Ash Hollow," 155.

73. Bettelyoun and Waggoner, *With My Own Eyes*, 63–64.

Chapter 7. Arms Raised, Palms Forward, Peace

1. Hanson, *Little Chief's Gatherings*, 107; G. Balch, Fort Laramie, to H. Balch, Sept. 18, 1855, Balch Papers; Beam, "Reminiscences of Early Days," 303.

2. Hanson, *Little Chief's Gatherings*, 107; Winship, Camp. No. 12 (Ash Hollow), to Hoffman, Fort Laramie, Sept. 4, 1855; Circular, Winship, Camp of Blue Water Creek, Sept. 4, 1855, LSSE.

3. Mattison, "Todd Journal," 115; Hanson, *Little Chief's Gatherings*, 107, which includes a plan by Warren of Fort Grattan; letter from Fort Laramie, Sept. 17, 1855, *Missouri Republican*, Oct. 27, 1855, in Watkins, "Notes," 282; Harney, Fort Laramie, to Thomas, New York, Sept. 26,

1855, LSSE; Van Vliet to Jesup, Sept. 3, 1855, RG 92, NA; G. Balch, Fort Laramie, to H. Balch, Sept. 18, 1855, Balch Papers. Carleton's *Prairie Logbooks*, 117–18, gave his recommended dimensions for a "turf fence," which reads quite similar to Warren's "fort."

4. Hanson, *Little Chief's Gatherings*, 107.

5. This version of Cokawin's surrender is from the Susan Bordeaux Bettelyoun Papers, NSHS, almost identical to another in Bettelyoun and Waggoner, *With My Own Eyes*, 64.

6. Mattison, "Todd Journal," 115; Winship, Camp on the Blue Water, to Cady, commanding battalion, Sixth Infantry, Camp near Ash Hollow, Sept. 8, 1855; Winship to Hendrickson, commanding, Fort Kearny, Sept. 8, 1855; Winship to Wharton, commanding, Fort Grattan, Sept. 8, 1855, LSSE; Ridgely, Camp at Fort Laramie, to Lawson, Washington, Sept. 17, 1855, LR, Officer of the Surgeon General, RG 112; Hanson, *Little Chief's Gatherings*, 107; G. Balch, Fort Laramie, Fort Laramie, to H. Balch, Sept. 18, 1855, Balch Papers; Anon. correspondent, Blue Water, Sept. 5, 1855, *Missouri Republican*, Sept. 27, 1855, in Watkins, "Notes," 280; Coyer, "Sweeny Letters," 240; Bandel, *Frontier Life*, 88. Four of the Oglala prisoners were the wife and three children of "Chanta-pe-tan-ya," or Visible Fire Heart. Warren, "Report of Sept. 4, 1855."

7. Mattison, "Todd Journal," 115.

8. Mattison, "Todd Journal," 115–16; Hanson, *Little Chief's Gatherings*, 107–9; Bandel, *Frontier Life*, 87; Harney to Thomas, Sept. 26, 1855, LSSE. The Sept. 11, 1855, quote about Chimney Rock and Court House Rock, now historic sites owned by the Nebraska State Historical Society, is from the "Todd Journal." The quote about the Grattan "masonry" marker came from G. Balch, Fort Laramie, to H. Balch, Sept. 18, 1855, Balch Papers. Surviving physical evidence of the site is slim, according to Paul L. Hedren, "Lieutenant John L. Grattan's Beltplate?" *Military Collector & Historian* 32 (Fall 1980): 130–32.

9. Twiss, Fort Laramie, to commissioner of Indian affairs, Oct. 1, 1855, in *Senate Executive Document No. 1*, Serial 810; Hanson, *Little Chief's Gatherings*, 108–9; Winship to Twiss, Sept. 18, 1855; Harney to Thomas, Sept. 26, 1855, LSSE; Chandless, *Visit to Salt Lake*, 95, reported that in September at Fort Laramie that he saw: "On the door of the store was posted a notice of pains and penalties to whoever should presume to trade with any of the Sioux nation, then at war with the

United States; also another notice that some persons had, for evil purposes, spread among peaceful Indians a false and wicked rumour that General Harney meant to kill every Indian he could catch, whether Sioux or not, and that such persons and all others were forbidden to publish this rumour under pain, &c."

10. Harry Anderson, "Harney v. Twiss, Nebr. Terr., 1856," *Westerners Brand Book, Chicago Corral* 20 (1963): 1–3, 7–8; Hoopes, "Twiss on the Upper Platte," 357–59; Price, *Oglala People*, 40–43. For more on Harney's views of Indian policy and Indian agents expressed before his meeting with Twiss, see Harney, Camp near Fort Leavenworth, to Thomas, New York, July 24, 1855; Winship, Fort Kearny, to Hoffman, Fort Laramie, Aug. 24, 1855; Winship, Camp No. 5 (on the Platte), to Hoffman, Aug. 27, 1855, LSSE.

11. Harney to Thomas, Sept. 26, 1855, LSSE; Mattison, "Todd's Journal," 116–17. Warren's journal provided the name of Grease, along with other details of the council. Hanson, *Little Chief's Gatherings*, 110.

12. Harney to Thomas, Sept. 26, 1855, LSSE. In this report, Harney revised the Blue Water statistics upward. "I felt warranted in granting these conditions, from the fact that I had already inflicted a severe chastisement upon them in killing some 100 of their people. . . ."

13. *Ibid.*

14. Hanson, *Little Chief's Gatherings*, 110.

15. Anon. correspondent, Fort Laramie, Sept. 19, 1855, *Missouri Republican*, Oct. 24, 1855, repr. *New York Times*, Oct. 27, 1855; Hanson, *Little Chief's Gatherings*, 108–9; Mattison, "Todd Journal," 116–17.

16. Hanson, *Little Chief's Gatherings*, 109; Mattison, "Todd Journal," 116–17 (Captain Todd was a member of the court); Winship, headquarters, Sioux Expedition, "Camp near Fort Laramie," to Cooke, "Camp above Fort Laramie," Sept. 16, 1855; Winship to Cooke, Sept. 17, 1855; Winship to Cooke, Sept. 18, 1855; Winship to Hudson, special judge advocate, Fort Laramie, Sept. 21, 1855; Winship to Cooke, Sept. 21, 1855; Harney, Camp in the Mauvaisses Terres, to Thomas, Oct. 10, 1855, LSSE; Anon. correspondent, *Missouri Republican*, Oct. 24, 1855. William Chandless was the source for the "execution" quote. Chandless, *Visit to Salt Lake*, 75. The primary source for the proceedings is Howe Court

Martial, Records of the Office of Judge Advocate General, RG 153, NA; since this was a general court martial, this record group also holds the files on the other soldiers—all enlisted men—who were tried at this time. The background of such judicial proceedings is discussed in John D. McDermott, "Crime and Punishment in the United States Army: A Phase of Fort Laramie History," *Journal of the West* 7 (Apr. 1968): 246–55.

17. Mendenhall testimony, Howe Court Martial. Others who came to bury Howe, not to praise him, were: (Lieutenant Drum) "I do not know whether the signal to advance was obeyed [by Howe] promptly or not, as I was not with the company at the time, or in sight of it." (Captain Steele) "This condition of things made the presence of a reserve very desirable; and toward the close of the charge, I much feared that we should lose many men, and I believe I did lose one, for want of a reserve, or organized body of troops, near so. Had there been a reserve immediately behind us, much of the time, which I spent in trying to keep together a few of my company, as a nucleus for others to rally upon, might have been devoted, more particularly, to encouraging the pursuit & destruction of the enemy." (Drum again) "If the order to Capt. Howe was to follow Col. Cooke immediately, I think there was delay. Seeing the company, or a portion of it, watering, and moving very slowly when I came up to it, I supposed they were on their way to our camp on Plat[t]e River. I knew nothing of any order, at this time, from Col. Cooke to join him immediately."

18. Winship to Dudley, Sept. 17, 1855; Winship to Wharton, commanding, Fort Grattan, Sept. 17, 1855; Winship to Commanding Officer, Fort Kearny, Sept. 17, 1855; Winship to M. Howe, Camp above Fort Laramie, Sept. 17, 1855; Winship to Cooke, Sept. 17, 1855; Winship to M. Howe, Sept. 18, 1855; Winship to Graham, commanding squadron, Second Dragoons, Sept. 19, 1855; Winship to Wharton, Sept. 19, 1855; Harney to Thomas, Sept. 26, 1855; Winship to Cooke, Sept. 26, 1855; Winship to Hoffman, Sept. 26, 1855; Winship to Hoffman, Sept. 28, 1855; Woods, Fort Pierre, to Hoffman, Fort Laramie, Oct. 26, 1855, LSSE; Hanson, *Little Chief's Gatherings*, 109–10; Mattison, "Todd Journal," 116–17; S. Starr, Fort Laramie, to E. Starr, Sept. 7, 1855, Bixby Collection.

19. Winship to Cooke, Sept. 18, 1855; Winship to Cooke, Sept. 21, 1855, LSSE; Mattison, "Todd Journal," 116–17. The freight train of

partner "Kincaid" may be one owned by the same Mr. "Kinkade" or "Kinkhead" who was so shabbily treated the year before.

20. Winship to Commanding Officer, Battalion Second Infantry, White River, or Fort Pierre, Sept. 20, 1855, LSSE; "Official Correspondence of Fort Pierre," 430; Gardner, Fort Pierre, to his mother, Oct. 18, 1855, Gardner Papers.

21. Charles E. Hanson, "The Fort Pierre–Fort Laramie Trail," *Museum of the Fur Trade Quarterly* 1 (Summer 1965): 3–7; James A. Hanson, "A Forgotten Fur Trade Trail," *Nebraska History* 68 (Spring 1987): 2–9.

22. Captain Winship's 1854 report mentioned the Fort Laramie–Fort Pierre trail. Lieutenant Balch added that Harney would be taking sixty-three wagons to Fort Pierre. G. Balch, "Camp on Bull Creek, N.T., 218 miles from Fort Laramie," to H. Balch, Oct. 13, 1855, Balch Papers. Hanson, *Little Chief's Gatherings*, 93–94, 109–10.

Pertinent sources that refer to this prior use by an army wagon train include: Jesup to Vinton, Mar. 23, 1855, in "Official Correspondence of Fort Pierre," 381; Van Vliet, Headquarters, Sioux Expedition, Fort Leavenworth, to Hoffman, Fort Laramie, May 7, 1855, LSSE; Anon. correspondent, *Missouri Republican*, Oct. 24, 1855, repr. *New York Times*, Oct. 27, 1855; Carlin, "Battle of Ash Hollow," in George W. Kingsbury, *History of Dakota Territory* 1 (Chicago: The S. J. Clarke Publishing Col, 1915): 62–63; and Girardi and Hughes, *Memoirs of Carlin*, chap. 1, "Frontier Service in the Old Army."

23. *Missouri Republican*, Oct. 24, 1855.

24. Winship to Hoffman, Sept. 28, 1855, LSSE. See also Harney to Thomas, Sept. 26, 1855, LSSE; Mattison, "Todd Journal," 116–17; Hanson, *Little Chief's Gatherings*, 110; G. Balch, Fort Laramie, to H. Balch, Sept. 18, 1855, with a Sept. 26 addendum, Balch Papers.

25. Twiss, Fort Laramie, to Cumming, superintendent of Indian affairs, St. Louis, Oct. 10, 1855, in *Senate Executive Document No. 1*, Serial 810.

26. Mattison, "Todd Journal," 117; Hanson, *Little Chief's Gatherings*, 110; Woods, Fort Pierre, to Hoffman, Fort Laramie, Oct. 26, 1855, LSSE; Morrison, *Memoirs of Henry Heth*, 133; Brian Jones, "Those Wild Reshaw Boys," in *Sidelights of the Sioux Wars*, ed. Francis B. Taunton (London: The English Westerners Society, 1967), 14. For more on

guarding the Platte Bridge that winter, see John D. McDermott, *Frontier Crossroads: The History of Fort Caspar and the Upper Platte Crossing* (Casper: City of Casper, Wyo., 1997) 10–12. For Harney's route, see Anonymous, "With Harney through the Bad Lands," *The Wi-iyohi, Monthly Bulletin of the South Dakota Historical Society* 14 (Sept. 1960): 1–4.

27. G. Balch, Camp near Fort Laramie, to H. Balch, Sept. 17, 1855, Balch Papers.

28. Mattison, "Todd Journal," 118–19.

29. Hanson, *Little Chief's Gatherings*, 111.

30. Mattison, "Todd Journal," 119; Hanson, *Little Chief's Gatherings*, 111; Beam, "Reminiscences of Early Days," 304; G. Balch, Camp on Bull Creek, Nebraska Territory, 218 miles from Fort Laramie, to H. Balch, Oct. 13, 1855, Balch Papers. Lieutenant Balch's letter left by express on that date to Fort Pierre.

31. Mattison, "Todd Journal," 119–20; Hanson, *Little Chief's Gatherings*, 111.

32. Mattison, "Todd Journal," 120, 122. See also Hanson, *Little Chief's Gatherings*, 111–12; Bandel, *Frontier Life*, 91; Beam, "Reminiscences of Early Days," 304. Fossils impressed the column that had earlier departed Fort Pierre, which also collected specimens. Gardner, Fort Pierre, to his mother, Oct. 18, 1855, Gardner Papers.

33. G. Balch, Camp near Fort Pierre, to H. Balch, Oct. 21, 1855, Balch Papers.

34. Harney, Camp in the Mauvaisses Terres, to Thomas, New York, Oct. 10, 1855; Winship, Camp in the Mauvaisses Terre, to Cady, commanding battalion, Oct. 10, 1855; Winship to Hoffman, commanding, Fort Laramie, Oct. 10, 1855, LSSE; Mattison, "Todd Journal," 121–24; Hanson, *Little Chief's Gatherings*, 112–13.

35. Mattison, "Todd Journal," 124–25; Hanson, *Little Chief's Gatherings*, 113; Harney, Headquarters, Sioux Expedition, Fort Pierre, N.T., to Thomas, New York, Oct. 19, 1855, "Official Correspondence of Fort Pierre," 397–98; G. Balch, Camp near Fort Pierre, to H. Balch, Oct. 21, 1855, Balch Papers.

36. Harney to Thomas, Nov. 9, 1855, LSSE.

37. Morrison, *Memoirs of Henry Heth*, 134; Meyers, *Ten Years in the Ranks*, chap. 4, "Fort Pierre and the Sioux Indians, 1855–1856." Military correspondence for that winter often mentioned the design,

manufacture, and use of "sleds" (and sleighs), including: Pleasonton to Starr, Nov. 16, 1855; Pleasonton to Cady, commanding battalion, Sixth Infantry, Missouri River above Fort Pierre, Dec. 3, 1855; Pleasonton to Capt. Henry W. Wessells, commanding battalion, Second Infantry, Fort Pierre, Dec. 5, 1855; Pleasonton to Starr, Dec. 5, 1855; Pleasonton to Starr, Dec. 13, 1855; Pleasonton to M. Howe, Jan. 8, 1856; Pleasonton to Capt. Parmenus F. Turnley, asst. quartermaster, Fort Pierre, Jan. 9, 1855, LSSE.

38. Harney to Thomas, Oct. 19, 1855; Harney to Thomas, Nov. 21, 1855; Harney to Thomas, Dec. 14, 1855; Harney, Camp on Ponca Island, Missouri River, to Thomas, Jan. 14, 1856, LSSE; Hanson, *Little Chief's Gatherings*, 113; G. Balch to H. Balch, Oct. 13, 21, 1855, Balch Papers; Record of events, "Official Correspondence of Fort Pierre," 430, listed the garrison as consisting of Harney, his staff, and the headquarters of the Sioux Expedition, plus 897 men in the camp of Second Dragoons, companies D and H (141 officers and men), E and K (111 officers and men), the Second Infantry at Fort Pierre, companies A, B, C, D, G, and I (410 officers and men); and the camp of Sixth Infantry, companies A, E, H, and K (235 officers and men). Francis B. Heitman, *Historical Register and Dictionary of the United States Army* 1 (Washington: U.S. Government Printing Office, 1903): 1050. A writer for the *Missouri Republican* of Dec. 19, 1855, expressed shock about Captain Winship's Dec. 13 death, having seen him, apparently in fine health, pass through town only a few days previous.

39. Woods, Fort Pierre, to M. Howe, commanding squadron, Second Dragoons, Nov. 3, 1855; Harney to Thomas, Nov. 9, 1855; Pleasonton to Starr, commanding dragoon camp, Missouri River, Nov. 16, 1855; Pleasonton to M. Howe, Nov. 21, 1855; Pleasonton to Starr, Dec. 8, 1855; Harney to Cooper, Febr. 22, 1856, LSSE; Mattison, "Todd Journal," 125; Van Vliet, "On the civilized side of the Mo.," to Turnley, Oct. 26, 1855, in "Official Correspondence of Fort Pierre," 400–1, 431; Gardner, Fort Pierre, to his mother, Oct. 18, 1855, Gardner Papers.

40. Meyers, *Ten Years in the Ranks*, 76–90, 94, 96–100. Corporal Bandel had similar experiences with the Indians, even going so far as exclaiming (in German), "I can now speak the language of the Sioux Indians better or almost as well as Polish." Bandel, *Frontier Life*, 73, 92.

41. Pleasonton to Starr, Dec. 12, 1855; Pleasonton to M. Howe, Steamer Grey Cloud, Missouri River, Jan. 9, 1855; Harney, Camp on

the Missouri near Ponca Island, to Thomas, Jan. 11, 1856; Harney, Ponca Island, to Cooper, Washington, Jan. 20, 1856; Harney to Cooper, Febr. 20, 1856; Harney to Cooper, Febr. 22, 1856; Harney to Cooper, Febr. 24, 1856, LSSE; "Proceedings of a General Court Martial Convened at the Dragoon Encampment near the mouth of the Big Sioux River, Minnesota Territory, June 26th, 1856," Court Martial File #HH661, Court Martial Case Files, 1809–1894, Records of the Judge Advocate General, RG 153, NA. Details of the Marshall Howe court martial are recalled in Turnley, *Reminiscences*, 156–57, 175–78. Harney had an earlier run-in with Marshall Howe during the expedition, if the memory of an old freighter can be trusted. Beam, "Reminiscences of Early Days," 303–4. For more on the military's switch from Fort Pierre to Fort Randall, see Robert G. Athearn, *Forts of the Upper Missouri* (Englewood Cliffs, N.J.: Prentiss-Hall, 1967), chaps. 3, 4.

42. Harney to Cooper, Jan. 20, 1856, LSSE.

43. Harney to Thomas, Nov. 9, 1855; Pleasonton, Fort Pierre, to Hoffman, Nov. 20, 1855; Harney to Thomas, Nov. 21, 1855; Pleasonton to Hoffman, Fort Laramie, Nov. 13, 1855, LSSE. In March 1856, word reached Harney that two more individuals implicated in the mail murders had surrendered at Fort Laramie, the "nephew of Red Leaf" and "the son of Black Heart," neither considered headmen. Harney to Thomas, Mar. 3, 1856; Pleasonton to Hoffman, Mar. 6, 1856, LSSE.

44. *New York Times*, Sept. 25, 1855. See also *New York Times*, Oct. 27, 1855, by telegraph from St. Louis, Oct. 25, which correctly reported that Chief Little Thunder had survived Blue Water, and *ibid.*, Oct. 1, 1855, from St. Louis, Sept. 29, which incorrectly reported, "Lieut. Heath [Heth] was killed at the battle of Ash Hollow." Heth later had a good chuckle about this in his autobiography. Morrison, *Memoirs of Henry Heth*, 129–32.

New York Times, Oct. 6, 1855, by telegraph from Washington, Oct. 5. This dispatch gave more details about the Indian relics that accompanied Harney's report: "The War Department has received a package of the papers taken from the Sioux at the recent battle of the Bluewater, among them is a Postmaster's blank—evidently taken from some one of the mail agents, whom they have robbed and murdered—and is covered with Indian hieroglyphics, apparently intended to detail some of the bloody deeds of the tribe. The massacre of Lieutenant

Grattan and his party, is evidently one of the subjects of this symbolic history. It is also believed to describe the murder of an emigrating party, composed in part of women. Among the articles captured were two scalps of white women; a small memorandum book in which some neat penman had noted the incidents of an overland journey; a letter from B. W. Leonard, dated Hermon [Hermann, Missouri?], July 6, 1855, doubtless taken from a captured mail; several rather good sketches of Indians fighting, and a portion of the clothing which had belonged to the soldiers of Grattan's party. There can be no doubt that the Indians from whom these things were taken are the same who massacred Grattan and his command."

45. *New York Times*, Oct. 6, 1855.

46. Ibid., Oct. 25, 1855, correspondence from Washington, Oct. 23.

47. *House Executive Document, No. 65*, Serial 853.

48. Pleasonton to Hoffman, Febr. 19, 1856; Harney to Cooper, Febr. 20, 1856; Harney to Thomas, Febr. 28, 1856; Pleasonton to Hoffman, Mar. 6, 1856; Harney to Cooper, Mar. 23, 1855, LSSE.

49. "Minutes of a council held at Fort Pierre, Nebraska Territory, on the 1st day of March, 1856, by Brevet Brigadier General William S. Harney, United States army, commanding the Sioux expedition, with the delegations from nine of the bands of the Sioux," in *Senate Executive Documents*, 34th U.S. Cong., 1st sess., 1855–1856, No. 94, Serial 859.

Harney's gratuitous comment about "leaving a door open" informs the following newspaper story: "We were told [an] excellent anecdote the other day of Gen. Harney by one of the officers who was with him at the battle of Ash Hollow, and afterwards at Fort Pierre. At the treaty held at the latter place . . . he stood a few steps in advance of his staff and was dictating to the interpreter what to say in his usual gruff and authoritative manner. . . . 'Ask them if they remember the fight at Ash Hollow.' (It will be remembered that a great number of the Indians made their escape through a pass in the hills that the General knew nothing of until too late.) 'Tell them that I left a place for them to escape through then, to prevent my braves from killing every one of them,' and he continued, turning his eyes over his shoulder to his staff, 'It's lucky for them that I didn't know where it was, or I'd have killed every damned redskin in the hollow.'" *Omaha Nebraskian*, Oct. 29, 1856.

50. Harney, Fort Pierre, to Cooper, Febr. 22, 1856; Pleasonton to Hoffman, Mar. 5, 1856; Harney to Thomas, Mar. 9, 1856, LSSE.

51. Pleasonton to Hoffman, Mar. 5, 1856; Pleasonton to Wharton, Mar. 5, 1856; Pleasonton to Capt. Henry W. Wessells, Fort Pierre, Mar. 6, 1856; Harney to Davis, Mar. 8, 1855, LSSE.

52. "Minutes of a council at Fort Pierre;" John S. Gray, "Honore Picotte, Fur Trader," *South Dakota History* 6 (Spring 1976): 201.

53. Harney to Davis, Apr. 22, 1856, LSSE; Davis to Pierce, May 31, 1856, letter attached to "Minutes of a council at Fort Pierre." Harney had "the man who killed the cow" and "the man who killed Gibson," both Miniconjous, placed under arrest and confined to the guardhouse. Harney to Davis, May 23, 1856, LSSE.

54. Meyers, *Ten Years in the Ranks*, 102–3; Harney to Jesup, Washington, May 17, 1856, LSSE.

55. Harney to Cooper, Mar. 9, 1856; Harney to Cooper, Apr. 4, 1856; Pleasonton to Starr, Apr. 21, 1856; Pleasonton to Andrews, asst. paymaster general, Steamer Genoa, Missouri River, May 22, 1856; Harney, Camped near old Fort Lookout, Missouri River, to Cooper, May 31, 1856; Harney, Camp near mouth of Big Sioux River, to Cooper, June 30, 1856, LSSE; "Official Correspondence of Fort Pierre," 431.

56. Harney, Camp near mouth of Big Sioux River, to Cooper, July 12, 1856; Harney, Fort Leavenworth, to Cooper, July 22, 1856, LSSE; Adams, *Prince of Dragoons*, 147.

57. Harney to Cooper, May 9, 1856; Pleasonton to Hoffman, May 10, 1856; Pleasonton to Heth, commanding, Platte Bridge, May 10, 1856; Harney, Camp near mouth of Big Sioux River, to Cooper, July 5, 1856, LSSE; Whitfield to Cumming, Oct. 2, 1854, in *House Executive Document No. 1*, Serial 777; Winship report of 1854. If the number of surviving overland accounts is any indication (they doubled in 1856 from the previous year), traffic significantly increased. Mattes, *Platte River Road Narratives*, 448–69.

58. For a succinct account of the first Cheyenne war, see Utley, *Frontiersmen in Blue*, 120–25. For the whole story, see Chalfant, *Cheyennes and Horse Soldiers*; Percival G. Lowe's, *Five Years a Dragoon (49 to 54) And Other Adventures on the Great Plains*, ed. Don Russell (Norman: University of Oklahoma Press, 1965), chap. 7. For details about the Cheyenne troubles on the North Platte River, see Stan Hoig, *The Western*

Odyssey of John Simpson Smith, Frontiersman, Trapper, Trader, and Interpreter (Glendale, Calif.: The Arthur H. Clark Co., 1974), 98–100; and McDermott, *Frontier Crossroads*, 12–13.

Chapter 8. Memory and Legacy

1. Anon. correspondent, *Missouri Republican*, Sept. 27, 1855, in Watkins, "Notes," 280.

2. David Finster, "The Hardin Winter Count," *Museum News* (W. H. Over Dakota Museum) 29 (Mar.–Apr., 1968): 43. See also James R. Walker, *Oglala Society*, ed. Raymond J. DeMallie (Lincoln: University of Nebraska Press, 1982), 142–43, where Harney is referred to as the "Wasp." An extremely useful list of Lakota winter counts, as well as a discussion of their value as historical documents, can be found in Linea Sundstrom, "Smallpox Used Them Up: References to Epidemic Disease in Northern Plains Winter Counts, 1714–1920," *Ethnohistory* 44 (Spring 1997): 341–43.

3. Mattes, *Platte River Road Narratives*, 455–69.

4. Journal of Helen McCowen Carpenter, copy in the Merrill J. Mattes Collection, National Frontier Trails Center. See also Sandra L. Myres, ed., *Ho For California!: Women's Overland Diaries from the Huntington Library* (San Marino, Calif.: Huntington Library, 1980), 93–188; Mattes, *Platte River Road Narratives*, 471.

5. Reminiscence of Emily McCowen Horton (sister of Helen McCowen Carpenter), in *Our Family* (n.p., 1922), typescript in Mattes Collection. See Mattes, *Platte River Road Narratives*, 475. In his earlier work, *Great Platte River Road*, Mattes had dated both of these accounts at 1856, not 1857.

6. LeRoy R. Hafen, ed., *The Utah Expedition, 1857–1858: A Documentary Account of the United States Military Movement under Colonel Albert Sidney Johnston, and the Resistance by Brigham Young and the Mormon Nauvoo Legion* (Glendale, Calif.: The Arthur H. Clark Company, 1982), 113–14.

7. Mattison, "Todd Journal," 114.

8. Ball, *Army Regulars on the Western Frontier*, chap. 8.

9. Kenderdine's *A California Tramp and Later Footprints* (Newton, Penn.: Philadelphia Press, 1888) is quoted in Mattes, *Great Platte River Road*, 333.

10. Bandel, *Frontier Life*, intro., chap. 4.

11. Meyers, *Ten Years in the Ranks*. For an account of his 1913 return, see ibid., 353–56; *Sioux City Journal*, Sept. 9, 1913.

12. Price, *Oglala People*, 128, 198; Thomas R. Buecker, *Fort Robinson and the American West 1874–1899* (Lincoln: Nebraska State Historical Society, 1999), 7, 213.

13. Bettelyoun and Waggoner, *With My Own Eyes*, 62.

14. Spotted Tail's confinement received considerable attention in Hyde, *Spotted Tail's Folk*, 76–82. Kingsbury, *History of Dakota Territory*, 67, gave an account of the Spotted Tail pardon: "The foregoing account of the cause of the famous Harney expedition was substantially furnished to President Franklin Pierce by an army officer, who wished to induce the President to pardon a number of the Indians who possibly would have been executed for their crimes committed during the first outbreak of hostilities. The President seemed to believe that the Indians had been 'more sinned against than sinning' and granted a full pardon, restoring them to all their annuities."

Spotted Tail's meeting the Cherokees came from D. C. Poole, *Among the Sioux of Dakota: Eighteen Months' Experience as an Indian Agent, 1869–70* (St. Paul: Minnesota Historical Society, 1988), 158. For more on the chief's career and untimely death, see James A. Hanson, *Famous Indians of Northwest Nebraska* (Chadron, Nebr.: Museum of the Fur Trade, 1983); and Richmond L. Clow, "The Anatomy of a Lakota Shooting: Crow Dog and Spotted Tail, 1879–1881," *South Dakota History* 28 (Winter 1998): 209–27.

15. Bettelyoun and Waggoner, *With My Own Eyes*, 154; biographies of Iron Shell and Hollow Horn Bear, Waggoner Papers, Museum of the Fur Trade; Henry W. Hamilton and Jean Tyree Hamilton, *The Sioux of the Rosebud: A History in Pictures* (Norman: University of Oklahoma Press, 1971), 289; the Iron Shell family served as major sources for Hassrick's, *The Sioux*, xiii. Paula Richardson Fleming and Judith Luskey, *The North American Indians in Early Photographs* (New York: Harper & Row, Publishers, 1986), 180, 189.

16. Hanson, *Little Chief's Gatherings*, 116, commenting on Hyde, *Red Cloud's Folk*, 121–22. See a correction, of sorts, in Hyde, *Spotted Tail's Folk*, 288.

17. *Omaha Daily Herald*, Apr. 24, 1873; *Omaha Daily Bee*, Apr. 28, 1873.

18. Bettelyoun and Waggoner, *With My Own Eyes*, 104; biography of Bear's Rib, Waggoner Papers; Sunder, *Fur Trade on the Upper Missouri*, 240; Robert M. Utley, *The Lance and the Shield: The Life and Times of Sitting Bull* (New York: Henry Holt and Company, 1993), 46–49.

19. Hyde, *Red Cloud's Folk*, 93–95; Hyde, *Spotted Tail's Folk*, 87–90; Reminiscence of Arthur Collister, *Douglas* (Wyo.) *Budget*, July 16, 1942. Mrs. "Twist" appeared on a Red Cloud Agency census ledger in 1876. Thomas R. Buecker and R. Eli Paul, eds., *The Crazy Horse Surrender Ledger* (Lincoln: Nebraska State Historical Society, 1994), 34.

20. Mattison, "Todd Journal," 92, 130.

21. Entries for Buford and Heth in Patricia L. Faust, ed., *Historical Times Illustrated Encyclopedia of the Civil War* (New York: Harper & Row, 1986), 89, 358. Buford has been the subject of a relatively recent biography by Edward G. Longacre, *General John Buford* (Conshohocken, Penn.: Combined Books, 1995).

22. Young, *West of Philip Cooke*, 270–71.

23. Entry for Cooke in Faust, *Historical Encyclopedia of the Civil War*, 164. Cooke's writings included, among others: *Scenes and Adventures in the Army* (1859); *Cavalry Tactics* (Washington: U.S. Government Printing Office, 1861); and *The Conquest of New Mexico and California: An Historical and Personal Narrative* (New York: G. P. Putnam's Sons, 1878).

24. Entry for Warren in Faust, *Historical Encyclopedia of the Civil War*, 803. See also Oliver Willcox Norton, *The Attack and Defense of Little Round Top*, Gettysburg, July 2, 1863 (New York: The Neale Publishing Company, 1913); and Taylor, *Gouverneur Kemble Warren*, chap. 6. A recent biography of Warren, which highlights the rough times he encountered after his Gettysburg heroics, is David M. Jordan, *"Happiness Is Not My Companion": The Life of General G. K. Warren* (Bloomington: Indiana University Press, 2001).

25. Schubert, *Explorer on the Northern Plains*, xvi–xxx; Schubert, *Vanguard of Expansion*, chap. 7.

26. Entry for Garnett in Faust, *Historical Encyclopedia of the Civil War*, 299–300. For a biographical sketch of Billy Garnett, see Donald F. Danker, "The Violent Deaths of Yellow Bear and John Richard, Jr.," *Nebraska History* 63 (Summer 1982): 137–38, in which Garnett was the principal informant for this episode.

27. Guy W. Moore, *The Case of Mrs. Surratt: Her Controversial Trial and Execution for Conspiracy in the Lincoln Assassination* (Norman: University of Oklahoma Press, 1954), 30, 52.

28. Adams, *Prince of Dragoons*, chap. 12.

29. Ibid., 240.

30. Ibid., chap. 13. One trader described how a Hunkpapa leader carefully treasured his commission from Harney in "a leathern pouch wrapped in a piece of calico." Henry A. Boller, *Among the Indians: Four Years on the Upper Missouri, 1858–1862*, ed. Milo Milton Quaife (Lincoln: University of Nebraska Press, 1972), 173–74.

31. Capt. Caleb H. Carlton, Fort Laramie, to his wife, Apr. 23, 1868, Caleb Carlton Collection, Manuscript Division, Library of Congress, Washington, D.C. For another example of the legendary Harney temper, fodder for anecdotes for years to come, see Beam, "Reminiscences of the Early Days," 300–1.

32. James C. Olson, *Red Cloud and the Sioux Problem* (Lincoln: University of Nebraska Press, 1965), chaps. 5, 6.

33. Utley, *Frontiersmen in Blue*, 281–97; Alvin M. Josephy, Jr., *The Civil War in the American West* (New York: Vintage Books, 1991), 302–12.

34. "Style of warfare" quote, *Rocky Mountain News* (Denver, Colo.), Nov. 14, 1865; "Peace with guns" quote, *Rocky Mountain News*, Jan. 9, 1868, commenting on a letter by A. K. McClure that appeared in the *Philadelphia Press*, Dec. 31, 1867; Curtis quote in Dunn, *Massacres of the Mountains*, 433–34; "More Sand Creek" quote, *Rocky Mountain News*, Nov. 27, 1865.

A couple of decades later, commentators began to make the distinction between Blue Water Creek and Sand Creek. Referring to Chivington at Sand Creek: "He had in mind also, General Harney's famous achievement at Ash Hollow in September 1855, and felt he had eclipsed the glory of that historic massacre, but forgot that Harney gave no orders to kill everything in sight, and hence saved himself the disgrace of an indiscriminate slaughter." Frank Hall, *History of the State of Colorado* 1 (Chicago: The Blakely Printing Company, 1889): 356.

35. Robert E. Morris, "Custer Made a Good Decision: A Leavenworth Appreciation," *Journal of the West* 16 (Oct. 1977): 5–11. The reaction of the press and the public to the Custer defeat occurred in the midst of the nation's 1876 Centennial celebration and is treated in Robert M. Utley, *Custer and the Great Controversy: Origin and Development of a Legend* (Pasadena, Calif.: Westernlore Press, 1962), chap. 2, "The Press," and Brian W. Dippie, *Custer's Last Stand: The Anatomy of an American Myth* (Lincoln: University of Nebraska Lincoln, 1994), chap. 1, "Myth and History: Custer and His Last Stand."

36. *Omaha Daily Herald*, July 15, 1876.

37. *Chicago Inter-Ocean*, Aug. 4, 1876, repr. of an interview in the *St. Louis Republican*. A decade earlier Harney had reminded the public of the government's failure in 1856 in almost the exact same words, "Had they executed the treaty I made with the Indians at Fort Pierre . . . we would not now be in this trouble." *Omaha Weekly Herald*, Aug. 22, 1867.

38. Logan Uriah Reavis, *The Life and Military Services of General William Selby Harney* (St. Louis: Bryan, Brand, 1878).

39. George Washington Manypenny, *Our Indian Wards* (Cincinnati: R. Clarke & Co., 1880), 159.

40. Adams, *Prince of Dragoons*, 47–51. Henry Heth later claimed, in a somewhat apocryphal story, to have used that famous temper to provoke Harney to attack Little Thunder's village. Morrison, *Memoirs of Henry Heth*, 127–28. See also the Carlin reminiscence in Kingsbury, *History of Dakota Territory*, 62.

41. This lack of formal Indian-fighting tactics is discussed by Jerome A. Greene in his foreword to Edward S. Farrow, *Mountain Scouting: A Handbook for Officers and Soldiers on the Frontiers* (Norman: University of Oklahoma Press, 2000), 3–8.

42. Stray reminiscent accounts of the First Sioux War, real and phony, dot the historical record, as the appendix to this book attests. Not all have been cited in the text, some for obvious reasons; they are clearly incorrect. For example, Stewart Van Vliet recalled: "Some years afterward, I was with Gen'l Harney in his Sioux Campaign, and we saw but one buffaloe on our march from the Missouri River to Ft. Lara-

mie." Not according to Captain Todd's daily journal. Van Vliet to J. Sterling Morton, Nebraska City, Nebr., in a July 10, 1896 letter in the J. Sterling Morton Collection, Nebraska State Historical Society Archives, Lincoln.

Some cannot be so easily dismissed. "Julia Clifford says that her father, Yuse, was an interpreter and scout for Lt. Gratton [*sic*] at Ft. Laramie, Wyoming; that he was killed at the fort when she was three years of age; that this is the story as her mother told it to her: One morning he came home and said to his wife that Lt. Gratton was determined to interfere about that Mormon cow; 'I am afraid you will be a widow before night.' The granduncle [?] had bought the cow from some Mormons who were passing through. The hoofs were worn smooth, and she was lame, so they traded her for a pair of leggins, a pair of moccasins, and a tanned deer skin, and they butchered the cow and someone reported to Lieut. Gratton that the cow had been stolen. The soldiers were drunk and fired on the Indians, and the Indians then butchered and killed the soldiers, and on this day Yuse was killed by the crazed Indians and had many arrows in his body." Letter from Julia Clifford, Martin, S. Dak., to Lulu Brown, Stockville, Nebr., Febr. 16, 1926, in Bayard H. Paine, *Pioneers, Indians and Buffaloes* (Curtis, Nebr.: The Curtis Enterprise, 1935), 36–37, 75–77.

Bibliography

Manuscript Materials

American Heritage Center, University of Wyoming, Laramie, Wyo.
    Remi A. Nadeau Collection.

Ash Hollow State Historical Park, Lewellen, Nebr.
    John M. Sullivan enlistment papers, compiled by Dennis Shimmin, Supt., and on file.

Bancroft Library, Berkeley, Calif.
    George T. Balch Papers.

Duke University, Durham, N.Carol.
    John T. Mercer Correspondence, U.S. Army Officers' and Soldiers' Miscellany Papers, William R. Perkins Library.

Fort Laramie National Historic Site, Fort Laramie, Wyo.
    Fort Laramie and Upper Platte Indian Agency Selected Documents, Fort Laramie Library.

Library of Congress, Washington, D.C.
    Caleb Carlton Collection, Manuscript Division.

Missouri Historical Society, St. Louis, Mo.
    Samuel H. Starr Correspondence, William K. Bixby Collection.

Museum of the Fur Trade, Chadron, Nebr.
    Biographies of Bear's Rib, Hollow Horn Bear, Iron Shell, and Spotted Tail, Josephine Waggoner Papers.

National Archives and Records Administration, Washington, D.C.
    RG 75, Records of the Office of Indian Affairs: Letters Received by the Office of Indian Affairs.
    RG 92, Records of the Office of Quartermaster General: Special File, "Sioux Expedition, 1855," Consolidated Correspondence File, 1794–1915.

RG 94, Records of the Office of the Adjutant General: Letters Received, Department of the West; Letters Received, Office of the Adjutant General; Report of a Board of Officers on the armament of the troops of the Expedition, Fort Pierre, Oct. 23, 1855; Returns of Expeditions.

RG 98, Records of the War Department, United States Army Commands: Letters Sent, Fort Laramie.

RG 112, Records of the Office of the Surgeon General: Letters Received, Office of the Surgeon General.

RG 153, Records of the Judge Advocate General: Proceedings of a General Court Martial Convened at Fort Laramie, N.T., Sept. 18th, 1855, Court Martial File #HH551; Proceedings of a General Court Martial Convened at the Dragoon Encampment near the mouth of the Big Sioux River, Minnesota Territory, June 26th, 1856, Court Martial File #HH661, Court Martial Case Files, 1809–1894.

RG 156, Records of the Office of the Chief of Ordnance: Letters Received, Office of the Chief of Ordnance.

RG 393, Records of the U.S. Army Continental Commands: Letters Received, Dept. of the West; Letters Sent, Fort Kearny; Letters Sent, Sioux Expedition, 1855–56, Dept. of the West.

National Frontier Trails Center, Independence, Mo.

Merrill J. Mattes Collection: Helen McCowen Carpenter Journal; James E. Enos Recollections; Emily McCowen Horton Reminiscence; Annie Dougherty Ruff Correspondence.

Nebraska State Historical Society Library–Archives, Lincoln, Nebr.

Susan Bordeaux Bettelyoun Collection.

Richard C. Drum Reminiscence.

Nathan A. M. Dudley Correspondence.

Robert W. Furnas Scrapbooks.

J. Sterling Morton Collection.

Eli S. Ricker Collection.

Addison E. Shelden Collection.

University of North Carolina, Chapel Hill, N.C.

Samuel Cooper, "Recollections of Incidents and Characters during Fifty Years of Military Service," Samuel Cooper Papers, Southern Historical Collection.

William M. Gardner Papers, Southern Historical Collection.

Wyoming State Archives, Cheyenne, Wyo.
    John Talbot obituary, clipping from a Cheyenne, Wyo., newspaper,
    July 1910.

Unpublished Materials
Carolyn Minnette McClellan, "The Sioux Expedition, 1854–1856,"
    Master's thesis, Washington University, St. Louis, Mo., 1945.
Timothy R. Nowak, "The Army's Use of Portable Cottages at Fort
    Pierre Chouteau during the Sioux Expedition, 1855–56," Paper
    presented at the annual meeting of the South Dakota State His-
    torical Society, Pierre, S.Dak., March 28, 1998.

Government Publications
House Executive Documents: Report of the Commissioner of Indian
Affairs, Nov. 25, 1854, 33rd U.S. Cong., 2nd sess., 1854–55, No. 1, Ser-
ial 777; Report of the Secretary of War, Dec. 4, 1854, 33rd U.S. Cong.,
2nd sess., 1854–55, No. 1, Serial 778; Reports from the Department of
the West, Serial 778; A report in regard to the expedition among the
Indians on the Upper Missouri, 34th U.S. Cong., 1st sess., 1855–56,
No. 65, Serial 853.

House of Representatives Reports: Letter from the Secretary of War,
transmitting information relating to an engagement between the
United States troops and the Sioux Indians near Fort Laramie, No. 63,
33rd U.S. Cong., 2nd sess., 1854–55, Serial 788.

National Archives Microfilm Publications: Report of an Inspection of
Forts Ripley, Ridgely, Snelling, Laramie, Kearney, Riley, Leavenworth,
and Atkinson, No. 567, roll 508; Letters Received by the Office of
Indian Affairs, M234, roll 889.

Senate Executive Documents: Exploration and Survey of the Valley of
the Great Salt Lake of Utah, Including a Reconnaissance of a New
Route through the Rocky Mountains, U.S. 32nd Cong., spec. sess.,
Mar. 1851, No. 3, Serial 608; Report of the Commissioner of Indian
Affairs, Nov. 26, 1855, 34th U.S. Cong., 1st sess., 1855–56, No. 1, Serial
810; Report of General Harney, Commander of the Sioux Expedition,
September 5, 1855, 34th U.S. Cong., 1st and 2nd sess., No. 1, Serial

811; Report of September 4, 1855, and Sketch of Battle Ground at Blue Water Creek, No. 76, Serial 811; Correspondence respecting the massacre of Lieutenant Grattan and his command by Indians, Report of the Secretary of War, July 10, 1856, 34th U.S. Cong., 1st sess., 1855–56, No. 91, Serial 823; Minutes of a council held at Fort Pierre, Nebraska Territory, on the 1st day of March, 1856, by Brevet Brigadier General William S. Harney, United States army, commanding the Sioux expedition, with the delegations from nine of the bands of the Sioux, 34th U.S. Cong., 1st sess., 1855–56, No. 94, Serial 859; Report of September 5, 1855, 34th U.S. Cong., 3rd sess., No. 58, Serial 881.

Newspapers

Chicago Inter-Ocean, 1876.
Council Bluffs (Ia.) *Chronotype*, 1855–56.
Douglas (Wyo.) *Budget*, 1942.
Frontier Guardian (Kanesville [Council Bluffs], Ia.), 1851.
Kansas Weekly Herald (Leavenworth), 1854–55.
Liberty (Mo.) *Weekly Tribune*, 1854.
Missouri Republican (St. Louis), 1849–55.
Nebraska Palladium (Bellevue), 1854.
New York Times, 1855.
Omaha Daily Bee, 1873, 1887, 1913.
Omaha Daily Herald, 1873, 1876, 1879.
Omaha Nebraskian, 1855–56.
Omaha Weekly Herald, 1867.
Philadelphia Press, 1867.
Rocky Mountain News (Denver), 1865, 1868.
Sheridan (Wyo.) *Enterprise*, 1907.
St. Louis Republican, 1876.
Sioux City (Ia.) *Journal*, 1913.

Books

Adams, George Rollie. *General William S. Harney: Prince of Dragoons*. Lincoln: University of Nebraska Press, 2001.
Athearn, Robert G. *Forts of the Upper Missouri*. Englewood Cliffs, N.J.: Prentiss-Hall, 1967.

Ball, Durwood. *Army Regulars on the Western Frontier, 1848–1861.* Norman: University of Oklahoma Press, 2001.

Bandel, Eugene. *Frontier Life in the Army, 1854–1861*, ed. Ralph P. Bieber. Glendale, Calif.: The Arthur H. Clark Company, 1932.

Barry, Louise. *The Beginning of the West: Annals of the Kansas Gateway to the American West, 1540–1854.* Topeka: Kansas State Historical Society, 1972.

Bettelyoun, Susan Bordeaux, and Josephine Waggoner. *With My Own Eyes: A Lakota Woman Tells Her People's History*, ed. Emily Levine. Lincoln: University of Nebraska Press, 1998.

Boller, Henry A. *Among the Indians: Four Years on the Upper Missouri, 1858–1862*, ed. Milo Milton Quaife. Lincoln: University of Nebraska Press, 1972.

Brooks, Juanita, ed. *On the Mormon Frontier: The Diary of Hosea Stout, 1844–1861.* Salt Lake City: University of Utah Press, 1964.

Buecker, Thomas R. *Fort Robinson and the American West 1875–1899.* Lincoln: Nebraska State Historical Society, 1999.

Buecker, Thomas R., and R. Eli Paul, eds. *The Crazy Horse Surrender Ledger.* Lincoln: Nebraska State Historical Society, 1994.

Carleton, J. Henry. *The Prairie Logbooks: Dragoon Campaigns to the Prairie Villages in 1844, and to the Rocky Mountains in 1845*, ed. Louis Pelzer. Chicago: Caxton Club, 1943.

Carriker, Robert C. *Father Peter John DeSmet: Jesuit in the West.* Norman: University of Oklahoma Press, 1995.

Chalfant, William Y. *Cheyennes and Horse Soldiers: The 1857 Expedition and the Battle of Solomon's Fork.* Norman: University of Oklahoma Press, 1989.

Chandless, William. *A Visit to Salt Lake: Being a Journey across the Plains and a Residence in the Mormon Settlements at Utah.* London: Smith, Elder, and Co., 1857.

Cooke, Philip St. George. *Cavalry Tactics.* Washington: U.S. Government Printing Office, 1861.

———. *The Conquest of New Mexico and California: An Historical and Personal Narrative.* New York: G. P. Putnam's Sons, 1878.

———. *Scenes and Adventures in the Army, or Romance of Military Life.* Philadelphia: Lindsay & Blakiston, 1859.

Cullum, George W. *Biographical Register of the Officers and Graduates of the U.S. Military Academy at West Point, N.Y., from Its Establishment in 1802 to 1890*. Boston: Houghton, Mifflin, 1891.

De Smet, Pierre J. *Western Missions and Missionaries: A Series of Letters*. New York: James B. Kirker, 1863.

Diffendal, R. F., Jr., R. K. Pabian, and J. R. Thompson. *Geologic History of Ash Hollow Park, Nebraska*. Lincoln: Conservation and Survey Division, University of Nebraska, 1982.

Dippie, Brian W. *Custer's Last Stand: The Anatomy of an American Myth*. Lincoln: University of Nebraska Lincoln, 1994.

Dunn, J. P., Jr. *Massacres of the Mountain: A History of the Indian Wars of the Far West*. New York: Harper & Brothers, 1886.

Farrow, Edward S. *Mountain Scouting: A Handbook for Officers and Soldiers on the Frontiers*. Norman: University of Oklahoma Press, 2000.

Faust, Patricia L., ed. *Historical Times Illustrated Encyclopedia of the Civil War*. New York: Harper & Row, 1986.

Fleming, Paula Richardson, and Judith Luskey. *The North American Indians in Early Photographs*. New York: Harper & Row, 1986.

Fletcher, Patricia K. A., Jack Earl Fletcher, and Lee Whiteley. *Cherokee Trail Diaries*. Sequim, Wash.: Fletcher Family Foundation, 1999.

Frazer, Robert W. *Forts and Supplies: The Role of the Army in the Economy of the Southwest, 1846–1861*. Albuquerque: University of New Mexico Press, 1983.

Garavaglia, Louis A., and Charles G. Worman. *Firearms of the American West, 1803–1865*. Albuquerque: University of New Mexico Press, 1984.

Girardi, Robert L., and Nathaniel Cheairs Hughes, Jr., eds. *The Memoirs of Brigadier General William Passmore Carlin, U.S.A.* Lincoln: University of Nebraska Press, 1999.

Goetzmann, William H. *Army Exploration in the American West, 1803–1863*. New Haven: Yale University Press, 1959.

Hafen, LeRoy R., ed. *The Utah Expedition, 1857–1858: A Documentary Account of the United States Military Movement under Colonel Albert Sidney Johnston, and the Resistance by Brigham Young and the Mormon Nauvoo Legion*. Glendale, Calif.: The Arthur H. Clark Company, 1982.

Hafen, LeRoy R., and Francis Marion Young. *Fort Laramie and the Pageant of the West, 1834–1890*. Glendale, Calif.: The Arthur H. Clark Co., 1938.

Hall, Frank. *History of the State of Colorado*. Chicago: The Blakely Printing Company, 1889.

Hamilton, Henry W., and Jean Tyree Hamilton. *The Sioux of the Rosebud: A History in Pictures*. Norman: University of Oklahoma Press, 1971.

Hanson, James A. *Famous Indians of Northwest Nebraska*. Chadron, Nebr.: Museum of the Fur Trade, 1983.

————. *Little Chief's Gatherings: The Smithsonian Institution's G. K. Warren 1855–1856 Plains Indian Collection and The New York State Library's 1855–1857 Warren Expeditions Journals*. Chadron, Nebr.: The Fur Press, 1996.

Hassrick, Royal B. *The Sioux: Life and Customs of a Warrior Society*. Norman: University of Oklahoma Press, 1964.

Hawkins, John Parker. *Memoranda Concerning Some Branches of the Hawkins Family and Connections*. Indianapolis: Privately printed, 1913.

Hedren, Paul L. *Fort Laramie in 1876: Chronicle of a Frontier Post at War*. Lincoln: University of Nebraska Press, 1988.

Heitman, Francis B. *Historical Register and Dictionary of the United States Army*. Washington: U.S. Government Printing Office, 1903.

Hodge, Frederick Webb, ed. *Handbook of American Indians North of Mexico*. Washington: U.S. Government Printing Office, 1912.

Hoig, Stan. *The Western Odyssey of John Simpson Smith, Frontiersman, Trapper, Trader, and Interpreter*. Glendale, Calif.: The Arthur H. Clark Co., 1974.

Hyde, George E. *The Pawnee Indians*. Norman: University of Oklahoma Press, 1974.

————. *Red Cloud's Folk: A History of the Oglala Sioux Indians*. Norman: University of Oklahoma Press, 1957.

————. *Spotted Tail's Folk: A History of the Brulé Sioux*. Norman: University of Oklahoma Press, 1974.

Jackson, W. Turrentine. *Wagon Roads West: A Study of Federal Road Surveys and Construction in the Trans-Mississippi West, 1846–1869*. New Haven, Conn.: Yale University Press, 1964.

Johnson, Paul D. *Civil War Cartridge Boxes of the Union Infantryman*. Lincoln, R.I.: Andrew Mowbray Publishers, 1998.

Jordan, David M. *"Happiness Is Not My Companion": The Life of General G. K. Warren*. Bloomington: Indiana University Press, 2001.

Josephy, Alvin M., Jr. *The Civil War in the American West*. New York: Vintage Books, 1991.

Kenderdine, Thomas. *A California Tramp and Later Footprints*. Newton, Penn.: Philadelphia Press, 1888.

Kingsbury, George W. *History of Dakota Territory*. Chicago: The S. J. Clarke Publishing Co., 1915.

Langellier, John P. *Army Blue: The Uniform of Uncle Sam's Regulars, 1848–1873*. Atglen, Penn.: Schiffer Military History, 1998.

Lass, William E. *From the Missouri to the Great Salt Lake: An Account of Overland Freighting*. Lincoln: Nebraska State Historical Society, 1972.

Lavender, David. *Fort Laramie and the Changing Frontier*. Washington: National Park Service, 1983.

Longacre, Edward G. *General John Buford*. Conshohocken, Penn.: Combined Books, 1995.

Lowe, Percival G. *Five Years a Dragoon (49 to 54) and Other Adventures on the Great Plains*, ed. Don Russell. Norman: University of Oklahoma Press, 1965.

Manypenny, George Washington. *Our Indian Wards*. Cincinnati: R. Clarke & Co., 1880.

Mattes, Merrill J. *The Great Platte River Road: The Covered Wagon Mainline Via Fort Kearny to Fort Laramie*. Lincoln: Nebraska State Historical Society, 1969.

———. *Platte River Road Narratives: A Descriptive Bibliography of Travel Over the Great Central Overland Route to Oregon, California, Utah, Colorado, Montana, and Other Western States and Territories, 1812–1866*. Urbana: University of Illinois Press, 1988.

McDermott, John D. *Frontier Crossroads: The History of Fort Caspar and the Upper Platte Crossing*. Casper: City of Casper, Wyo., 1997.

———. *A Guide to the Indian Wars of the West*. Lincoln: University of Nebraska Press, 1998.

Meyers, Augustus. *Ten Years in the Ranks, U.S. Army*. New York: The Stirling Press, 1914.

Moore, Guy W. *The Case of Mrs. Surratt: Her Controversial Trial and Execution for Conspiracy in the Lincoln Assassination*. Norman: University of Oklahoma Press, 1954.

Morrison, James L., Jr., ed. *The Memoirs of Henry Heth*. Westport, Conn.: Greenwood Press, 1974.

Myres, Sandra L., ed. *Ho For California!: Women's Overland Diaries from the Huntington Library*. San Marino, Calif.: Huntington Library, 1980.

Nadeau, Remi. *Fort Laramie and the Sioux Indians*. Englewood Cliffs, N. J.: Prentiss-Hall, 1967.

Norton, Oliver Willcox. *The Attack and Defense of Little Round Top, Gettysburg, July 2, 1863*. New York: The Neale Publishing Company, 1913.

Olson, James C. *Red Cloud and the Sioux Problem*. Lincoln: University of Nebraska Press, 1965.

Paine, Bayard H. *Pioneers, Indians and Buffaloes*. Curtis, Nebr.: The Curtis Enterprise, 1935.

Parkman, Francis, Jr. *The Oregon Trail*. New York: Penguin Books, 1985 repr. of 1849 edit.

Paul, R. Eli, ed. *Autobiography of Red Cloud: War Leader of the Oglalas*. Helena: Montana Historical Society Press, 1997.

Peterson, Jacqueline. *Sacred Encounters: Father De Smet and the Indians of the Rocky Mountain West*. Norman: University of Oklahoma Press, 1993.

Poole, D. C. *Among the Sioux of Dakota: Eighteen Months' Experience as an Indian Agent, 1869–70*. St. Paul: Minnesota Historical Society Press, 1988.

Price, Catherine. *The Oglala People, 1841–1879: A Political History*. Lincoln: University of Nebraska Press, 1996.

Prucha, Francis Paul. *The Sword and the Republic: The United States Army on the Frontier, 1783–1846*. New York: Macmillan Publishing Company, 1969.

Reavis, Logan Uriah. *The Life and Military Services of General William Selby Harney*. St. Louis: Bryan, Brand, 1878.

———. *St. Louis: The Future Great City of the World*. St. Louis: C. R. Barns, 1876.

Rodenbough, Theophilus F. *From Everglade to Canyon with the Second United States Cavalry: An Authentic Account of Service in Florida,*

Mexico, Virginia, and the Indian Country, 1836–1875. Norman: University of Oklahoma Press, 2000.

Sage, Rufus B. *Rocky Mountain Life, or Startling Scenes and Perilous Adventures in the Far West, during an Expedition of Three Years [1841 to 1844].* Lincoln: University of Nebraska Press, 1982.

Sandoz, Mari. *Crazy Horse, the Strange Man of the Oglalas.* Lincoln: University of Nebraska Press, 1992.

Schoolcraft, Henry R. *Information Respecting the History, Condition and Prospects of the Indian Tribes of the United States.* Philadelphia: Lippincott, Grambo & Company, 1853.

Schubert, Frank N. Introduction to *Explorer on the Northern Plains: Lieutenant Gouverneur K. Warren's Preliminary Report of Explorations in Nebraska and Dakota, in the Years 1855–'56–'57.* Washington: U.S. Government Printing Office, 1981.

————.*Vanguard of Expansion: Army Engineers in the Trans-Mississippi West, 1819–1879.* Washington: U.S. Government Printing Office, 1980.

Schubert, Frank N., ed. "March to South Pass: Lieutenant William B. Franklin's Journal of the Kearny Expedition of 1845," *Engineer Historical Studies*, No. 1. Washington: U.S. Government Printing Office, 1980.

Schuler, Harold H. *Fort Pierre Choteau.* Vermillion: University of South Dakota Press, 1990.

Scott, H. L. *Military Dictionary: Comprising Technical Definitions; Information on Raising and Keeping Troops; Actual Service, Including Makeshifts and Improved Materiel; and Law, Government, Regulation, and Administration Relating to Land Forces.* New York: D. Van Nostrand, 1864.

Settle, Raymond W., ed. *The March of the Mounted Riflemen: First United States Military Expedition to Travel the Full Length of the Oregon Trail from Fort Leavenworth to Fort Vancouver, May to October, 1849.* Glendale, Calif.: The Arthur H. Clark Company, 1940.

Steffan, Randy. *The Horse Soldier, 1776–1943: The United States Cavalryman; His Uniforms, Arms, Accoutrements, and Equipments*; Vol. 2, *The Frontier, the Mexican War, the Civil War, the Indian Wars, 1851–1880.* Norman: University of Oklahoma Press, 1978.

Sunder, John E. *The Fur Trade on the Upper Missouri, 1840-1865*. Norman: University of Oklahoma Press, 1965.

Tate, Michael L. *The Frontier Army in the Settlement of the West*. Norman: University of Oklahoma Press, 1999.

Taylor, Emerson Gifford. *Gouverneur Kemble Warren: The Life and Letters of an American Soldier, 1830–1882*. Boston: Houghton Mifflin Company, 1932.

Turnley, Parmenus Taylor. *Reminiscences of Parmenus Taylor Turnley: From the Cradle to Three-Score and Ten*. Chicago: Donahue & Henneberry, 1892.

Unruh, John D., Jr. *The Plains Across: The Overland Emigrants and the Trans-Mississippi West, 1840–60*. Urbana: University of Illinois Press, 1979.

Utley, Robert M. *Custer and the Great Controversy: Origin and Development of a Legend*. Pasadena, Calif.: Westernlore Press, 1962.

———. *Frontiersmen in Blue: The United Army and the Indian, 1848–1865*. New York: Macmillan Publishing Company, 1967.

———. *The Indian Frontier of the American West, 1846–1890*. Albuquerque: University of New Mexico Press, 1984.

———. *The Lance and the Shield: The Life and Times of Sitting Bull*. New York: Henry Holt and Company, 1993.

Walker, James R. *Oglala Society*, ed. Raymond J. DeMallie. Lincoln: University of Nebraska Press, 1982.

Werner, Fred H. *With Harney on the Blue Water: Battle of Ash Hollow, September 3, 1855*. Greeley, Colo.: Werner Publications, 1988.

Whiteley, Lee. *The Cherokee Trail: Bent's Old Fort to Fort Bridger*. Denver: The Denver Posse of the Westerners, 1999.

Young, Otis E. *The West of Philip St. George Cooke, 1809–1895*. Glendale, Calif.: The Arthur H. Clark Co., 1955.

Articles

Anderson, Harry. "The Controversial Sioux Amendment to the Fort Laramie Treaty of 1851," *Nebraska History* 37 (Sept. 1956): 201–20.

———. "Harney v. Twiss, Nebr. Terr., 1856," *Westerners Brand Book, Chicago Corral* 20 (1963): 1–3, 7–8.

Anonymous. "With Harney through the Bad Lands," *The Wi-iyohi, Monthly Bulletin of the South Dakota Historical Society* 14 (Sept. 1960):1–4.

———, ed. "Official Correspondence Relating to Fort Pierre," in *South Dakota Historical Collections* 1 (1902): 381–440.

Beam, D. C. "Reminiscences of Early Days in Nebraska," *Transactions and Reports of the Nebraska State Historical Society* 3 (1892): 292–315.

Bek, William G., trans. "From Bethel, Missouri, to Aurora, Oregon: Letters of William Keil, 1855-1870, Parts I-II," *Missouri Historical Review* 48 (Oct. 1953–Jan. 1954): 23–41, 141–53.

Bray, Kingsley M. "Lone Horn's Peace: A New View of Sioux-Crow Relations, 1851–1858," *Nebraska History* 66 (Spring 1985): 28–47.

———. "The Oglala Lakota and the Establishment of Fort Laramie," *Museum of the Fur Trade Quarterly* 36 (Winter 2000): 2–18.

———. "Teton Sioux Population History, 1655–1881," *Nebraska History* 75 (Summer 1994): 65–88.

Brown, Randy. "Buried in Ash Hollow," *Overland Journal* 8 (No. 3, 1990): 18–25.

Butscher, Louis C., ed. "An Account of Adventures in the Great American Desert by His Royal Highness, Duke Paul Wilhelm von Wurttemberg," *New Mexico Historical Review* 17 (July–Oct, 1942): 181–225, 294–344.

Clow, Richmond L. "The Anatomy of a Lakota Shooting: Crow Dog and Spotted Tail, 1879–1881," *South Dakota History* 28 (Winter 1998): 209–27.

———. "General William S. Harney on the Northern Plains," *South Dakota History* 16 (Fall 1986): 229–48.

———. "Mad Bear: William S. Harney and the Sioux Expedition of 1855–1856," *Nebraska History* 61 (Summer 1980): 132–51.

———. "William S. Harney," in Paul Andrew Hutton, ed., *Soldiers West: Biographies from the Military Frontier*. Lincoln: University of Nebraska Press, 1987.

Coyer, Richard Joseph, ed. "'This Wild Region of the Far West': Lieutenant Sweeny's Letters from Fort Pierre, 1855–56," *Nebraska History* 63 (Summer 1982): 232–54.

Dains, Mary K. "Midwestern River Steamboats: A Pictorial History," *Missouri Historical Review* 66 (July 1972): 589–605.

————. "Steamboats of the 1850s–1860s: A Pictorial History," *Missouri Historical Review* 67 (Jan. 1973): 265–82.

Danker, Donald F. "The Violent Deaths of Yellow Bear and John Richard, Jr.," *Nebraska History* 63 (Summer 1982): 136–51.

Drum, Richard C. "Reminiscences of the Indian Fight at Ash Hollow, 1855," *Collections of the Nebraska State Historical Society* 16 (1911): 142–50.

Finster, David. "The Hardin Winter Count," *Museum News* (W. H. Over Dakota Museum) 29 (Mar.–Apr., 1968): 1–57.

Fletcher, Jack E., and Patricia K. A. Fletcher. "The Cherokee Trail," *Overland Journal* 13 (No. 2, 1995): 21–33.

Garavaglia, Louis A., and Charles G. Worman. "Frontier Forts Counted on Minie," *The American Rifleman* 125 (Apr. 1977): 32–34.

Gray, John S. "Honore Picotte, Fur Trader," *South Dakota History* 6 (Spring 1976): 186–202.

Greene, Jerome A. "Foreword," in Edward S. Farrow, *Mountain Scouting: A Handbook for Officers and Soldiers on the Frontiers*. Norman: University of Oklahoma Press, 2000.

Hanson, Charles E., Jr. "Geminien P. Beauvais," in LeRoy R. Hafen and Ann W. Hafen, eds., *The Mountain Men and the Fur Trade of the Far West*. Glendale, Calif.: The Arthur H. Clark Co., 1965–72.

————. "The Fort Pierre–Fort Laramie Trail," *Museum of the Fur Trade Quarterly* 1 (Summer 1965): 3–7

Hanson, James A. "A Forgotten Fur Trade Trail," *Nebraska History* 68 (Spring 1987): 2–9.

Harvey, Robert. "The Battle Ground of Ash Hollow," *Collections of the Nebraska State Historical Society* 16 (1911):152-64.

————. "Report of the Committee on Marking Historic Sites," in *Annual Report of the Nebraska State Historical Society for the Year Ending December 31, 1909* (1909): 22, 25–28.

Hedren, Paul L. "Lieutenant John L. Grattan's Beltplate?," *Military Collector & Historian* 32 (Fall 1980): 130–32.

Hill, Burton S. "Thomas S. Twiss, Indian Agent," *Great Plains Journal* 6 (Spring 1967): 85–96.

Hoopes, Alban W. "Thomas S. Twiss, Indian Agent on the Upper Platte, 1855–1861," *Mississippi Valley Historical Review* 20 (Dec. 1933–34): 353–64.

Jones, Brian. "Those Wild Reshaw Boys," in Francis B. Taunton, ed., *Sidelights of the Sioux Wars*. London: The English Westerners Society, 1967.

King, James T. "Forgotten Pageant: The Indian Wars in Western Nebraska," in R. Eli Paul, ed., *The Nebraska Indian Wars Reader, 1865–1877*. Lincoln: University of Nebraska Press, 1998.

LeCheminant, Wilford Hill. "A Crisis Averted: General Harney and the Change in Command of the Utah Expedition," *Utah Historical Quarterly* 51 (Winter 1983): 30–45.

Mattison, Ray H., ed. "The Harney Expedition Against the Sioux: The Journal of Capt. John B. S. Todd," *Nebraska History* 43 (June 1962): 89–130.

McCann, Lloyd E. "The Grattan Massacre," *Nebraska History* (Mar. 1954): 1–25.

McDermott, John D. "Crime and Punishment in the United States Army: A Phase of Fort Laramie History," *Journal of the West* 7 (Apr. 1968): 246–55.

———. "James Bordeaux," in LeRoy R. Hafen and Ann W. Hafen, eds., *The Mountain Men and the Fur Trade of the Far West*. Glendale, Calif.: The Arthur H. Clark Co., 1965–72.

Miller, George L. "The Fort Pierre Expedition," *Transactions and Reports of the Nebraska State Historical Society* 3 (1892): 110–19.

———. "The Military Camp on the Big Sioux River in 1855," *Transactions and Reports of the Nebraska State Historical Society* 3 (1892): 119–24.

———. "Personal and Other Notes of the Early Days," *Transactions and Reports of the Nebraska State Historical Society* 4 (1892): 194–98.

Morris, Robert E. "Custer Made a Good Decision: A Leavenworth Appreciation," *Journal of the West* 16 (Oct. 1977): 5–11.

Munkres, Robert L. "Ash Hollow: Gateway to the High Plains," *Annals of Wyoming* 42 (Apr. 1970): 5–43.

Nowak, Timothy R. "From Fort Pierre to Fort Randall: The Army's First Use of Portable Cottages," *South Dakota History* 32 (Summer 2002): 95–116.

Oliva, Leo E. "Fort Atkinson on the Santa Fe Trail, 1850–1854," *Kansas Historical Quarterly* 40 (Summer 1974): 212–33.

Paul, R. Eli. "Frontier Forts," in David J. Wishart, ed., *Encyclopedia of the Great Plains*. Lincoln: University of Nebraska Press, forthcoming.

Paul R. Eli, ed. "Battle of Ash Hollow: The Recollections of General N. A. M. Dudley," *Nebraska History* 62 (Fall 1981): 373–99.

———. "George Wilkins Kendall and a Party of Pleasure Seekers on the Prairie, 1851," *Nebraska History* 64 (Summer 1983): 35–80.

Sandoz, Mari. "Some Oddities of the American Indian," in *Hostiles and Friendlies: Selected Short Writings of Mari Sandoz*. Lincoln: University of Nebraska Press, 1959, 79–86.

Soderberg, Elizabeth. "Fort Pierre Sutler, 1855," *Military Collector & Historian* 49 (Summer 1997): 50–57.

Sundstrom, Linea. "Smallpox Used Them Up: References to Epidemic Disease in Northern Plains Winter Counts, 1714-1920," *Ethnohistory* 44 (Spring 1997): 305–43.

Thayer, John M. "My Very First Visit to the Pawnee Village in 1855," *Proceedings and Collections of the Nebraska State Historical Society* 15 (1907):119–27.

Vaux, William. "Report from Fort Laramie, Oct. 1, 1854," in *The Spirit of Missions* 22 (1855):40–41.

Wade, Arthur P. "Forts and Mounted Rifles Along the Oregon Trail, 1846–1853," *Kansas Quarterly* 10 (Summer 1978): 3–15.

Watkins, Albert, ed. "Notes on the Early History of the Nebraska Country," *Publications of the Nebraska State Historical Society* 20 (1922): 1–379.

White, Richard. "The Winning of the West: The Expansion of the Western Sioux in the Eighteenth and Nineteenth Centuries," *Journal of American History* 65 (Sept. 1978): 319–43.

Whiteley, Lee. "The Trappers Trail: 'The Road to Fort Laramie's Back Door'," *Overland Journal* 16 (Winter 1998–99): 2–16.

Wilson, Frederick T. "Old Fort Pierre and Its Neighbors," *South Dakota Historical Collections* 1 (1902): 263–311.

Withers, Ethel Massie, ed. "Experiences of Lewis Bissell Dougherty on the Oregon Trail, Part II," *The Missouri Historical Review* 24 (July 1930): 550–67.

Wright, Norman E. "Odometers," *Overland Journal* 13 (No. 3, 1995): 14–24.

Acknowledgments

The one person who I wish could have read this book is Dennis Shimmin, the longtime superintendent of Ash Hollow State Historical Park, Lewellen, Nebraska. In 1977, as my first special assignment with the Nebraska State Historical Society, I collaborated with Dennis on developing the museum exhibits for his new visitor center at the park. He took me, a novice to the area's history, on my first tour of the battlefield along Blue Water Creek. It culminated with our discovery of what I now think was a remnant of "Hudson's Hole," that last sheltering overhang for a few of Little Thunder's people. While I was obsessively looking for snakes—the hilltop we were scrambling about was known locally as "Rattlesnake Butte"— Dennis jumped down, poked around a bit, and came up with a treasure, a smashed minie ball and one obviously from the September 3, 1855, fight. We later put the bullet on display in the visitor center, where I saw it again in 2002.

During the interim, Dennis and I remained interested in the Blue Water fight. I went on and edited for publication an officer's battlefield reminiscence, and continued to gather more information on the First Sioux War; he kept walking the site and also transcribed the entire series of letters sent by the commander of the Sioux Expedition. Dennis shared a copy of those few hundred pages of transcription not long before his death in 1998. This transcription helped immeasurably. His generosity in sharing information, as well as the help and generosity of other individuals hereafter recognized, have been instrumental in my undertaking and completing this book.

John McDermott and James Hutchins shared much of their research discoveries in the military records of the National Archives, plus set me on the trail for more. Jack also read and discussed the manuscript, as did Thomas Buecker, Jerome Greene, Paul Hedren, and Frank Schubert. I also profited from discussions with Kingsley Bray, James Hanson, Robert Larson, John Ludwickson, Douglas McChristian, James Potter, and Douglas Scott on their related research, and with Charles Rankin on editorial matters, great and small. From all these gentlemen, I have also benefitted from long, valued friendships.

Newfound friends and renewed acquaintances helped me when I visited, especially in 2001 and 2002, the many archives, libraries, historical sites, and historical societies that figure in this project. They include: Jeff Uhrich and Vivian Kallsen, Ash Hollow State Historical Park, Nebraska Game and Parks Commission, Lewellen, Nebraska; Gail Potter, Museum of the Fur Trade, Chadron, Nebraska; Barbara Larsen and Reed Whitaker, National Archives—Central Plains Region, Kansas City, Missouri; Michael Musick, National Archives, Washington, D. C.; John Mark Lambertson and David Aamodt, National Frontier Trails Center, Independence, Missouri; Richard Sommers, United States Army Military History Institute, Carlisle Barracks, Pennsylvania; and Kenneth Lohrentz, Anschutz Library, University of Kansas, Lawrence.

Staff members of the following historical societies, long dedicated to public service, were especially helpful: the Kansas State Historical Society, Topeka; the State Historical Society of Missouri, Columbia; and the Nebraska State Historical Society, Lincoln. The library of Fort Laramie National Historic Site, Fort Laramie, Wyoming, with its volumes of transcribed military records, is to be commended, together with those archivists, historians, and librarians, past and present at the aforementioned institutions, who have created the findng aids that make research visits so productive. I also thank the University of Oklahoma Press crew, first Chuck Rankin, followed by Caroline Dwyer, Diana Edwards, Candice Holcombe, Greta Mohon, and Marian Stewart.

Some individuals gave exceptional support and receive my special thanks. Frank and Irene Schubert, Alexandria, Virginia, always provided a warm welcome and a comfortable place to stay during many research trips to Washington, sometimes in the company of one of the friends above. Their generous hospitality also included stimulating conversation and a genuine interest in my work. Similar hospitality came from Tom and Kay Buecker, Crawford, Nebraska, and Brent and Carmen Carmack, Bill and Sue Munn, and Steve and Mary Jo Ryan, all of Lincoln, Nebraska. I also drew upon the drafting skills of Dell Darling of Lincoln, Nebraska, whose work graces this book. Since moving to the Kansas City metropolitan area, I have enjoyed the support of Bill and Janice McCollum, Kansas City, Missouri.

My greatest supporter and advocate remains my wife, Lori Cox-Paul, who also served as the first reader and commentator of the manuscript. To her and to all, thank you.

Index